MW00830476

APPLYING RESTORATIVE JUSTICE TO
CAMPUS SEXUAL MISCONDUCT

APPLYING RESTORATIVE JUSTICE TO CAMPUS SEXUAL MISCONDUCT

A Guide to Emerging Practices

Edited by Kaaren M. Williamsen and

Erik S. Wessel

Foreword by Ryan C. Holmes, Tamara Greenfield King,
and Jennifer Meyer Schrage

Routledge
Taylor & Francis Group

NEW YORK AND LONDON

Published in 2023 by Routledge
605 Third Avenue, New York, NY 10017
4 Park Square, Milton Park, Abingdon, Oxon OX14 4RN

Routledge is an imprint of the Taylor & Francis Group, an informa business.

© 2023 Taylor & Francis Group

All rights reserved. No part of this book may be reprinted or reproduced or utilised in any form or by any electronic, mechanical, or other means, now known or hereafter invented, including photocopying and recording, or in any information storage or retrieval system, without permission in writing from the publishers.

Trademark Notice: Product or corporate names may be trademarks or registered trademarks, and are used only for identification and explanation without intent to infringe.

ISBN: 9781642673845 (hbk)
ISBN: 9781642673852 (pbk)
ISBN: 9781003443018 (ebk)

DOI: 10.4324/9781003443018

CONTENTS

PART THREE: FACILITATION FOCUS

PART FOUR: REFLECTIONS ON IMPLEMENTATION

I n our collective experience as campus leaders, educators, scholars, and practitioners serving in higher education over the past 2 decades, we have sat at many tables with and looked into the eyes of real students in crisis to offer support as they navigated the aftermath of sexual misconduct on a college campus, including those who identified as survivors, complainants, respondents, and bystanders. Over the years, the external regulatory guidance and associated counsel dictating how to facilitate a response process respectful of legal obligations shifted dramatically, and it was always complex, often contradictory and never fully centered on student development and the higher learning mission. In every case, regardless of the local and national political and legal landscape, these students we sat next to, those reporting and responding, were afraid, in pain, confused and seeking paths to healing and a voice in a process that our formalistic policies and paradigms could not offer. Still, to this day, these are the cases that are replayed in our minds as we reflect on our careers and the real purpose of our work.

These experiences, among others, are what brought us together with many other educators across the field of campus conduct and conflict management to coauthor *Reframing Campus Conflict: Student Conduct Practice through a Social Justice Lens* in 2009 and again in 2020 for the second edition retitled *Reframing Campus Conflict: Student Conduct Practice Through the Lens of Inclusive Conflict Excellence* (Stylus). Both editions were inspired by scholarship and an ongoing shared movement across our profession advocating for a fuller spectrum of resolution options (Schrage & Thompson, 2008) for responding to student conduct incidents in ways that aligned with procedural, restorative, social and transformative justice, or the lenses of inclusive conflict excellence (Schrage & Giacomini, 2020). We desired to make the work about the students, healing, and education rather than rules, policies, and punishments.

Applying Restorative Justice to Campus Sexual Misconduct builds upon this ongoing shared movement in our profession. In every chapter, it is evident that the editors and the authors in this publication bring deep wisdom, insight, reflections, innovation, and practical solutions gained from years of experience at the frontlines of responding to sexual misconduct on campus.

The work represented in these chapters is a testament to the power of intellect and creativity. In the face of shifting and massive Title IX regulations that veered toward increased formalism with each year and unprecedented political pressures over the past decade, these authors and practitioners continued to innovate and advocate for more restorative approaches, successfully calibrating systems and processes to make space for a fuller spectrum of resolution options in sexual misconduct response.

Title IX of the Education Amendments of 1972 (United States Department of Justice, n.d.), made it the law of the land that "no person in the United States shall, on the basis of sex, be excluded from participation in, be denied the benefits of, or be subject to discrimination under any educational program or activity receiving Federal financial assistance." Coauthored by U.S. Representative Patsy Takemoto Mink, the very law designed by the first woman of color elected to Congress and meant to prohibit discrimination against women has often become an instrument of marginalization as campuses in fear of litigation have been hesitant to use adaptive and restorative pathways designed to center the voices and the needs of students. The lenses of inclusive conflict excellence help us to see all students as "our" students, those responding, those reporting, reeling and seeking healing from it. Principled practitioners must be equipped to provide the necessary care, concern, compassion, and education specific to the situation. Our systems must be more student-centered in their outcomes. The authors in this work have provided content to support the possibilities of positive personal and community transformation, even in situations of sexual misconduct. This book offers real strategies and solutions to the higher education practitioners and leaders invested in using inclusive conflict excellence in sexual misconduct response. For the sake of students and our campus communities, we hope it finds its way to the desks of every policy developer, implementer and all of those who give counsel to the educators at the frontlines doing this very difficult work.

References

Schrage, J. M., & Giacomini, N.G. (Eds.). 2020. Introduction. In *Reframing campus conflict: Student conduct practice Through the lens of inclusive excellence* (pp. 1–4). Stylus.

Schrage, J. M., & Thompson, M. C. (2008, June). *Using a social justice model for conflict resolution to ensure access for all students.* Paper presented at the Donald D. Gehring Academy for Student Conduct Administration, Salt Lake City, UT.

United States Department of Justice. (n.d.). *Title IX of the education amendments of 1972.* 20 U.S.C.D. 1681–1688. Title 20: Education. Chapter 38 discrimination based on sex or blindness. https://www.justice.gov/crt/title-ix-education-amend ments-1972

Ryan C. Holmes, EdD, (he/him) president emeritus, Association of Student Conduct Administration; contributor, *Reframing Campus Conflict and Thought*; partner with resolv ED. LLC.

Tamara Greenfield King, JD, (she/her) president emeritus, Association of Student Conduct Administration and contributor, *Reframing Campus Conflict and Thought*; partner with resolv ED. LLC.

Jennifer Meyer Schrage, JD, (she/her) coeditor and contributor, *Reframing Campus Conflict and Thought*; partner lead with resolv ED. LLC.

ACKNOWLEDGMENTS

We worked on this book from the state of Michigan, both of us working at the University of Michigan which is located on the traditional territory of the Anishinaabe people. In 1817, the Ojibwe, Odawa, and Bodewadami Nations made the largest single land transfer to the University of Michigan. This was offered ceremonially as a gift through the Treaty at the Foot of the Rapids so that their children could be educated. We acknowledge this connection to the land and to the many global indigenous teachings that are at the root of restorative practices. We honor and acknowledge these connections and teachings.

We would like to thank all the contributors to this edited book. Your passion and commitment to this work shines through and we are so grateful that you took time out of your busy lives to contribute to this project. This was a collective labor of love, and we are thrilled to be able to combine all our voices to help move this work forward.

We would also like to thank Jennifer Meyer Schrage and Nancy Geist Giacomini whose foundational work *Reframing Campus Conflict: Student Conduct Practice Through a Social Justice Lens* (2009) influenced and inspired both of us in profound ways. Your work helped to open the door for our work and this book. Thank you, thank you.

We would also like to thank Mary Koss, whose research and groundbreaking RESTORE program inspired many (including practitioners in this book) to think another way to respond to sexual harm was possible. Your work inspired me (Kaaren) to completely change my career trajectory and I am so grateful for your leadership, vision, and dedication.

We would also like to thank our colleagues, collaborators, teachers, and mentors in higher education and in this movement we call restorative justice. We are grateful to be in this work together.

A big thank you also to Amanda Smith for her amazing organizational skills, editing skills, and late-night hours. We could not have done this without you.

And finally—we thank and dedicate this to our students. You inspire us, motivate us, and give us hope.

INTRODUCTION

Erik S. Wessel and Kaaren M. Williamsen

The prevalence of campus sexual misconduct is starkly illustrated by multiple institutional and national surveys. The relative consistency of these data across public and private college communities is a sobering reminder of the depth of harm experienced with gut-wrenching regularity. The 2019 American Association of Universities (AAU) survey of 33 college campuses found that 13% of all student survey respondents indicated experiencing some form of nonconsensual sexual contact (Cantor et al., 2020). Rates for undergraduate women (25.9%), TGQN and undergraduate students (22.8%) represent a staggering number that is symptomatic of broader and deep-rooted societal concerns. (The AAU Survey [Cantor et al., 2020] uses the acronym *TGQN* to capture gender identities shared by students in this survey. This includes transgender woman, transgender man, nonbinary/genderqueer, gender questioning, and gender not listed.)

Yet, the number of people seeking formal assistance from their institutions is consistently low. A 2017 study found that, out of their sample of 834 female students at a midwestern university, 34% reported being sexually assaulted; however, only 6% reported it to any campus official, and only 2% filed formal complaints (Holland & Cortina, 2017). The AAU survey sheds some light on why this is, finding that students choose not to report sexual assault for a variety of reasons; including (a) a belief that the behavior they experienced was not serious enough to report, (b) a belief that they could "handle it themselves," (c) because they "felt embarrassed or ashamed," (d) because they "did not want the person to get in trouble," (e) because "the event happened in a context that began consensually," (f) a belief that "I didn't think these resources would give me the help I needed" (Cantor et al., 2020). Clearly, the data show that needs are going unmet in our communities. Of those who have experienced some of the most traumatic harm in our communities, some hold to their own view of the experience, others want to maintain their own agency to respond as they wish, and some survivors want to maintain control of what consequences might come.

To all of this diversity of need and complexity of circumstance, we have historically offered a singular campus approach that looks more and more like an adversarial criminal court with each passing day. This investigatory approach, which includes the opportunity for a live hearing, cross-examination, and a decision by an independent fact-finder, remains the central (and required by regulation) resolution pathway, and this option may be exactly the process by which some survivors choose to seek justice. However, when we know that the supermajority of sexual harm in our community is going unreported—does that not beg the question, at the very least, as to whether there might be additional ways of seeking to offer justice in community? Perhaps we should not immediately assume that one person's vision of justice comports to another. Should we not be seeking to return as much agency back to those who have had power taken from them? Not all will agree on all methods of seeking justice, but should we not provide options and empower those who are most directly affected to make that call for themselves?

Having worked with the college student population in the field of student conduct and conflict resolution for nearly a decade and a half, I (Erik) have facilitated investigations and formalized community accountability procedures that aimed to end the harassment, prevent it from recurring, and remedy the effects. I am, however, fairly confident in stating that even where we may have succeeded in the first two, the imperative to "remedy the effects" on the survivor of campus sexual misconduct (CSM) has remained elusive. As further anecdotal evidence to this observation, I've personally never heard a practitioner in the Title IX field who would represent they were confident in their process actually meeting individual student or even community needs. This fundamental realization brought me back around to a continually evolving restorative mindset. Maintaining the singular procedural status quo became less tenable in my own recognition of incongruence with my own personal and professional values. Therefore, leaning to a restorative framework and clearly articulating the case to others has become a clear imperative.

In advancing this work with colleagues at the University of Michigan, I find myself fortunate to stand on the shoulders of those who have paved the way. The foundational restorative framework employed at the University of Michigan goes back many years, but today's work largely draws from the foundational spectrum model of conflict resolution pathways developed by Jennifer Meyer Schrage and Monita Thompson (2008). Much of the applied restorative practice found in the University of Michigan's sexual and gender-based policy and procedure draws its inspiration from the spectrum model—which itself has its roots in ancient and indigenous peacemaking practices. Therefore, although the application of a restorative approach remains a fledgling practice in higher education, in particular as connected to sexual and gender-based misconduct, the roots of restorative justice (RJ) run deep in the history of humanity. It is this legacy that gives me hope and confidence in the wisdom of restorative approaches to create the necessary conditions for human needs to be met—to truly achieve the aims of Title IX in remedying the effects of CSM.

When Schrage and Giacomini released the first edition of *Reframing Campus Conflict* in 2009, the optimism they reflected was rooted in the observed movement away from policy established firmly in a legal framework (Giacomini & Schrage, 2009) In the second edition, they reflected further on this shift from a "one size fits all standardization . . . quasi-courtroom proceedings in the name of due process" and to an embrace of "educational, collaborative and inclusive approaches" (Schrage & Giacomini, 2020a, p. 11). The Title IX landscape exists under the heavy burden of externally imposed standardization that in many ways suffers from much the same limiting and rigid foundational procedural justice frameworks. However, in recent years, externally imposed regulations have recognized the imperative to provide a greater degree of agency to those most directly affected by sexual and gender-based misconduct. The idea of working collaboratively with those most directly affected is a fundamental restorative construct which intersects conceptually with the idea of inclusive excellence. Drawing from the foundational guiding principles originally developed by the American Association of Colleges and Universities, Schrage and Giacomini (2020a) noted, "Inclusive conflict excellence brings together in a shared frame the social, restorative, transformative, and procedural" (p. 30) to most effectively understand, envision and operationalize. Building upon the lenses of inclusive excellence model (Schrage & Giacomini, 2020a) and the multidimensional inclusive learning assessment model (Wessel & Karel, 2020), Figure I.1 offers a way to conceptualize the multifaceted nature of working toward inclusive excellence through envisioning, building, operationalizing, and sustaining restorative and equitable policy, procedure, and practice.

Conceptual Frames

In this framework model we attempt to visualize the componentry to increasingly equitable process as viewed through the lens of inclusive excellence. As we twist the prism it is important that we explore application of

Figure I.1. Inclusive excellence foundational framework for restorative responses to campus sexual and gender-based misconduct.

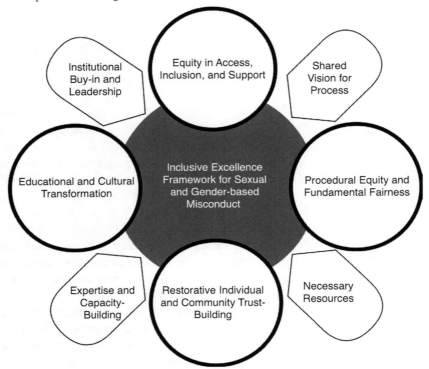

Note. This figure is inspired by the lenses of inclusive conflict excellence, developed by N. Giacomini and J. Schrage with M. Thompson (2020) as well as adapted from Wessel and Karel (2020).

restorative frameworks through the following primary frames: Equity in access, procedural equity, restorative trust-building, and educational/cultural transformation.

> *Equity in access, inclusion, and support.* Perhaps the cornerstone to inclusive policy and practice is equitable opportunity. Equity, of course, is not to be confused with equality. Not every individual or community will present with sameness of need. Instead, equity envisions fundamental support that attends to the uniqueness of need expressed among those who are party to the harm.
> *Procedural equity and fundamental fairness.* Procedural equity is built through community engagement in the development of fundamentally fair and transparent processes.
> *Restorative individual and community trust-building.* Trust is built in the context of relationships. Trust is the nature of believing that

what is committed to will be done in good faith. Communities who build processes that are compliant, coherent, and creative WITH their communities tend to instill trust.

Educational and cultural transformation. Transformation occurs at the confluence of individual and community education, reflection, application, evaluation, and creating a new way of being. Transformation by definition is a dramatic change, and the restorative approach to sexual and gender-based misconduct requires traversing through understanding to deep reflection. It requires applying new knowledge and understanding while evaluating what has been learned and, finally, turning that process into building something new. Perhaps in this context something new is a transformed conceptualization of healthy relationships in community.

Administrative Frames

Adding some additional complexity to the model, it will be important to consider several administrative frames from a systems perspective. These are institutional buy-in and leadership, shared vision, resources, as well as expertise and building capacity for the work.

Institutional buy-in and leadership. As hierarchical organizations, buy-in and support from those who possess institutional authority and decision-making power will be important for long-term sustained advancement of a restorative program.

Shared vision for process. The degree to which a vision for a restorative approach can be clearly, concisely, and broadly communicated will be critical to building shared community understanding, trust, and support.

Necessary resources. Higher education has invested a mountain of time, talent, and treasure into current policy and procedures with results that objectively do not demonstrate success. Although it is cost-neutral for each of us as practitioners to develop our own restorative mindset and begin to think and apply restorative approaches to current practices, building and sustaining inherently restorative procedures requires investment.

Expertise and capacity-building. The restorative practitioner is a highly skilled facilitator of process—and takes time and investment to develop. In this book, we will devote attention across several chapters to building individual and community capacity to respond to sexual violence in increasingly restorative ways.

In this work, we will look through the prism of restorative responses to sexual and gender-based misconduct on campus. Each chapter will provide further focus on access, inclusion, and support. We will explore educational and cultural transformation for social change. We will delve deeper into the necessary balance of procedural equity, fundamental fairness, and support. And we will explain the ways in which a restorative approach might more fully promote justice by first building trust between individuals and communities. This work is designed to aid the restorative practitioner in thinking through critical elements for building a fundamentally restorative process, including leadership buy-in and coalition building, casting a vision that the community can embrace, ensuring that an implemented restorative approach has fidelity backed by sustainable expertise, and creative and realistic resource procurement and development for a successful process.

Moving Toward a Restorative Approach

When I (Kaaren) first heard about RJ and its focus on understanding and repairing harm, I experienced an epiphany. It suddenly became clear why so many survivors did not want to use our carefully crafted investigation and hearing-based campus adjudication system. Judith Herman (2005) wrote that

> The wishes and needs of victims are diametrically opposed to the requirements of legal proceedings . . . Indeed if one set out intentionally to design a system for provoking symptoms of traumatic stress, it might look very much like a court of law. (p. 574)

We had unwittingly done just that on our campus, as had most colleges and universities around the country. In 2009, I started a journey to help me answer the question, "What if we started with the goal of healing in mind; what would our campus processes look like? What if we then layered in learning and behavior change, and then made it all compliant—what would the process look like?" What if? Restorative justice seemed to offer an alternative.

Professor Mary Koss (2010), a groundbreaking sexual assault researcher and RJ innovator, explained that following an assault survivors have survival needs (safety, shelter, emotional support, financial help, etc.) and justice needs. Understanding justice needs helps us to understand why traditional adversarial justice processes often leave survivors wanting. She explained,

> According to SVs [survivor/victims], satisfying their justice needs rests on the extent to which they: (1) contribute input into key decisions and remain informed about their case, (2) receive response with minimal delay, (3) tell their story without interruption by adversarial and sometimes hostile questioning, (4) receive validation, (5) shape a resolution that meets their material and emotional needs, and (6) feel safe. (pp. 221–222)

An RJ response, by design, has a greater opportunity to meet these needs. Koss's RESTORE (Responsibility and Equity for Sexual Transgressions Offering a Restorative Experience) project was a pioneering RJ program for sexual offenses in the United States; research on the program showed promising results, where survivors and those responsible for causing harm reported high satisfaction with the restorative process (Koss, 2010).

The RESTORE project inspired me and others to see how we might bring an RJ approach to college and university campuses. The 2011 Dear Colleague Letter (Ali, 2011) did not mention RJ; however, it did include a prohibition of the use of mediation for sexual assault. This served as a chilling effect to most schools in using anything other than a formal investigatory approach to respond to complaints of CSM. However, the limitations of the adversarial model were starting to become clear to activists, survivors, and administrators. In 2015, writer Deborah Copaken Kogan reflected on her own sexual assault the night before her college graduation:

> It's hard not to wonder now, from my perch of more than a quarter-century later, staring at the pinched look on my face in the photos from that rainy graduation morning, why there hadn't been a third option besides either pressing charges or doing nothing, neither of which felt like an appropriate reaction to what had happened to me in that bed. What if there had been a way for me to report the date rape to the administration, to define that crossing of boundaries in front of my rapist and a panel of well-trained adults, and to express, in a safe forum, my extreme disgust with his actions in such a way that my rapist would have been forced to at least listen to and ponder the hurt he'd caused, followed by sensitivity training and reeducation? (para. 32)

Similarly, in 2018 Sofie Karasek (cofounder of End Rape on Campus) wrote a *New York Times* op-ed Times calling for additional approaches:

> Over time, many student activists have become disillusioned with an emphasis on punitive justice—firings, expulsions and in some cases, prison sentences. We've seen firsthand how rarely it works for survivors. It's not designed to provide validation, acknowledgment or closure. It also does not guarantee that those who harmed will not act again. As the campus sexual assault movement, and now #MeToo, has made clear, sexual injustices, from harassment to rape and assault, are deeply ingrained in American society, involving people from all walks of life. We cannot jail, fire or expel our way out of this crisis. We need institutional responses to sexual harm that prioritize both justice and healing, not one at the expense of the other. (paras. 4–5)

I also focused on this concern in my own dissertation research (Williamsen, 2017), for which I interviewed 21 campus administrators involved in their CSM response process, including Title IX coordinators, student conduct officers, and advisors/advocates to students going through the campus process. What I heard from research participants was a collective concern about the limitations of the traditional investigative approach to responding to CSM, and all but one shared an openness for expanding RJ options for cases of student sexual misconduct. They longed for a more compassionate alternative—one that lived up to their goals and was responsive to the needs of survivors. An RJ framework offers this kind of compassionate response.

After the last case I had as a Title IX coordinator, the complainant debriefed the hearing with me; she shared that even though the respondent had been suspended, she was devastated by the process. She told me that she now had two traumas to heal from—the rape and the hearing. I knew from my own research and from conversations with other survivors that she was not alone in this feeling. I also knew other campus administrators heard similar stories and felt the devastation of causing more harm with their carefully crafted procedures; they were also clamoring for additional options. For the past several years I've worked with colleagues to offer training for campus administrators in using RJ for CSM. I see that familiar look of frustration, pain, and desperation in the faces of the administrators in the training circle (or Zoom boxes) and see lightness and relief when they realize that there can be another way. That other way (an RJ response) is not perfect, and is not right for every case, but I have seen it meet needs, contribute positively to healing for survivors, and spur learning and self-reflection among those responsible for causing harm that I have not seen accomplished by an adversarial justice approach.

RJ invites a shift in focus from *what policy was broken* to *what harm was done* (Zehr, 2015). A policy focus tends to be institution focused—its policies were violated and the complainant is a witness to that violation, reporting it to the school. The school then investigates the allegations, decides if its policies were violated and, if so, decides what actions to take. When we start with a focus on harm, we go down a different path. We seek to understand the harm—who was harmed and in what ways? What needs do they now have, and how might their harm be repaired and their needs met? This shift to a *harm focus* offers a fundamentally different starting point. The focus is on the harmed party—they experienced a violation and are seeking help addressing the harm.

In the past 5 years, schools have started to expand their response options. The language used to describe an RJ–based option varies; it is often encompassed in processes called *alternative resolution, informal resolution, remedies-based resolution*, and *adaptable resolution* (McMahon et al., 2022). A study of early adopters of RJ for CSM found that a handful of schools started to formally (and informally) offer restorative options before the Department of Education, Office for Civil Rights Title IX regulations were clear on the subject (McMahon et al., 2022). There are many lessons to be learned from these early adopters, some of which are shared in chapter 1 by Williamsen and McMahon. They offer additional insights from these early adopters and identify guideposts to aid campus officials who are looking to expand their response options. Part One of this book focuses on observations of and lessons learned from those who have implemented RJ (and or alternative)–based responses. Chapter 2, by Jacoby and Wessel, explores the philosophical and practical aspects of policy creation, while chapter 3, by Cerdera and Lopez, addresses common concerns to using restorative approaches to campus sexual and gender-based misconduct.

Part Two builds upon the foundational observations of these restorative applications and the policy-focused underpinnings of restorative practice applied to campus sexual and gender-based misconduct. In chapter 4, Naidu and Karp share an overview of common restorative practices; in chapter 5, Jacoby and Zichi explore necessary procedural elements and documentation mechanisms. Part Two concludes with chapter 6, by Tabachnick and Wilgus, which advances specialized interventions for individuals who have caused harm through sexual and gender-based misconduct.

Having outlined potential restorative options, essential procedural mechanisms, and post-process specialized intervention, we then turn to a focus on facilitation in Part Three. In chapter 7, McMahon and Anderson describe the ways in which a facilitator embodies an RJ approach, attending to self, people, and systems, with particular attention to identities and power dynamics. Chapter 8, by Landrum, focuses on the ways in which the RJ practitioner is most effective in working restoratively with both complainants and respondents. And finally, this section concludes in chapter 9 with McMurphy's reflection and case studies on the use of supported dialogues. In Part Four, we begin in chapter 10 with Landrum's reflection on adaptable resolution, healing, and justice and conclude with a collection of reflections on institutional implementation from administrators, RJ facilitators, restorative consultants, facilitators of psychoeducational interventions, and a student survivor who experienced an RJ process. This is a new and emerging field within higher education, and these reflections offer an on-the-ground perspective on efforts to meet individual and community needs created by sexual and gender-based violence in our communities.

A Note About Language

The language we use matters, and we have intentionally given space to variation of voice, perspective, and language. The authors–practitioners in this book represent a variety of academic and professional backgrounds, including higher education, student conduct, advocacy, Title IX, social work, and law, and the language used reflects this. Therefore, not all sections will utilize the same terminology, but where language differs between chapters it is intentional to the content of that particular chapter, and each author will explain the use of specific terms. With this recognition we would also like to offer a note on the variation of language you will see throughout the book. First, we use the term *sexual misconduct* to encompass the range of sexual and gender-based misconduct that colleges and universities respond to, including sexual assault and sexual harassment. In addition, the terms such as *complainant* and *respondent* are often used in chapters that focus on policy and procedure, as these are the terms most commonly used in regulatory documents and related campus policies. Some chapters will use identity-oriented terms, such as *survivor*.

We feel it is important to intentionally acknowledge this difference and recognize that this variation of terms has utility in understanding and recognizing the complexity associated with campus sexual and gender-based misconduct work. Further, as RJ applications to sexual and gender-based misconduct continue to advance, we will also see the terms *harmed party* and *responsible party* or *person responsible for causing harm* entering our vocabulary. As McMahon et al. (2022) observed, there is also variation in terminology for processes other than traditional investigatory processes; these include *alternative resolution*, *adaptive* or *adaptable resolution*, *informal resolution*, and *remedies-based resolution*. Each of these terms conveys the common connotation of a voluntary, remedies-based, facilitated process that is focused on the repair of harm, identifying and meeting needs, and the cocreation of the conditions necessary for accountable future engagement in the college and university community.

References

Ali, R. (2011, April 4). *Dear colleague letter*. U.S Department of Education, Office for Civil Rights, Office of the Assistant Secretary. https://www2.ed.gov/about/offices/list/ocr/letters/colleague-201104.html

Cantor, D., Fisher, B., Chibnall, S., Harps, S., Townsend, R., Thomas, G., Lee, H., Kranz, V., Herbison, R., & Madden, K. (2020). *Report on the AAU campus climate survey on sexual assault and misconduct*. Association of American Universities.

https://www.aau.edu/sites/default/files/AAU-Files/Key-Issues/Campus-Safety/Revised%20Aggregate%20report%20%20and%20appendices%201-7_(01-16-2020_FINAL).pdf

Copaken Kagen, D. (2015, May 13). Entering the mind of my rapist: An exercise in extreme empathy. *The Nation.* https://www.thenation.com/article/archive/entering-mind-my-rapist-exercise-extreme-empathy/

Giacomini, N. G., & Schrage, J. M. (2009). Building community in the current campus climate. In J. M. Schrage & N. G. Giacomini (Eds.), *Reframing campus conflict: Student conduct practice through a social justice lens* (pp. 7–21). Stylus.

Giacomini, N. G., & Schrage, J. M. (Eds.). (2020). Transforming the climate and culture of campus communities through inclusive conflict excellence. In *Reframing campus conflict: Student conduct practice through a social justice lens* (2nd ed.; pp. 7–40). Stylus.

Herman, J. (2005). Justice from a victim's perspective. *Violence Against Women, 11*(5), 571–602. https://doi.org/10.1177/1077801205274450

Holland, K. J., & Cortina, L. M. (2017). "It happens to girls all the time": Examining sexual assault survivors' reasons for not using campus supports. *American Journal of Community Psychology, 59*(1–2), 50–64. https://doi.org/10.1002/ajcp.12126

Karasek, S. (2018, February 22). I'm a campus sexual assault activist: It's time to reimagine how we punish sex crimes. *New York Times.* https://www.nytimes.com/2018/02/22/opinion/campus-sexual-assault-punitive-justive.html

Koss, M. P. (2010). Restorative justice for acquaintance rape and misdemeanor sex crimes. *Restorative Justice and Violence Against Women, 29*(9), 218–238. https://doi.org/10.1177/088626051351153

McMahon, S. M., Williamsen, K. M., Mitchell, H. B., & Kleven, A. (2022). Initial reports from early adopters of restorative justice for reported cases of campus sexual misconduct: A qualitative study. *Violence Against Women* [Advance online publication]. https://doi.org/10.1177/10778012221108419

Schrage, J. M., & Giacomini, N. G. (Eds.). (2020). *Reframing campus conflict: Student conduct practice through the lens of inclusive excellence.* Stylus.

Schrage, J. M., & Thompson, M. C. (2008, June). *Using a social justice model for conflict resolution to ensure access for all students.* Paper presented at the Donald D. Gehring Academy for Student Conduct Administration, Salt Lake City, UT.

Wessel, E., & Karel, A. (2020). Cultural responsiveness in student conduct and conflict resolution assessment. In J. M. Schrage & N. G. Giacomini (Eds.), *Reframing campus conflict: Student conduct practice through a social justice lens* (2nd ed., pp. 295–307). Stylus.

Williamsen, K. M. (2017). *"The exact opposite of what they need": Administrator reflections on sexual misconduct, the limitations of the student conduct response, and the possibilities of restorative justice* [Doctoral dissertation]. University of Minnesota. https://conservancy.umn.edu/bitstream/handle/11299/190564/Williamsen_umn_0130E_18323.pdf?sequence=1

Zehr, H. (2015). *The little book of restorative justice: Revised and updated.* Simon & Schuster.

PART ONE

PHILOSOPHY AND GETTING STARTED

I

A RESTORATIVE JUSTICE APPROACH TO CAMPUS SEXUAL MISCONDUCT

Restorative Guideposts and Insights From Early Adopters

Kaaren M. Williamsen and Sheila M. McMahon

Guideposts may be found at the intersections of two or more roads. In this chapter, we discuss the importance of guideposts in the careful work of applying restorative approaches to campus sexual misconduct (CSM). The guidance provided here for getting started with a restorative response to CSM is based on a combination of recent qualitative research by the chapter authors; our collective professional experiences; and the wisdom from the writers, researchers, and restorative justice (RJ) practitioners who light the way toward the uses of RJ in cases of CSM.

Overview of Research: Description of Practices/Approach

We began our study of 10 early adopters of RJ for CSM (representing seven different institutions, and one former administrator, now a consultant) in 2019, and our findings yielded a wealth of information about the implementation of restorative approaches, including variations of practice across institutions (McMahon et al., 2022). While each campus-based RJ leader in our study referenced RJ, most used other language to formally describe their respective campus policies regarding reported cases of sexual harm, including *alternative resolution*, *adaptable resolution*, and *informal resolution*. Many early adopters also referenced other practices that influenced their restorative response programs, including mediation, dispute resolution, and conflict resolution practices. To account for the variations and to most accurately describe what we found, we are introducing the phrase *restorative justice–informed approaches* (RJIAs) to describe the approaches we found in our study. Who facilitated these RJIAs also varied; facilitators included full-time professionals (hired to do RJ and conflict resolution work), conduct officers, ombudspeople, Title IX coordinators, faculty/staff volunteers, an external consultant, and a senior student affairs practitioner. Practices included restorative shuttle agreements (no in-person meeting between the parties), circles, conferences, and dialogues. For the most part, facilitators also followed a basic restorative flow: intake with each party, preparation with each party, restorative engagement, and follow-up. All RJIAs were voluntary for the parties and were designed to allow the parties to engage in a process to best meet their needs. For some institutions, these processes culminated in the creation of a formal agreement (sometimes called a *restorative agreement* or *resolution*) to be approved by the Title IX coordinator. The facilitator typically provided some follow-up to the parties, including monitoring the restorative agreements to ensure completion. While the restorative practices varied, the goals were consistent—to offer a process in which the parties could collectively identify ways to address harm and prevent its recurrence, with the needs of the survivor at the center of the process and outcomes. Table 1.1 summarizes the diverse approaches used by early adopters as they implemented RJIAs for CSM on their respective campuses.

While each of these RJIAs developed separately, there were themes that emerged, and we offer five guideposts to consider when developing RJ on your own campus. These guideposts, explored in more detail below, included the following: (1) Understanding CSM and sexual violence more broadly, (2) Understanding RJ philosophy and practices, (3) Listening and responding to campus community needs, (4) Understanding and navigating national and local context, and (5) Reimagining campus response to CSM.

Guidepost 1: Understanding CSM and Sexual Violence More Broadly

In their groundbreaking research project and book *Sexual Citizens: Sex, Power, and Assault on Campus*, Hirsch and Kahn (2020) highlighted that most research and writing on campus sexual assault focuses on addressing toxic masculinity and the adjudication of cases, while their research examined the "social drivers of assault" (p. xi). This includes culture, relationships, friendships, and communication surrounding incidents between two people.

TABLE 1.1

Restorative Justice Informed Approaches by Early Adopters

Who (RJ facilitators for CSM cases)	• Designated restorative facilitator • Student conduct officers • Ombudspeople • Title IX coordinators • Faculty/staff volunteers • External consultants • Senior student affairs professionals
What (RJIA practices)	• RJ circles • RJ dialogues • RJ conferences • RJ shuttle agreements • RJIA, including aspects of mediation, dispute resolution, and conflict resolution approaches
When (pathways to RJ for CSM)	• Complainant requests process and Title IX coordinator approves • At one institution, the ombudsperson offered an informal restorative dialogue process, outside the formal reporting or Title IX process. (We note that this research was conducted before the 2020 Title IX regulations, which required schools to have a formal complaint before engaging in "informal resolutions.")
Where	• In person • Via Zoom • Shuttle (never any visual or verbal communication between the parties) • Some combination of all of the above
How (restorative flow)	• Intake with each party • Preparation with each party • Voluntary restorative engagement • Finalizing restorative agreement (if an agreement is reached) • Title IX coordinator approves agreement (or makes suggested edits for review by the parties) • Follow-up on the agreement

Note. RJ = restorative justice; CSM = campus sexual misconduct; RJIA = restorative justice–informed approaches.

They encouraged a public health approach to incidents that "expands the focus from the individual and how they interact to systems (Hirsch and Kahn, p. xi)." This approach not only includes meaningful individual interventions but also includes a specific focus on understanding and changing context and culture to prevent sexual assault. A restorative approach to addressing campus sexual assault creates the space for context and culture to come to the surface to be addressed. Participants in our study (McMahon et al., 2022) emphasized the importance of culture and context, sharing that most assaults happen between people who knew each other or at least are in the same social circles. This fact is also a factor that explains why there are so few formal reports to the Title IX coordinator. The American Association of Universities' 2019 Campus Climate study (Cantor et al., 2020) on CSM asked students why they chose not to report, and among the most common reasons were "I thought I could handle it myself," "It wasn't serious enough," and "I didn't want to get the person in trouble" (Cantor et al., 2020). These reasons do not negate their distress, but they do deter someone from seeking assistance. Indeed, Hirch and Kahn (2020) explained, "What happened when people actually did have contact with authorities—security, police, or the central office responsible for investigating and evaluating cases? Sadly, the answer was: not much that was good for the person who reported" (p. 214). They elaborated:

> The person who reported their experiences of being assaulted is likely to feel like they're being doubted. They have to go over details again and again. . . . The process drags on. Our legal system uses what scholars call an adversarial process. This is not an accident; it was designed so that the parties involved argue before a neutral evaluator, each seeking to advance their own interest. There is little about the process that pushes both parties toward a shared understanding. Instead, people are forced to advocate. It is contentious by design. And when the stakes include getting expelled, or being suspended, and then returning to face the label of 'rapist" or "predator". . . (or, for the person filing the complaint, being called a "psycho" or "liar"), the process becomes even more adversarial. (p. 215)

Participants in our study echoed the critical importance of understanding the dynamics of campus sexual violence before undertaking any response, especially one deemed trauma informed and/or restorative. This means dispensing with an oversimplified view of the victim–survivor and instead honoring the impact of harm and the need for a resolution that offers justice as defined by that survivor (Herman, 2015). RJ facilitators must also take seriously the complex interplay among CSM, power, marginalized identities, and complex social relations among college students when designing a restorative process in the aftermath of sexualized harm (Hirsch & Khan, 2020).

Case Study

When I (Kaaren) served as a Title IX coordinator there were several cases where I was able to use what our policy called *remedies-based solution*, and one case, in particular, illustrates the importance of understanding context. In this case, a young woman, Kate (not her real name) experienced unwanted touching and kissing while dancing with a young man, Calvin (not his real name). They knew each other and had many mutual friends. She came to see me because she wasn't sure what to do. I asked her what she was hoping for, and she said "I just want to know what he was thinking."

Through a shuttle conversation (where I spoke individually with each party and relayed information back and forth), it became clear that Kate was actually only at the party because of pressure from their friends; she had also reluctantly agreed to dance with Calvin because she didn't want to disappoint him or their friends. Calvin interpreted her dancing with him as a sign that she liked him; he also noticed she was uncomfortable but thought that was because of the crowded dance floor. Through their shuttle conversation, they began to understand where things went wrong—he mistook her discomfort as not wanting to be in the middle of the crowded dance floor, while she was actually uncomfortable with his continual touching and kissing. To alleviate what he thought was her discomfort on the dance floor, he led her to an equally dark, but uncrowded, hallway. She became more uncomfortable and fearful and eventually just pulled away and left. In our conversations, we were able to unpack the assumptions, mistakes, and miscues, but we also talked about the context—the party space. Each of them described a scene where the music was so loud the two of them couldn't actually hear each other, and so dark they couldn't actually see each other. Consent was hard to establish in a space like that. In this case, repair not only included individual accountability and actions, but requests to the party hosts to create a party space that allowed for easier communication between partygoers. While this case did not end with a formal agreement (this was before our policy made the space for one), it does illustrate the importance of context in understanding the incident and in how to approach repair.

Looking back, I wish I had also created a space to discuss each student's "sexual project," as Hirsch and Kahn (2020) described as "the reasons why anyone might seek a particular sexual interaction or experience" (p. xiv). They explained that these reasons can range from pleasure, to wanting to fit in, to creating a relationship, exploration of identity, or "proving" an identity (Hirsch & Kahn, 2020). With this framing the students may have been able to better understand what transpired that night, in the context of their friends, not wanting to disappoint people, and trying to figure out their own desires and how to communicate them.

Hirsch and Kahn (2020) argued that most young people are wildly unprepared to communicate in their sexual encounters (or in their sexual projects, as they described):

> The young people in whose world we immersed were frequently figuring out their sexual projects through trial and error, to no small degree because no one had spent much time talking to them about what a sexual project might be. . . . Hungry for guidance, young people gleaned lessons from elsewhere: from their peers who are similarly in the dark, or from pornography. (pp. xv–xvi)

Restorative interventions can make space for communication about the impact of culture and context, which can help guide students to meaningful reflection on their own sexual project.

Guidepost 2: Understanding RJ Philosophy and Practices

RJ can be defined as an inclusive, collaborative response to harm, crime, or wrongdoing. Originating in indigenous communities, RJ is a philosophy rooted in the notion that "I am because we are" (Davis, 2019, p. 17). Within this paradigm, relationships form the basis of decision making rather than a predetermined rule book. As Zehr (2015) explained, RJ is focused on addressing harm to people and relationships. The invitation to build and repair relationships is voluntary, respects needs for safety, and creates a container in which taking responsibility for causing harm becomes not only possible but meaningful. The processes associated with RJ philosophy invite individuals most connected to an incident to work together to identify harm, establish ways to repair it, and build trust to ensure that it doesn't happen again. These meaning-making processes are contextual and relevant to the realities, needs, and concerns of the parties involved.

In our experience, this grounding in the repair aspect of RJ is often what resonates most with Title IX practitioners. Traditional investigative and adversarial resolution options are designed to identify whether or not an incident violated a school's policy, and the tools for redress often do not include repair to the harm done to people and relationships. While administrators often want these processes to do just that, they are left with processes that, by and large, don't meet the needs of the parties seeking their assistance, nor do they meaningfully contribute to healing for survivors or behavior change for respondents (Williamsen, 2017). The impact of this adversarial process can be devastating (Hirsch & Kahn, 2020; Williamsen, 2017). Rather than turning away from hurtful institutional responses to CSM, the restorative practitioners in our study turned toward the harm at all levels of their institutions to find pathways forward that best served the needs of their students.

For example, a seasoned campus-based restorative practitioner, explained, "It [RJ for CSM] originally started out of an interest in serving students of diverse and multiple identities, recognizing a one size fits all approach doesn't work." While they initially did not offer RJ for sexual misconduct, she explained that after the institution updated its policies in accordance with new Title IX guidance, students immediately began to request restorative options for CSM cases. This is understandable, as restorative approaches to harm shift the paradigm of crime/punishment to one of acknowledging impact and repairing harm. While RJ processes are multipartial (the facilitator attends to all participants' needs and respects the diverse positionalities of participants), the starting point for a process are the harms and needs experienced by the survivor. Giving voice and choice to the harmed party through the RJ process offers an opportunity for that person to regain a sense of personal agency and power.

As noted in the "Overview of Research: Description of Practices/ Approach" section of this chapter, many of the early adopters of RJ for CSM used a variety of restorative practices that we refer to as *RJIAs*—processes informed by RJ and also beyond the scope of RJ. For example, one early adopter described educational sanctions that their office sometimes assigned to responsible parties. While these activities may have been very helpful in that student's learning, they were not necessarily a result of an agreement made in a restorative process between the harmed party and the responsible party. So, while the education modules were intended to serve a restorative purpose, they were not the result of an RJ circle or a conference agreement process led by the identified needs of the harmed party.

One of the hardest parts of using RJ as a philosophy and set of practices in response to CSM may be that it requires us as administrators to be open to the possibility that harmed parties (often students) may request RJ or other restorative practices even in situations that we ourselves would prefer to avoid and/or only use a traditional adjudication model. For example, one study participant described institutional limitations on the availability of RJ for sexual assault within the context of intimate relationships on their campus. This framing of RJ as unavailable for complex CSM cases, not as a result of the harmed parties' desires but as a result of administrators' fears about the process, takes us back to Guidepost 1. It is critical that RJ processes are led by persons with significant understanding of CSM and of RJ to ensure that any evaluation of readiness for an RJ process is done by persons well informed about the potential for abuse and also the possibilities of repair within the context of these cases. In chapter 8, Landrum explores working restoratively with complainants and respondents, including assessing readiness for an RJ process.

Guidepost 3: Listening and Responding to Campus Community Needs

RJ is not just a set of practices, but also a philosophy. This philosophy takes into account that harms create needs, and solutions come from those identified needs. As we discussed in the section on Guidepost 2, harms are resolved by addressing the needs of the harmed parties, including the ripple harms that affect members of the broader campus community, as well as by understanding the conditions that informed the actions of the responsible party. This process requires facilitators to lead with deep listening, without defensiveness; it also requires listening for community harms, needs, and concerns. One of the early adopters we interviewed in our study described the ways in which she listened to her campus community and then, with them, created a restorative option for responding to incidents of CSM. Essentially, she used RJ principles, such as voluntariness, equity, and multi-partiality, to create a restorative campus process for addressing CSM.

Listening to and addressing concerns is an important step in building community support and buy-in for RJIAs. One practitioner reflected on the importance of emphasizing RJIAs as adding another option, rather than replacing the existing investigative resolution process:

> For people who maybe are having a tough time getting institutional buy-in or even talking with parents or support people or attorneys . . . reminding everyone that by including an alternative process or restorative justice, you're adding more options. You're not taking them away . . . just because this is an option doesn't mean that all of our cases are going through that or investigation is now off the table. No, we're just saying, you know, for those that feel, an investigation is not the right form of addressing the behavior, here's another option that might be right for you.

Another early adopter described how she listened to her students' concerns about adopting RJIAs for CSM, recalling a time when she presented to a student organization:

> I went to this student organization and somebody was like "This is easy. This is meaningless. RJ is the easy way out." And I said to them, "OK, let's think about the things that have been hardest for you in your student experience or in your life. The hardest thing you ever had to do, like to

volunteer, check out some community service hours, or write a paper, or that kind of thing, or go to a meeting? And they were like, "No, no, no, no." And I said "OK. What are the harder things?" And then they started to come up with these human pieces, like grief, or forgiveness, or confronting a fear. And all of those things happen in an RJ circle. So the emotional power, the emotional labor that's required of sitting face to face with somebody who you hurt or who harmed you. It's absolutely not an easy way out, and justice can be fulfilled through restorative justice. . . . having not participated, they didn't know that anything, even in theory suspension or expulsion could come from an RJ circle; anything is on the table. It's not just, you have the conversation and life goes on. There's a process. There's a process and then an outcome, and then life goes on.

This guidepost is a gentle reminder to use the restorative process to build RJIAs on your campus; listen for needs from your community and introduce a new way of communicating and responding. When we are able to model a restorative approach, we are creating the conditions for campus community members to expand their imaginations about what is possible for healing individuals, groups, and institutions.

Guidepost 4: Understanding and Navigating National and Local Context

Among early adopters, the successful implementation of restorative justice happened when practitioners understood their context, both locally and nationally, and knew how to successfully navigate both. U.S. institutions of higher education are called to grapple with the swinging pendulum of federal policy with regard to CSM. Early adopters of RJIAs in our study recognized the importance of policy constraints while at the same time found ways to move beyond compliance to center the needs of the parties with restorative options.

The practitioners in our study were mindful of the ever-changing federal regulations related to responding to campus sexual misconduct; they were also aware of a growing movement for allowing RJ responses to sexual misconduct. This growing movement started to show up in national conversations and publications. In 2017, the American Bar Association's Criminal Justice Section's Task Force on College Due Process Rights and Victim Protections released a recommendations document and encouraged schools to consider alternatives: "Where appropriate, the Task Force encourages schools to consider non-mediation alternatives to resolving complaints that are research or evidence-based, such as Restorative Justice processes" (p. 3). The 2018 National Academics of Sciences, Engineering, and Medicine Report on the Sexual Harassment of Women also mentioned restorative options and recommended that funders support research into the efficacy of restorative options. In early 2020, the National Association of Student Personnel Administrators released a research brief for campus administrators on the use of RJ for CSM, providing detailed recommendations on implementation (Karp & Williamsen, 2020).

While the national conversations were steadily growing, individual practitioners were doing their best to offer meaningful alternatives on their campuses, responding to individual requests for something different. These "champions," as McMahon et al. (2022) referred to them, were able to understand their own specific campus context and harness resources to begin to offer RJ-informed options.

While practitioners in our study mentioned being at times constrained by a lack of support from senior administration, or a lack of skilled facilitators, these champions were able to move to implementation in spite of these challenges. Each of these champions understood their local context— identifying opportunities, resources, and colleagues who could assist—and found or nurtured supporters in key positions on campus. One practitioner intentionally reached out to the director of the campus advocacy and prevention office to get their support, knowing that support from that leader would be crucial for success on campus. Another practitioner collaborated with colleagues in other offices to bring an RJ facilitator training to campus; this allowed her to get more people on campus introduced to the practices and philosophy while identifying individuals who might be able to assist with cofacilitating restorative processes.

Another practitioner, a Title IX coordinator, was frustrated that while many reports of sexual misconduct were made to her office, very few chose to move forward with their traditional investigative resolution process. She had heard about alternative processes and reached into her community to explore options that might work for their campus. She spent a summer working with students (including survivors who had chosen NOT to move forward) to design a process they would have used. By the fall, she had written this new process into policy, and students began to request it. She knew her local context and had built relationships along the way that helped her success:

> So I had a lot of people that had a lot of faith in this, from our general counsel, to our campus police, to our local prosecutor's office. I know sometimes people talk about hiccups or roadblocks. I didn't have that. . . . [I] created the structure for us to utilize that was vetted by all the appropriate people, had buy-in and approval from all the appropriate people, including

students. And I utilized students . . . both advocates as well as students that had been in that situation where they told me they didn't want to move forward but wanted something else. So I asked them if they would feel comfortable coming in and talking to me about this new process. From those conversations, I made tweaks along the way until we were comfortable with it. And then that's what we wrote into policy.

In this example, the practitioner not only understood her context but also worked with her community to design an RJ-informed process that spoke directly to their needs and requests.

Guidepost 5: Reimagining Campus Responses to CSM

Perhaps the most important guidepost is the need to collectively reimagine both prevention and response to CSM in ways that honor students' experiences, acknowledge interpersonal and institutional power differentials, and involve flexible restorative processes that are designed with and for the needs of the parties in each RJ process. This means including persons responsible for harm as well as those impacted in the development of a restorative process.

A restorative approach to incidents of CSM starts at intake and impacts our structures. In our study, successful early adopters brought key stakeholders together to discuss and plan how they would respond to reports of CSM, including how they would treat the harmed party. One early adopter described her RJIA implementation efforts this way:

Yeah, for us that was successful on the back end because we got all the buy-in on the front end. So it worked really well for us. I had recently gotten information from our climate survey, so I was able to use that data in supporting conversations with upper level administration. My colleagues in advocacy and counseling understood the need for it because they were getting the same questions. Police understood a need for something as well. So I kind of utilized everyone's different perspective in the way that they would interact with victims, or we call them report letters, through our process, to make sure that we were building something that worked well for everybody.

This RJIA implementer brought in all of the people and offices, including representatives from the criminal–legal system, to discuss what a restorative response to sexual harm would look like. She leveraged relationships and data to build a restorative response system, one that included restorative case management.

A restorative approach to case management begins with harms and needs first. Because harmed parties are often concerned about different things (e.g., Why me? Who else knows about this? How will this process impact the responsible party? Am I safe? Will my friends believe me?) the strategies used to address the harm, such as educational training, flow from the identification of harms and needs first.

While RJ and RJIA are often described as approaches to ameliorate harm, RJ practices, such as community-building circles, can also be used to build relationships among students, faculty, and staff. The following case study illustrates this use.

Case Study on Prevention

When I (Sheila) was an administrator at a university, I was on a student affairs behavioral response team that routinely received reports of high numbers of alcohol-related hospital transports during the first week of school. These situations tended to involve first-year students who wanted to belong, so they drank at parties with orientation leaders and other upper class students and ended their evenings with alcohol poisoning.

I gathered the orientation leaders (OLs) and resident advisors (RAs) during their summer training. Instead of using a didactic approach, I gathered the students in circles (a team of students from my office had received previous training to prepare them to function as small-group facilitators). Each small group was invited to use a circle process to convene about their experiences as OLs/RAs, connect about what they had experienced themselves as incoming students new to the university, share concerns about how peer pressure and heavy alcohol consumption might adversely impact the incoming students after the impending orientation period, and collaborate on strategies to welcome first-year students in ways that honored their well-being and kept them safe. It was the first year in colleagues' memories that we had so few students transported to the hospital for alcohol misuse. Several OLs and RAs later reported to the student leaders from my office that the circles had given them time to reflect on how they wanted to welcome new students and the kinds of experiences they wanted to share (notably, these experiences did *not* include a trip to the hospital emergency room).

Implementing RJ/RJIAs in response to CSM is not a one-time event nor a static policy in the student handbook. Rather, it is an invitation for key campus stakeholders to engage in an ongoing journey of reading the guideposts together; learning and unlearning with impacted parties and the campus community; and building a restorative campus that can hold space for care, repair, accountability, and support.

Conclusion

We embarked on this research with early adopters to learn how RJ was being used for cases of CSM and to glean lessons from the administrators who first implemented these processes. Being an early adopter comes with risks; some of our participants implemented RJ processes before the 2020 regulations that explicitly allowed it, and others were willing to create something untested to attempt to better meet the needs of their community. These early adopters tended to be leaders (champions), and they were motivated to add a process because of their dissatisfaction with their current offerings and from direct requests from students. Through the insights from these early adopters and from our own professional experience, we offer these guideposts as important points to consider when considering or building an RJ-based approach to CSM.

References

American Bar Association, Criminal Justice Section, Task Force on College Due Process Rights and Victim Protections. (2017, June). *Recommendations for colleges and universities in resolving allegations of campus sexual misconduct.* https://www.americanbar.org/content/dam/aba/publications/criminaljustice/due_process_tf_recommendations.pdf

Cantor, D., Fisher, B., Chibnall, S., Harps, S., Townsend, R., Thomas, G., Lee, H., Kranz, V., Herbison, R., & Madden, K. (2020). *Report on the AAU climate survey on sexual assault and sexual misconduct.* Association of American Universities.

Davis, F. E. (2019). *The little book of race and restorative justice: Black lives, healing, and US social transformation.* Simon & Schuster.

Herman, J. L. (2015). *Trauma and recovery: The aftermath of violence—From domestic abuse to political terror.* Hachette.

Hirsch, J. S., & Khan, S. (2020). *Sexual citizens: Sex, power, and assault on campus.* W. W. Norton.

Karp, D., & Williamsen, K. M. (2020). *Five things student affairs administrators should know about restorative justice and campus sexual harm* [Issue brief]. National Association of Student Personnel Administrators.

McMahon, S. M., Williamsen, K. M., Mitchell, H. B., & Kleven, A. (2022). Initial reports from early adopters of restorative justice for reported cases of campus sexual misconduct: A qualitative study. *Violence Against Women* [Advance online publication]. https://doi.org/10.1177/10778012221108419

National Academies of Sciences, Engineering, and Medicine. (2018). *Sexual harassment of women: Climate, culture, and consequences in academic sciences, engineering, and medicine.* National Academies Press. https://doi.org/10.17226/24994.

Williamsen, K. M. (2017). *"The exact opposite of what they need": Administrator reflections on sexual misconduct, the limitations of the student conduct response, and the possibilities of restorative justice* [Doctoral dissertation]. University of Minnesota.

Zehr, H. (2015). *The little book of restorative justice: Revised and updated.* Skyhorse.

2

BUILDING RESTORATIVE PRINCIPLES INTO CAMPUS POLICIES

Chelsea Jacoby and Erik S. Wessel

Institutional policies set expectations across campus regarding behavior; align operations; and convey roles, responsibilities, and established procedures. Well-crafted policies can help to not only maintain compliance but also communicate and uphold institutional values, practices, and philosophies. However, for policy to be effective, it must be tailored to adequately reach its appropriate audience. As such, institutional offices/departments—especially those responsible for implementing sexual misconduct policy—must work to devise language that is clear, easily understood, and manageable. Furthermore, it is important to disseminate just the right amount of information to those who are/will be directly impacted by the content. At the end of the day, if campus community members and other key stakeholders understand a policy, they are more likely to follow it and help to uphold it.

This chapter will lay the foundational building blocks for weaving restorative justice (RJ) principles and practices into campus sexual misconduct policies. Overall, this chapter will provide an overview of the life cycle of policy development, including recommendations regarding action steps to take when drafting and ultimately implementing the policy. This chapter will offer beneficial policy language as well as guiding principles and recommendations to consider for generating buy-in among stakeholders. But first, let's examine the pressing need to incorporate informal resolution options into institutional policy, particularly those grounded in RJ practices, at this current juncture.

Federal Guidance, Regulation, and Restorative Policy Imperatives

Colleges and universities, collectively referred to as *institutions of higher education* (IHEs), serve as excellent examples of microcosms of the broader society. IHEs often reflect many of the same social structures, culturally based expectations of social conduct, and patterns of interaction that we see in the larger society (Sweet, 2001). Deliberation on the topic of sexual violence and discrimination has commenced for almost 50 years yet continues to be a perpetual and growing concern nationwide (Hill & Kearl, 2011; Mansell et al., 2017). Similar to the broader context of society, these concerns have been identified as some of the most pervasive issues impacting IHEs (Edwards et al., 2015; Fedina et al., 2018; Fisher, 2000; Kilpatrick et al., 2007; Krebs et al., 2007). First, we must begin by conceptualizing the policy-making process at the federal level before we can turn to a deeper dive of policymaking at an institutional level.

Title IX of the Education Amendments of 1972 (Pub. L. 93-218; hereafter *Title IX*) states that "No person in the United States shall, on the basis of sex, be excluded from participation in, be denied the benefits of, or be subjected to discrimination under any education program or activity receiving Federal financial assistance," (para. 2). Under Title IX, all IHEs that receive federal funds are required to implement compliance policies and procedures to prevent, mitigate, and resolve issues involving and resulting from discrimination, including sexual violence. In 1972, Title IX was enacted as a way for the federal government to overtly recognize and prohibit discrimination on the basis of sex in public institutions that receive federal funding. In the years following the 1972 legislation, Congress entrusted the Department of Education's (DOE's) Office for Civil Rights (OCR), formally known as *Health, Education, and Welfare*, with enforcing Title IX regulations in institutions that receive federal funds. As stated in the U.S. Federal Register (U.S. Department of Education, 2018), "In the four decades following its enactment, no Title IX regulations have been promulgated to address sexual harassment as a form of sex discrimination; instead, the DOE has addressed this subject through a series of guidance documents" (para. 26) disseminated by the OCR (Nondiscrimination on the Basis of Sex in Education Programs or Activities Receiving Federal Financial Assistance, 2018). This held true until 2020, when the DOE initiated a rule-making process ultimately resulting in the current regulations around Title IX.

Prior to 2020, the OCR regularly published "Dear Colleague" letters (DCLs) as a means of ensuring that institutions and the general public understand how the decisions, such as those around Title IX, apply to all institutions of learning, including IHEs (Hepler, 2013; U.S. Department of Education, n.d.). These documents were essentially guidelines for institutions to follow, rather than a prescribed formula, to offer insight around how IHEs can adjust their own policies and practices to enhance civil rights protections and uphold their legal obligations (U.S. Department of Education, n.d.). Throughout the guidance, the OCR emphasized that, in cases involving sexual harassment, institutions must offer resolution options that are prompt and equitable. Under the Obama Administration, there were targeted efforts that demonstrated a broad, comprehensive response to strengthen Title IX guidance and reduce violence against women, one in particular being the issuance of the OCR's pivotal 2011 Dear colleague Letter (DCL; U.S. Department of Education, 2011). This particular DCL placed IHEs on notice and demanded they do better to resolve students' reports of sexual assault and protect their rights throughout the process. As a result, students, perhaps now feeling more empowered, began filing more complaints through OCRs against their institutions that allegedly mishandled their Title IX cases. In addition, dozens of accused and/or disciplined students sued their IHEs, claiming that their own rights had been violated (Saul & Taylor, 2017). Additional guidance had also been issued in a U.S. Department of Education (2014) DCL and Q&A that offered further detail on how to maintain federal compliance.

Overall, some perceived the guidance within the DCLs, especially the 2011 release, to be a step in the right direction and felt that it provided a means to hold IHEs accountable for mishandling Title IX cases while providing the motivation and support that IHEs needed to implement prompt and impartial processes to resolve incidents of sexual violence. On the other hand, others felt that the Obama-era guidance lacked an appropriate level of due process and inequitably favored victims/survivors, which ultimately compromised the rights of the accused. Although the DCLs aimed to offer recommendations, many IHEs interpreted them as the letter of the law out of fear that the DOE may rescind federal funding for noncompliance. This guidance-based structure remained the underpinnings of institutional Title IX policymaking until September 7, 2017, when Trump Administration Secretary of Education, Betsy DeVos, issued interim guidance that withdrew the guidance in the 2011 and 2014 DCLs and signaled a dramatic shift in policy expectations and federal enforcement of regulations governing campus sexual assault (Camera, 2017). Over a year after the guidance was rescinded, the DOE published a draft of their proposed Title IX regulations in the Federal Register, which officially commenced the federal rule-making process, including a comment/review period and compilation of finalized changes, and it officially published the Final Title IX Rule (regulation) on May 6, 2020.

What we can see here is that over the past several years the guidelines/mandates surrounding sexual harassment/violence have been in a perpetual state of flux. This is further demonstrated through another set of proposed regulations released under the Biden Administration on June 23, 2022 (U.S. Department of Education, 2022a), and a new comment period was initiated. Living in this constant state of change makes it increasingly more challenging for institutions to understand, implement, and meet their obligations to maintain compliance. Objectively, this regulatory environment is not only inefficient but ultimately creates confusion, distrust, and hesitancy among Title IX professionals around what constitutes best practices (since the regulations seem to change before best practices can even be established). For students, the confusion, distrust, and hesitancy are often grounded in the perceived (and oftentimes very real) complexity and insecurity around reporting their experience. Consideration of the student experience is paramount, and the current state of federal regulations has given further credence to considering a range of resolution options to recognize the substantial variability of interests and unique needs that often go unmet through formal investigative Title IX procedures and the adversarial hearings that follow. The formal grievance process, especially under § 106.45 of the Final Rule, is incredibly prescriptive—its objective is to determine whether or not institutional policy had been violated. This process almost entirely ignores what harms may have been caused/experienced and what it may take to meet real expressed needs and achieve repair to the extent possible. For those in search of the latter, they may be left with limited options, if any at all, if their institution's policy offers only a singular pathway for resolution. Ultimately, to not offer some element of procedural choice may prove to be particularly problematic, especially given the trends on a national and societal level to both ensure and redefine accountability centered on the needs of those most directly harmed.

Over the past several years we've seen a rise of activism across the United States. Whether it be movements such as #MeToo, Black Lives Matter, Stop AAPI Hate, or various others, they all have their unique focus, but all share the common goal of dismantling oppressive systems and cultural practices. These movements are in search of not just change, but justice. A notion that many of these movements have helped amplify is that justice often extends far beyond what we'd traditionally define as "punishment" and can embody restoration and healing. In an article about why RJ may be critical to explore at this time, Virden (2022) eloquently summarized this point:

> One of the most commonly used adages in equity and justice spaces is intent vs. impact. It requires a focus on the impact of actions as opposed to the intent behind them. This is often an extremely difficult shift for people to make, especially people with privileged identities. Because restoration is not interested in finding out "who dunnit?" and punishing them, and because restoration doesn't believe in "canceling" anybody, restoration diffuses much of the defensiveness that comes with conversations around race [and arguably sex, gender, and other marginalized identities] and allows us to center impact. (para. 16)

Colleges/universities are not immune to the social concerns, external pressures, and cultural shifts seen throughout society. However, the directionality of cultural "signposts" should be interpreted as moving toward a need-centric positionality where concurrent educational and compliance mandates are not seen as mutually exclusive. At the end of the day, the students we serve may not be experts in federally compliant policy, but their insight is critically instructive as we endeavor to provide procedural resources that prevent, protect, and remedy the effects of sexual and gender-based discrimination within our communities. Apparent to all is the fundamental reality that traditional investigative approaches and adversarial hearing processes aren't going to meet the multiplicity of needs represented in our communities. Restorative approaches, therefore, represent a necessary evolution to campus sexual and gender-based misconduct resources in higher education.

Procedural "North Star": Due Process, Equity, and Education

In the preceding we have endeavored to make the case that the evolutionary directionality of federal regulations has been, perhaps unintentionally, pointing us toward a restorative orientation to procedural diversification. Before we turn our attention to the specifics of this evolution, it is important that we find our common center: that is—in our view—fundamentally fair and equitable due process and keen attention to our collective educational mandate. As practitioners in this work, it is incumbent upon all of us to continually orient ourselves to the principles that guide us. We are right to ask, "What is our North Star"? In the space of sexual and gender-based misconduct on campus, our response would rightly be fundamental fairness in policy and practice that is marked by equitable process by design. This, of course, is emblematic of the ideal, but in practice it is more complex.

For instance, in our efforts to achieve fairness, it is observed that many of our policies and procedures seem to prioritize equality. Past federal guidance in this space and the regulation that followed has certainly prioritized affording equal rights. At a glance, such an approach may seem reasonable and necessary; however, what effect, if any, does it have on achieving fundamental fairness and equity? In other words, what effect do we have on meeting actual needs, which are often not the same between those involved? To put it succinctly, the problem lies in the observation that sameness (equality) in a campus community response risks ignoring the deep complexity of experienced needs—which require movement toward equity. *Equality* and *equity*, often erroneously used interchangeably, are actually quite different as equity requires a full examination of needs, the return of agency to those most directly harmed, and community responses that are adaptable to achieve the full measure of due process while centering opportunities for repair of harm to the extent possible. It is in this prioritization of need that we find a fundamental divergence between justice rooted in procedural fairness and justice rooted in repair.

How, then, shall we conceptualize the concepts of due process and equity in this context? It is here suggested that they are most appropriately viewed as equal parts to a complete circle. Under Title IX, the field of higher education has fixated on adherence to equal access to due process as the gold standard for fundamental fairness. However, as we have largely uniformly observed, outcomes achieved more often than not do not "protect every student's right to equal access to educational opportunities"—the ultimate goal of Title IX as described by U.S. Secretary of Education Miguel Cardona (2021, para. 1). At least, the lived experience of the students involved do not often lend to a perception of preserved educational opportunity. The problem here is that so much of work in Title IX is fully focused on strict adherence to compliance. Our policies and procedures are finely tuned to make every attempt at achieving effective compliance. However, have we completed the circle by identifying whether or not our policy and procedure is effective at meeting individual and community needs? And ultimately capable at achieving any true form of "justice"? Truly, this is a fundamental question for each of us to ponder as practitioners who care deeply about the student and the communities we serve.

Community Needs Assessment

To start completing this circle, we must deeply understand the unique needs of our campus community. Before we can begin proposing solutions and resolution options for our campus to repair harm or identifying whether our policies and procedures are effective at meeting our campus' needs, we first and foremost have to identify community needs. And to do that, a helpful place to start is with a needs assessment.

The U.S. Department of Education (2016) seemed to concur with this recommendation in their five-step needs assessment cycle. These five steps include:

1. Identify local needs
2. Select relevant evidence-based interventions
3. Plan for implementation
4. Implement
5. Examine and reflect

Following the general pattern previously described, a needs assessment, when done effectively, can provide "process that helps local stakeholders and system leaders understand how the pieces of a complex educational system interact, uncovering strengths and challenges that will inform growth and improvement" (Cuiccio & Husby-Slater, 2018, p. 24). In this case, conducting a needs assessment could help your institution gauge the perceptions among your campus stakeholders on whether your current policies/procedures are working well, what may need improvement, and interest in/openness to utilizing informal resolution options to address/repair harm caused by sexual violence. To start, it's important to conceptualize the guiding questions that the needs assessment should address and determine whose voices/opinions need to be included—both in terms of who your audience will be and who is best suited to assist with the implementation/analysis of the assessment—and then how to best capture the voices of your designated audience.

As we think about continual forward progress toward equity through community needs-oriented policy and practice, it stands to reason that the voices of our communities—although perhaps lacking in technical regulatory knowledge—hold a wealth of knowledge regarding the ways in which your community might be an integral part of the solution to the core issues. For instance, as you listen to the voices of your campus community, they might express that a singular pathway for resolution—although perhaps federally compliant—does not account for community members who have experienced harm but for whom a hearing with adversarial cross-examination does not meet their needs or interests. They may also express strengths and opportunities for improvement within your established policies and procedures.

To capture such critical perspectives from your campus, perhaps you may find it beneficial to disseminate a climate survey across campus that targets these issues, or maybe through conducting focus groups, or maybe even both. When determining what approach to take, you should be conscientious about what data-gathering methods your campus may respond to best that will help generate high-quality data. It's important to have a comprehensive understanding of your campus' unique needs and what resolution options would meet those needs, but what is arguably just as important, if not more, is knowing and recognizing whether your campus embodies enough trust in your institution to carry out those policies, practices, and resolution options effectively without causing them additional harm. These factors related to what's commonly referred to as potential *institutional betrayal* (Stader & Williams-Cunningham, 2017) would also be important to gather, measure, and analyze throughout this need assessment process.

Research shows that when students trusted their university support system (e.g., campus police, administrators) they were more likely to report concerns about violence (Sulkowski, 2011). This is also important to note because earning this level of trust from campus community members can be challenging, particularly at a time in society where our mainstream media are full of examples of institutional wrongdoing, specifically, cases involving of campus sexual assault. Numerous high-profile cases have seen the spotlight over the past few years, and cases such as these have drawn attention to instances where IHEs' personnel and/or policies/procedures may have discouraged reporting of violations, or made reporting unnecessarily difficult, blamed the victim for their experience, and failed to implement appropriate sanctions to hold the accused accountable (Stader & Williams-Cunningham, 2017). These pitfalls are not unique to just these institutions. These types of cases have helped establish a narrative about campus sexual violence as a whole and the role IHEs play in that. When an IHE fails to appropriately respond to reports of sexual violence, it can lead to a silencing effect that discourages future reporting and can result in institutional betrayal. Because of the perceptions guiding so many of these conversations taking place nationally, and just how common they have become, it is possible that even if an individual's campus may not have been featured in the headlines, campus community members may still be hesitant to engage with their institution's process out of fear of betrayal. This fear may also be rationalized as research has found that the trauma experienced by students can be exacerbated by the institution's failure to respond, or inadequacy of responding, because they have an expectation of safety and trust from the institution (Smith & Freyd, 2013). Impacts of the presence of institutional trust, or lack thereof, could arguably have tremendous trickle-down effects, including whether parties would feel comfortable participating in resolution processes offered, even informal options.

It is important that members of the community feel comfortable reporting and are willing to do so. However, that may all be for naught if neither faculty/staff nor students effectively know how to report and can describe what happens following the report. To avoid inflicting any form of institutional betrayal, whether perceived or real, efforts must be placed in making information about the option and process of reporting and ensuring that what resolution options are available and what they entail are transparent, understandable, and readily accessible to all members of the campus community and beyond. This can be done by having an effectively written policy that outlines this information, but efforts need to extend beyond just that singular document. Institutions should consider ways to make this type of information publicly available, such as sharing it on their websites (e.g., the office of Title IX or a similarly situated office), during trainings for both faculty/staff and students, and reinforcing it throughout the year in a variety of ways, both in person (e.g., tabling events, marketing campaigns, Q&A sessions, open forums) and electronically via social media platforms.

For example, The College of New Jersey (TCNJ) hosts an expo-style event each year called THRIVE, which is a day-long event dedicated to promoting health and wellness strategies and resources to all members of the TCNJ campus community. The Office of Title IX & Sexual Misconduct was one of the many departments to host a table for the event and maximized that opportunity to review the available resources, supports, and resolution options through their office, and it placed specific emphasis on their Alternative Resolution (AR) process, which is nonpunitive in nature and is grounded in restorative practices. As campus community members approached the table, they were presented with an overview of the AR process and were then asked three questions. Community members were asked their level of awareness of the institution's AR process, whether they perceived it to be an acceptable method for addressing sexual misconduct, and whether they would consider using the process themselves and/or recommend it to others. This informal survey of the community suggested there was low awareness but a strongly positive perception of an alternative resolution process. These data, while anecdotal in nature, helps demonstrate the importance of adequately communicating these processes as viable options to your campus community.

At TCNJ, the AR process has been formally integrated into policy and has been available to address incidents of sexual misconduct since 2017, the resolution option is mentioned on various resources, website pages, and the office's social media account, yet an overwhelming majority of people who stopped by the table indicated that they'd never heard of it before.

This highlights the need for intentional and creative marketing strategies to successfully reach your pertinent stakeholders because you may end up dedicating a considerable amount of time to create these resolution options only for no one to end up utilizing them because they simply don't know about them.

Generating Buy-In

Because the fundamentals of informal resolution can be, initially, contrary to the dominant narratives on addressing sexual and gender-based misconduct, the vitality of a strong informal resolution program is dependent, in large part, on support from internal and external stakeholders. With the recognition that circumstances where harm occurs vary, and the expressed needs of those who have been harmed are also on a continuum, establishing partnerships with key campus stakeholders, including campus and local individual support and law enforcement resources, is a fundamental practice to build trust and reduce complications throughout the informal resolution process. Ideally, it is through these partnerships that interorganizational and interpersonal trust is developed.

To more fully understand the process of institutional trust-building through partnership, it is recommended to first survey the existing institutional partnership landscape and then move to identification of critical stakeholder partnerships which need to be built or strengthened. The Edward Ginsberg Center at the University of Michigan developed the partnership continuum depicted in Figure 2.1.

Figure 2.1. Toward a culture of partnership.

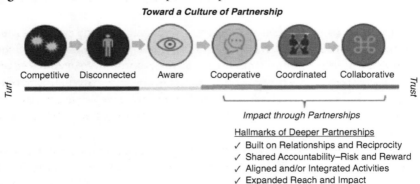

Toward a Culture of Partnership

Competitive   Disconnected   Aware   Cooperative   Coordinated   Collaborative

Turf ← → Trust

Impact through Partnerships

Hallmarks of Deeper Partnerships
✓ Built on Relationships and Reciprocity
✓ Shared Accountability–Risk and Reward
✓ Aligned and/or Integrated Activities
✓ Expanded Reach and Impact

Note. Developed by Mary Jo Callan and the Ginsberg Center at the University of Michigan.

In this model, created in the Department of Student Life at the University of Michigan, the definition of a partnership is paraphrased as mutual cooperation between stakeholders who agree to work in coordination to advance a mutually shared vision through reciprocity, accountability, a shared assumption of risk, and alignment/integration of work. Drawing upon this model as a guide, early efforts toward policy creation will benefit from identification of stakeholder groups into clear strategic partnership categories. Questions to ask might include the following:

- *Competitive*: Which stakeholder groups might represent competing initial interests? And how might we invite them into dialogue early in the process to build shared understanding.
- *Disconnected*: Which stakeholder groups may benefit from awareness and/ or provide important insight and support, even if not directly engaged in the process?
- *Aware*: Which stakeholder groups need to be aware of such efforts to ensure success?
- *Cooperative*: Which stakeholder groups need to be engaged in the distribution of work, even if peripheral to the process?
- *Coordination*: Which stakeholder groups need to have shared responsibility for the process and product, need to be engaged in regular systematic two-way communication, and have greater investment/distribution of shared work?
- *Collaboration*: Which stakeholder groups need to develop structurally connected efforts, frequent two-way communication, and have shared ownership of the policy and process?

Buy-In at the Community Level

Colleges and universities are complex organizations, and no institution is like the other. Each institutional culture and the people and perspectives that inhabit the organization are going to influence the strategy required to explore meaningful enhancement toward increasingly equitable and needs-centered policies and practices. That said, there are elements that cut across communities of higher education. For instance, colleges and universities generally have three main stakeholder groups—faculty, staff, and students. The engagement of each of these main stakeholder groups is essential to generating policy and procedural buy-in—and yet, an all-too-common institutional approach is to convene a working group of policy experts who are typically drawn from the administrative staff stakeholder group and not necessarily representative of the overall campus community. Now, for clarity, the critique here is not in the convening of expertise. With the ever-increasing complexity of regulatory requirements, harnessing community expertise will remain quite necessary. That said, if we have learned anything from this most recent societal moment it is that our communities have a propensity to distrust processes and outcomes where opportunities for engagement and representation are perceived to be limited. Given that, and again drawing upon the stakeholder partnership model, an important question to consider is: Where do you need to foster support for integrating processes/programs grounded in RJ into your policies? Is it student affairs administrators? Legal counsel? Campus safety? Student government? All of the above? At most institutions it will not be possible to include all voices at the community level. However, building coalitions of invested and trusted stakeholders across the community spectrum is imperative. If these stakeholders, who represent trusted messengers in their stakeholder subgroups, feel respected, heard, and engaged then that narrative of trust will begin to permeate more broadly and mitigate the potential for community mistrust.

Buy-In at the Administrative Level
Not all policy contributors or implementers are also policy decision-makers. In fact, many are not. Therefore, those most closely associated with the work often need to cultivate buy-in up the administrative hierarchy. Although each institution has its own hierarchical cultural norms, a few tactics drawn from the business and industry are recommended. In a 2015 article, the *Harvard Business Review* provided some helpful insight (Ashford & Detert, 2015):

Tailor your proposal: Know your decision-maker audience. Grafting your proposal onto their vision and values while making a compelling community needs-based business case will be important for decision-maker buy-in critical for successful implementation.

Frame the issue: Ensure that your approach (and proposal) clearly explains how it supports a critical strategic institutional goal.

Manage expectations: though we may be invested in establishing a full spectrum of restorative resolution pathways, such an approach may not be strategic in securing initial decision-maker investment. Building out from a modest initial investment after a pilot test and proof of concept is a common successful strategy.

Consider careful timing: Advancement of policy and procedure is often a long-term investment. Savvy practitioners seek clarity on institutional priorities and utilize existing compatible institutional efforts to position their proposal for success—even if that success is realized across years instead of weeks or months.

Involve others: Who are the influential thought leaders within the community that might join you in championing efforts toward policy and procedural change?

Adhere to institutional norms: What are the decision-making norms at your institution? Is your leadership data driven? Savvy practitioners and policy crafters know the conventions and norms that drive decisionmaking.

Adopt a solution orientation: You've already framed the issue (the what), now provide a solution (the how). Offer a measured, well-articulated, and stakeholder-/partnership-oriented approach to the issue.

Adapt to decisions: Sometimes after careful planning, efforts are met with a "no," or, more likely, a "not now." Knowing the difference and seeking further clarity is important when framing potential next steps. Taking the time to evaluate the proposal, reframe the moment, reflect on what is learned, and recommit to the effort is critical for long-term institutional buy-in efforts. Perhaps the timing wasn't quite right. Or, perhaps there are individuals with influence who need to be brought on to champion the efforts. Organizational decision making is rarely linear and therefore requires us to adapt.

Incorporating Informal Resolution Options Into Institutional Policy

Having walked the important road of institutional buy-in and decision-making, we turn to the artful task of crafting policy and procedural language that provides the foundational underpinnings for RJ processes and RJ-informed procedures. Policies need to provide just the right level of information to the individuals specifically affected by the content: not too much for it to be overly complex and overwhelming, but not too little that the room left open for interpretation can create unrealistic expectations and opportunities for institutional liability. This is particularly true when working to incorporate informal resolution processes into formalized policy given how ambiguous these processes can appear to be due to their individualized nature. Here we offer some generalized recommendations to work toward that "just right" position for policy and procedure:

- *Less is often more.* But make sure the "less" is clear and concise. Expect to go through multiple revisions, building upon stakeholder reflections, feedback, and guidance.
- *Use balanced language.* Embrace language that establishes definitive expectations but affords the opportunity for flexibility.

- *Maximize the voices of your relevant stakeholders.* They will be the ones expected to abide by and/or uphold this policy, so their insight and expertise is crucial.
- *Consider questions for restorative policy creation.* It may be helpful to consider specific questions initially proposed by Karp (2015) and adapted here to be more reflective of "policy" that integrates restorative practices rather than a RJ "program", including:
  - What kind of RJ process or processes resonate best with your campus culture or with the kinds of cases on which your program will focus? Conferencing, circles, shuttle negotiation?
  - In what ways can you infuse RJ principles into current disciplinary practices and procedures?
  - What opportunities or constraints currently exist in your policy (and/or code of conduct) for implementing an RJ process?
  - Where will the process/resolution option be housed and facilitated? Title IX and/or student conduct office(s)? Residential life? A distinct conflict resolution center/department?
  - Staffing:
    - Do you have the right staff to effectively implement an RJ process/resolution option?
    - Is your staffing model adequate to allow the process to be sustainable?
    - Who will coordinate the resolution process? Could the coordinating responsibilities be added to a current position?
    - Who will facilitate cases: staff, faculty, graduate students, undergraduate students?
    - Can you connect/collaborate with a local RJ program or other institutions? Are there possible partnerships with faculty or academic departments (higher education management, law, criminal justice, conflict analysis, peace studies, social work, etc.)?
  - Financial burden:
    - How much will implementation of the resolution process cost initially and to then facilitate each case thereafter?
    - What costs do you need to consider?
    - Do you have financial support?
    - How will the designated area cover the necessary costs?
  - What resources are currently available, and what may you need to obtain?

Necessary Elements/Guidelines for Restorative Process Participation

Through many iterations of guidance and regulation, the DOE has slowly built up a tolerance for alternative, restorative procedures that can reasonably and accurately be described as "needs-based remedies." Despite what we see as continued unnecessary and inaccurate conflation or RJ/practice with the concept and process of mediation, the department—in its most recent Q&A document in July 2021—reaffirmed schools *may* (but are not obligated to) offer "informal resolution process[es]" so long as they met certain conditions (U.S. Department of Education, 2021). The three conditions—footnoted in the Q&A—are

1. The provision of written notice to both parties disclosing information regarding the specific allegations, requirements for informal resolution, any consequences resulting from participation, and records which will be maintained or could be shared,
2. Voluntary written consent to participate obtained from both parties, and
3. Is not a matter involving allegations of harassment of a student by an employee of the institution. (34 CFR 106.45[b][9])

The DOE has herein outlined the floor, however, that may not represent the full measure of due diligence in fully considering the appropriate use of procedure outside of the traditional investigative adversarial adjudication process. Additional considerations are necessary. Here we offer a few practical questions to consider as policymakers and decision makers:

1. *Decision-making data:* In what ways, and through what mechanisms, do our policy and procedure allow for collection of sufficient data to make an informed decision on whether an informal process would be appropriate?
2. *Policy/procedure communication:* In what ways do our policy and procedure allow for parties, particularly the complainant initially, to learn about all resolution option pathways in order to make an informed decision on how to proceed?
3. *Complainant request:* With full knowledge of resolution option pathways available to them, is the complainant requesting a noninvestigative/nondisciplinary approach?
4. *Respondent consent:* With full knowledge of their options and clarity on the voluntary, nondisciplinary and remedies/needs-based nature of a

noninvestigative resolution pathway, is the respondent(s) expressing their written consent to participate?

5. *Attention to power balance and equity:* Do we believe the parties would be able to participate in a process equitably, given imbalances of power that might exist? The DOE expressed concern about using a noninvestigatory approach where the matter involved a relationship of real and/or perceived power (i.e., employee/student). As facilitators of a noninvestigative resolution process with a focus on RJ, it is imperative to be attentive to dynamics of power imbalance that might tip the balance away from equitable engagement and opportunity for a fundamentally fair process and outcome.

6. *Escalating concern:* Does the institution have knowledge of previous reports or disciplinary history involving the respondent?

7. *Fact pattern of violence:* Was the alleged prohibited conduct perpetrated with a weapon or resulted in egregious bodily harm that may indicate a potential risk to the greater campus community?

8. *Likely not to create more harm:* Do we have reasonable assurance the process would be able to mitigate the potential for further victimization?

9. *Jurisdiction:* Does the institution have jurisdiction over the alleged behavior and involved respondent in particular?

10. *Consensus to proceed:* Do we have a consensus (and perhaps approval) among key stakeholders, including, but not limited to, the complainant, respondent, and the Title IX coordinator? Following agreement to participate in your initial intake process for noninvestigative alternative/ adaptable resolution procedures, are the parties able to achieve a consensus on how to proceed? Some institutions may employ a single AR pathway, such as a shuttle negotiation process that works toward an agreed-to resolutions outcome. Others, however, may employ several possible resolution pathways. In either frame, it is necessary that the parties agree to the process by which resolution (and potentially written agreement) will be sought.

Another element that can be difficult to sort out, but is critical to the success of any resolution process—in particular, interpersonal approaches, such as facilitated dialogue or a restorative circle or conference—is the current state of mental and emotional wellness of those who would participate. In other words, just because a process is appropriate doesn't mean that the time for that process is right. A judgment on whether the time is right for initiating a noninvestigating/nondisciplinary alternative/adaptable resolution process must be made in close consultation with campus and community expertise. This may include consultation with the community/ local counseling and psychological services and/or other campus student support resources.

Exceptions For Use or RJ/Informal Resolution

It may be reasonable to ask, "Are there any bright lines as to where the use of a restorative or noninvestigative approach is precluded?" However, although for some the answer might seem clear cut, we suggest that upon further review the answer to the question is not so simple. As a society, we like to put things into easily understood categories, right or wrong, yes or no. However, more often than not lived experience is just more complicated than that, and an oversimplification ultimately leads to disservice. That said, we suggest a few requirements and recommendations for reasonable caution can be made in this regard and are as follows:

- *Guard against real or perceived coercion:* The use of a noninvestigative restorative resolution process must be initiated without coercion with fully written consent from all involved parties. This is not just a sound recommendation but also a federal requirement under the 2020 Title IX Final Rule.
- *Guaranteed equity of process, not outcomes:* Parties should be clear that equity of process is guaranteed; however, specific outcomes are never guaranteed. As such, where desired outcomes are not reasonably possible, caution should be exercised in using an RJ process. Rather, it is incumbent on the facilitator to continue engaging in preprocess work with the involved parties to further define interests that underlie held positions to try and identify areas of overlapping interest from which a mutual agreement might be built.
- *Reasonable policy check and balance:* Incorporate reasonable checks and balances into your policy for the use of a noninvestigative restorative resolution process, such as facilitator discretion to discontinue/not proceed and Title IX coordinator approval of initiation and outcomes.
- *Mindful of community positionality:* We recommend adapting your policies and procedures in incremental and reasonable ways to meet community need while being mindful of what your specific community is ready for and able to deliver on. A particular restorative approach should never be used when either the community doesn't have trust in it or you don't have confidence in your ability to deliver on it with credibility and without the potential for creating more harm.

Pressure Cooking Your Policy and Procedures

After compiling an initial draft of your updated policy, it's strongly recommended that you take the time to "pressure cook" it. Pressure cooking policy is to walk the whole way around it and view it from multiple perspectives. Having drafted your policy following substantial process garnering stakeholder buy-in and perspective, taking this critical step to tie up all the loose ends will ideally benefit from the collective insight of the many. Through this process you'll want to read through that document forward and backward and ensure that you've identified/addressed potential loopholes and obstacles to enforcement. In other words, you'll want to make sure that the draft policy is both functional and avoids as much institutional liability and community/individual future harm as possible. Through your own review process, what can be helpful is that each time you review the policy you intentionally and consciously do so through a different lens. For example, you can ask yourself, "How might I interpret this document if I were a _____?" and fill in the blank with various stakeholder roles, such as complainant, respondent, parent, defense attorney, and even a representative from the DOE. The following are several questions/considerations for the policy and procedure review process and subsequent implementation preparation:

- Does this make sense to the various audiences who will need to understand this?
- Are there ways to scale back the legal jargon that may be included to make the document more accessible?
- Are there portions of the policy that we anticipate changing down the road under a different federal administration? If so, do we have a process in place institutionally that will afford us the opportunity to make such changes?
- "If this . . . then what"—does this process play out like we intended it to? Are there gaps/holes remaining?
- Is this process feasible to carry out? Does it allow for your accountability framework to be upheld?
- If this process were to be carried out, would it be equitable for both parties?
- What factors or circumstances may arise that may impact the intended procedure and are they ways that disruptions can be mitigated?
- How will you launch and market the availability of the resolution option/process?

- What will be your referral streams? How can referrals be promoted?
- How would you implement training for the resolution process, and who will need to receive such training?
- How will you assess the effectiveness of the resolution process, once implemented?

Throughout these pressure cooking efforts, it will be important to clarify policy and procedural safeguards that should be explicitly written into policy versus what should be internal standard operating procedures that do/should not be formalized in this type of document. In other words, what should be publicly facing (recognizing that there are various audiences this will include—students, employees, parents, attorneys, etc.), and what should be kept internal? Documents/procedures kept internally will be easier to modify/adapt to align with best practices, but bear in mind there will be a need to find a happy balance between keeping items internal and sharing publicly for transparency.

Conclusion

With keen historical knowledge around federal guidance and regulation coupled with the present (and likely future) regulatory environment, we offer you encouragement to venture out of the traditional procedural constructs. Although traditional formal procedures will remain, they represent but one legitimate pathway for addressing sexual and gender-based harm in our communities. The policy pathway forward will look different at each institution, but the road map presented here offers an inclusive, and inherently equitable, approach to building increasingly supportive systems through generating stakeholder buy-in and cultivating partnerships for success.

References

Ashford, S. J., & Detert, J. (2015). Get the boss to buy in. *Harvard Business Review, 93*(1), 16.

Callan, M. (n.d.). *Toward a culture of partnership (model)*. Figure 2.1. University of Michigan.

Camera, L. (2017, September 22). Trump administration rescinds Obama-era campus sexual assault guidance. *U.S. & World News Report*. https://www.usnews .com/news/education-news/articles/2017-09-22/trump-administration-rescinds-obama-era-campus-sexual-assault-guidance

Cardona, M. (2021, June 23). *Secretary Cardona: Title IX the "strongest tool" in protecting educational opportunities free from sex discrimination.* https://www .ed.gov/news/press-releases/secretary-cardona-title-ix-strongest-tool-protecting-educational-opportunities-free-sex-discrimination

Cuiccio, C., & Husby-Slater, M. (2018). *Needs assessment guidebook supporting the development of district and school needs assessments.* State Support Network. https:// oese.ed.gov/files/2020/10/needsassessmentguidebook-508_003.pdf

Education Amendments of 1972, § 506 and Titles VIII and IX. P.L. 92-318, 7 U.S.C. 301. https://www.govinfo.gov/content/pkg/COMPS-11127/uslm/COMPS-11127 .xml

Edwards, K. M., Moynihan, M. M., Rodenhizer-Stampfli, K. A., Demers, J. M., & Banyard, V. L. (2015). Campus community readiness to engage measure: Its utility for campus violence prevention initiatives—Preliminary psychometrics. *Violence and Gender, 2*(4), 214–224. https://doi.org/10.1089/vio.2015.0028

Fedina, L., Lynne Holmes, J., & Backes, B. L. (2018). Campus sexual assault: A systematic review of prevalence research from 2000 to 2015. *Trauma, Violence, & Abuse, 19*(1), 76–93. https://doi.org/10.1177/1524838016631129

Fisher, B. (2000). *The sexual victimization of college women.* U.S. Department of Justice, Office of Justice Programs, National Institute of Justice. https://www .ncjrs.gov/pdffiles1/nij/182369.pdf

Hepler, C. (2013). A bibliography of Title IX of the education amendments of 1972. *Western New England Law Review, 35*(2), 441–511. https://digitalcommons.law .wne.edu/lawreview/vol35/iss2/6

Hill, C., & Kearl, H. (2011). *Crossing the line: Sexual harassment at school.* American Association of University Women. https://www.aauw.org/app/uploads/2020/03/ Crossing-the-Line-Sexual-Harassment-at-School.pdf

Karp, D. (2015). *Little book of restorative justice for colleges and universities: Revised and updated.* Skyhorse.

Kilpatrick, D. G., Resnick, H. S., Ruggiero, K. J., Conoscenti, L. M., & McCauley, J. (2007). *Drug-facilitated, incapacitated, and forcible rape: A national study.* National Criminal Justice Reference Service.

Krebs, C. P., Lindquist, C. H., Warner, T. D., Fisher, B. S., & Martin, S. L. (2007, December). *The Campus Sexual Assault (CSA) Study—Final report* (Document 221153). National Institute of Justice, U.S. Department of Justice. https://www .ncjrs.gov/pdffiles1/nij/grants/221153.pdf

Mansell, J., Moffit, D. M., Russ, A. C., & Thorpe, J. N. (2017). Sexual harassment training and reporting in athletic training students. *Athletic Training Education Journal, 12*(1), 3–9. https://doi.org/10.4085/12013

Nondiscrimination on the Basis of Sex in Education Programs or Activities Receiving Federal Financial Assistance. (2018). Federal Register 61462. (November 29, 2018). 34 CFR Part 106.

Saul, S., & Taylor, K. (2017, September 22). Betsy DeVos reverses Obama-era policy in campus sexual assault investigations. *New York Times.* https://www .nytimes.com/2017/09/22/us/devos-colleges-sex-assault.html

Smith, C. P., & Freyd, J. J. (2013). Dangerous safe havens: Institutional betrayal exacerbates sexual trauma. *Journal of Traumatic Stress, 26*(1), 119–124. https://doi.org/10.1002/jts.21778

Stader, D. L., & Williams-Cunningham, J. L. (2017). Campus sexual assault, institutional betrayal, and Title IX. *The Clearing House, 90*(5–6), 198–202. https://doi.org/10.1080/00098655.2017.1361287

Sulkowski, M. L. (2011). An investigation of students' willingness to report threats of violence in campus communities. *Psychology of Violence, 1*(1), 53. https://doi.org/10.1037/a0021592

Sweet, S. (2001). *College and society: An introduction to the sociological imagination.* Pearson.

Title IX, 34 CFR part 106. 2022. https://www2.ed.gov/about/offices/list/ocr/docs/t9nprm.pdf

U.S. Department of Education. (n.d.) *Office for civil rights—Sex discrimination.* https://www2.ed.gov/about/offices/list/ocr/sexoverview.html

U.S. Department of Education, Office for Civil Rights (2011, April 4). *Dear colleague letter: Sexual violence.* https://www2.ed.gov/about/offices/list/ocr/letters/colleague-201104.pdf

U.S. Department of Education, Office for Civil Rights (2014, April 29). *Questions and answers about TItle IX and sexual violence.* https://www2.ed.gov/about/offices/list/ocr/docs/qa-201404-title-ix.pdf

U.S. Department of Education. (2016). *Non-regulatory guidance: Using evidence to strengthen education investments.* https://www2.ed.gov/policy/elsec/leg/essa/guidanceuseseinvestment.pdf

U.S. Department of Education, Office for Civil Rights (2018). *Final rule.* Federal Register. 83 FR 61462. https://www.federalregister.gov/documents/2018/11/29/2018-25314/nondiscrimination-on-the-basis-of-sex-in-education-programs-or-activities-receiving-federal

U.S. Department of Education, Office for Civil Rights (2020). Final Rule. Federal Register. 85 FR 30026. https://www.federalregister.gov/documents/2020/05/19/2020-10512/nondiscrimination-on-the-basis-of-sex-in-education-programs-or-activities-receiving-federal

U.S. Department of Education, Office for Civil Rights (2021). *Questions and answers on Title IX regulations on sexual harassment.* https://www2.ed.gov/about/offices/list/ocr/docs/202107-qa-titleix.pdf

U.S. Department of Education. (2022, June 28). *Questions and answers on the Title IX regulations on sexual harassment (July 2021).* https://www2.ed.gov/about/offices/list/ocr/docs/202107-qa-titleix.pdf

Virden, R. (2022, January 14). *Three reasons we need restorative justice now.* The Good Men Project. https://goodmenproject.com/featured-content/3-reasons-we-need-restorative-justice-now-kpkn/

3

WHAT ABOUT DUE PROCESS?

Addressing Common Concerns and Questions About Using Restorative Justice in Cases of Campus Sexual and Gender-Based Misconduct

Pablo Cerdera and Elise Lopez

This chapter will address the most common concerns raised about using restorative justice (RJ) for campus sexual misconduct cases. This includes risks of participation for respondents and complainants and the risks associated with an institution taking a nondisciplinary response. Also discussed are strategies to mitigate legal concerns and risks, Insights and tips about addressing common concerns also are provided.

Introduction

Although there is a significant amount of theoretical literature and trainings on the use of RJ in higher education for cases of sexual and other gender-based harm, it is in many ways still early in its practical use. Few institutions have attempted it, and even as recently as 2019 such approaches were not formally sanctioned by federal guidelines. It is only natural, then, that there is a common set of questions about this approach. It is our firm belief, rooted in our experience as RJ practitioners and researchers in the area of sexual harm, that these practices can be implemented in ways that are deeply beneficial to all members of the campus community. This chapter will raise and attempt to address many of the most common philosophical, process, and legal concerns around RJ in cases of sexual misconduct. It is our hope that these answers will help you feel more confident in these practices and in your efforts to help establish them on your campus. Additionally, we hope that this chapter will equip the reader with basic language to help begin to answer the types of questions that may arise from colleagues who are not versed in this area.

The Restorative Justice Philosophy

Restorative justice is not just a set of practices, it is a way of thinking about and approaching crime or harm. Understanding the philosophical under-pinnings of restorative justice is important when trying to address common questions that arise about the use of restorative justice practices.

What Does RJ Have to Do With Accountability for Responsible Parties?

When we say "responsible parties" we are referring to the participant(s) in the process who are taking accountability for the harm or harms which have occurred. Accountability is coequal to safety and support in its importance in a restorative process. Punitive approaches to justice often equate account-ability with punishment—in the restorative worldview, accountability is an internal process that cannot be imposed from without.

Many practitioners and advocates (Creative Interventions, 2012; Mingus, 2019; Sered, 2019) state that meaningful accountability requires responsible parties to do the following:

- acknowledge that they caused harm through their actions
- acknowledge that they had agency in these harmful actions
- work to understand the impact that their actions had on others
- take steps to repair the harm, to the extent possible, based on the needs of those affected
- notice patterns in their life that led to them making these harmful decision(s)

In other words, the truest accountability is changed behavior. When pursued with fidelity, the restorative process supports responsible parties in the messy and nonlinear process of taking meaningful accountability. It challenges them to let go of their defensiveness, listen deeply to the people they have harmed, and ultimately do the difficult work of accepting the reality of their actions and taking steps to meet the needs of the people they have harmed. This can be a transformational process for students who have caused harm and can have a lasting positive impact on them as they continue to move through the world.

Won't Most Responsible Parties Just Agree to RJ as a Quick "Get Out of Jail Free Card"?

Sometimes people voice the concern of "false" accountability—individuals saying the right thing but not truly believing what they are saying. While it is impossible to assert that this never happens, it is less common than many fear. The process of hearing directly from someone who you have harmed about the impact of your actions tends to cut through defenses, on conscious and unconscious levels. Additionally, what a responsible party says is only part of their accountability process. They also work to cocreate concrete and actionable accountability plans that often involve ongoing learning, reflection, and material and symbolic acts of repair. It is up to the harmed party whether the words and actions as a whole constitute meaningful redress based on their needs.

A critical component of minimizing the possibility that a reported party would disingenuously agree to RJ is to ensure that there is a codified process that includes a monitored period whereby the individual actively engages in a redress plan. As noted in other chapters, RJ as an accountability process option cannot simply be a meeting with a verbalized apology. The process cannot appear to be, or be, an "easy way out."

What About Justice for Victims?

Justice for victims is often envisioned as being based in a punitive response. A central question, however, is who gets to envision and define what justice should be? Does this rest in the hands of the policy and/or decisionmaker, or might it best be situated in the hands of those most directly affected by violence? In 1994, the Violence Against Women Act was first passed as part of the Omnibus Crime Bill (VAWA, 1994). In doing so, it shaped not only services, but public perceptions that the best route for addressing sexual harm would be through the criminal legal system. Additionally, the concurrent heavy social discourse focus on "stranger danger" encouraged the idea that sexual harm is primarily perpetrated by serial rapists. The reality is that most rapes are committed by a person known to the victim/survivor, such as an intimate partner, classmate, coworker, or friend (RAINN, 2022).

Research has shown that because most rapes are perpetrated by acquaintances, people who are sexually assaulted often do not want an adversarial, punitive response that involves the person getting in trouble and potentially going to jail or prison. The justice desires of victims–survivors are not always lock-ups, expulsions, or apologies (McGlynn et al., 2012). Rather, they report wanting (a) the person to admit responsibility and validate the harm they caused, (b) for the person's harmful behavior to change, and (c) an accountability process that doesn't let the person off "with a slap on the wrist" but that monitors that person's progress toward change. Victims–survivors who chose an RJ diversion program within the criminal legal system have reported these same justice desires and reported high levels of satisfaction at the end of the accountability process (Koss, 2014). This is just one example of how victims–survivors' voices can be used to rethink the question of "What is justice for victims?" It is imperative that we expand our menus of services to include those voiced by victims, rather than those that have been imposed on them from decades of reliance on a criminal legal system that most victims are reluctant to utilize.

What About Retraumatizing Victims–Survivors?

A commonly expressed concern is that RJ may be retraumatizing to reporting parties, particularly when the restorative approach could involve direct interaction with the person who harmed them. Given the reality that sexual harm is highly correlated to trauma, it is essential to consider the possibility of causing further harm in this context. In many cases, the simple reality is that trauma is already present—working with sexual harm in any capacity means working in a space fraught with trauma. We cannot change the lived experience of the students who come to us for help. Instead, our role is to provide structure and support that help those directly impacted to navigate as safely as possible through trauma, toward healing, repair, and accountability.

The reality is that retraumatization most often occurs in justice processes when people feel their experience is being ignored, invalidated, or diminished. It is not simply the act of revisiting a traumatic experience that is retraumatizing—many of the students we work with are already spending a lot of time talking or thinking about their traumatic experiences—rather, it is the repeated experience of powerlessness or loss of control, reconjured feelings of distress and lack of safety that can deepen the wounds caused by trauma.

This stands in contrast to many student's experiences with or expectations from the investigative process. As many of us know from anecdotal experiences, students often fear or feel that their agency and control is removed once a formal Title IX investigation begins. These experiences of loss of agency in the investigative process have also been documented in studies and surveys, including prominently in the 2021 "Know Your IX" survey (Nesbitt & Carson, 2021).

Restorative processes, implemented with fidelity, are structured to maximize agency and minimize risk of reenacting or reinforcing the trauma of victimization. For example, one way that RJ processes can increase agency and support all parties in their feelings of safety with RJ is to offer an array of methods by which RJ conferences could take place. Some survivors want to have a moderated, face-to-face meeting with the person who harmed them in a safe environment. Others may want more distance, such as through a live video call. Still other reporting parties may not want a meeting in real time; in these instances, shuttle communication can offer a route for the RJ experience to still occur.

What About Consistency and Fairness?

Traditional investigatory processes emphasize consistency as a self-evident virtue; that is, the process should look the same for everyone, with commonly prescriptive sanctions depending on the type and severity of the conduct violation. It is widely perceived that fundamental fairness is equated to repeatability, evenhandedness, and equality in outcomes. These are understood to be the benchmarks that Title IX investigatory processes should strive to meet. Therefore, at first glance, given this widely accepted framework it is understandable that the much more adaptable and participant-oriented process of RJ would raise concerns.

We suggest that one way to address this concern is through an intentional shift from the benchmarks of *equality* to the fundamentals of a process marked by *equity*. The adoption of a fundamentally equitable process is to shift our focus from consistency in sanctioning outcomes to consistency in attention to values, needs, goals, and supportive processes. As many Title IX professionals know through experience, consistent processes with consistent sanctions can have wildly inconsistent impacts on stakeholders based on individuals' material positioning, social supports, mental/emotional needs, and things like the quality of representation retained by each party. On the other hand, the flexible and individualized approach of RJ can help ensure that the process matches the needs of the participants and can therefore help promote more consistent outcomes with regard to meaningful accountability, healing, and participant satisfaction.

What About Protecting the Community From Dangerous People?

There is a common but erroneous belief that the majority of campus rapes are committed by a small number of men. Longitudinal research shows that most campus sexual assaults are not perpetrated by serial rapists; rather, most of these rapes are committed by someone who does it once or twice, and in a time-limited way (e.g., only in the first year of college, but for some reason not after that; Swartout et al., 2015). In other words, most campus rapes are being committed by otherwise "normal" everyday people. This does not diminish the seriousness of the offense, but it does mean that we need to shift our thought process around what it means to keep campus safe.

Often the burden of proof in an investigation means that these same "dangerous people" will not be found responsible, or only found responsible after a long and arduous process that puts them on the defensive and encourages denial and deflection. In many cases, someone who did cause the harm but wasn't found responsible feels vindicated and justified—potentially increasing their capacity to do harm in the future.

Finally, we must remember, as you likely know from your own work, that most individuals who behave in ways that harm others are not monsters. That said, although not the norm, sometimes misconduct is perpetrated serially by an individual, or an assault is so heinous that a necessary protective measure for an individual or a community is temporary or permanent exclusion. In any scenario, however, exclusion from student status alone does not solve the problem of violence in community. Further, a student removed from a campus community or from campus entirely is still going to be part of other communities. When it is safe to do so, when a reporting party desires it, and when the reported party is amenable to taking responsibility for the harm caused, an RJ process can help to put that person on a path toward not causing future harm. People who cause harm, even serious harm like sexual violence, are able to learn and grow and avoid causing similar harm in the future while becoming part of the healing process for the person/people they harmed most directly.

This potential for increased awareness, learning, and behavior change is especially salient for the college student population, most of whom developmentally are late-stage adolescents. Developmentally, they are still quite malleable in terms of thoughts, beliefs, attitudes, and behaviors. As professionals at institutions of higher education, it is imperative that, whenever possible, we consider whether and how our sanctions are educational. Further, sanctions to change behavior should not only address gaps in knowledge or change in attitudes but include skill-building for behavior change.

What About When Survivors Don't Want to "Forgive" the People Responsible?

Despite its reputation, RJ is not oriented toward forgiveness as an end. Howard Zehr (2002) articulated the core goals of the restorative process as being "to involve, to the extent possible, those who have a stake in a specific offense and to collectively identify and address harms, needs, and obligations, in order to heal and put things as right as possible" (p. 37) with a focus on meaningful accountability. Forgiveness is not a core element of this process, nor is reconciliation. The goal of a restorative process is to address harm in a manner that makes it easier for all involved to move forward in a good way. When forgiveness happens, it is a happy side effect of a deep engagement with harm and accountability, and it is motivated by the harmed party and their own healing needs.

Process

A philosophical understanding of RJ is helpful in answering some of the big questions, but what about the specific, in-the-weeds questions? When trying to propose, create, or implement a new RJ program it can be helpful to be prepared to answer some common implementation questions.

What About Getting Buy-In From Key Campus Stakeholders?

We recommend that a pitch to key campus stakeholders (e.g., Title IX officers, campus safety officers, conduct officers) conduct staff, and decisionmakers should anticipate and address commonly held perceptions and concerns upfront. Some items to cover are discussed in the following sections.

Myth of RJ as "Soft on Crime"

There is a common misconception that RJ is simply a conference where the responsible person apologizes to the survivor-victim. This implies that responsible persons would disingenuously consent to RJ in order to get out of sanctions. Highlight that RJ is a formal process that requires admission of responsibility by the reported party, consent by and preparation of both parties, a conference or something similar to acknowledge the harm done, and a time-bound accountability plan the responsible person would complete. If a responsible person does not participate adequately in or complete the accountability plan, the case would follow the typical conduct processes for when a student found responsible does not comply with their assigned sanctions. Similarly, if an RJ process is begun but the reported party decides (or shows) early on that they actually do not take responsibility for the misconduct, then the case can revert to the traditional conduct accountability process.

Safety

Project RESTORE (Responsibility and Equity for Sexual Transgressions Offering a Restorative Experience) was the first RJ for sex crimes program to be empirically evaluated. Individuals were referred by prosecutors. The program was highly structured and required voluntary participation from the victim–survivor and for the reported person to be willing to take responsibility for the harm done. The evaluation of the program showed high rates of satisfaction and feelings of safety from both victims–survivors and responsible persons. We can be cautiously optimistic that RJ, when implemented thoughtfully and with fidelity, can be utilized safely for cases of sexual harm.

Time Commitment and Burden

Developing an RJ track within or alongside the existing conduct process is time intensive. Acknowledge this from the beginning. Continue by noting that once the program is implemented, it may reduce burden for investigators and conduct boards. RJ by nature reduces or eliminates the large amount of time it takes to conduct adversarial investigations. This includes eliminating the fact-finding process, which can take months, report writing, presentation to hearing boards, and determination of responsibility.

Appeals

Conduct process appeals often contend that the determination of responsibility (or not) was unfair, the investigation was not thorough, or that the sanctions are inappropriate for the conduct violation determined. With RJ, victims–survivors and responsible persons participate in RJ only on a voluntary basis. Policies that include an RJ-informed pathway should also include an off-ramp for any participant to discontinue their participation and elect to pivot to another pathway for resolution, including a formal investigative process. Further, it is important to point out that because there is already buy-in from the students involved, and no expectation of or process for determination of guilt, the need for appeals is negated through voluntary participation, shared decision making on process and outcome, and voluntary transparent agreement on resolution.

Frustration With Victims

Law enforcement and student conduct workers are sometimes frustrated by victims–survivors who report an assault but do not want to move forward with a formal investigation or filing of charges. Notifying students during the reporting process, particularly when they have called law enforcement, that there may be an RJ option available instead of the formal adversarial process, could result in higher victim–survivor cooperation in resolving cases.

Isn't RJ Resource-Heavy Beyond Our Capacity?

While implementing a new RJ program may seem to be beyond the capacity of many offices, with adequate training and preparation, an office may be able to integrate restorative options with existing staff. Not all restorative options require in-person meetings, and staff may be able to shift from time-intensive investigations to RJ facilitation with the same resources.

Training

Engaging in RJ processes responsibly requires a core group of well-trained and experienced facilitators. It is advisable to have this team spend time facilitating other kinds of restorative processes on campus before they attempt to facilitate cases of sexual harm; the RJ process and philosophy should be well integrated before facilitating such complex cases. The facilitators must be trained in both RJ facilitation and sexual violence–related and trauma-informed support. It is highly recommended that at least one person has the coordination of RJ processes as the primary responsibility of their job, wherever they sit in the organizational structure.

Preparation

It is also advisable to prepare certain documents and protocols before diving into this practice. Ensuring that the Title IX team and the office of general counsel are involved, draft an agreement-to-participate form, model language for agreement forms, and a standardized intake document. In addition, it is highly advisable to have strong relationships with and buy-in from whatever counseling services, chaplain's offices, student resource centers, student health centers, and any other key stakeholders you have on your campus so that you are readily able to make referrals and offer appropriate support to students. This last step is also important to ensure that these campus partners are familiar with RJ and can share appropriate information.

The length of time a case takes can vary widely based on the circumstances and, more importantly, the needs of the parties. In the simplest and least emotionally demanding cases, expect to have an intake meeting and several preconference meetings with each participant, in addition to meeting with every support person involved prior to moving to the joint session. When using the restorative conferencing approach the process typically consists of one or two 2-hour facilitated sessions. Cases can take anywhere from a month to 6 months or longer to resolve, followed by ongoing outreach. Typically, the facilitator of the process would follow up with both participants immediately after the conference, and then again later that month, then 3 and 6 months later to ensure that the agreement is being followed and that no additional supportive measures or processes are needed.

The above is written with the assumption that it is deemed prudent to hold an in-person face-to-face conference between the parties. For clarity, it is acknowledged that in some situations it is unsafe or unwise to allow the parties to speak directly with one another based on the physical and psychological safety needs. In these cases, a shuttle facilitation process may be preferred to minimize risk of further harm. In utilizing such an approach the facilitator would shuttle elements of the conference individually with each party and report back to each what is heard from the other while working toward a potential agreement designed to meet needs. Shuttle facilitation often stretches over several meetings—normally ranging anywhere from four to 10, depending on the complexity of the needs that arise.

These figures can sound daunting, but it is important to consider the time and resources required to conduct a thorough investigation into an allegation of sexual harm as well as to follow a case through a process of hearing and/or appeal. It is our belief that the energy that would otherwise be devoted to an investigation can instead be marshaled to honor the needs of the students involved. Any effort to offload the process of investigation and adjudication by prioritizing restorative processes is ill advised. However, the time and energy spent on shepherding a successful restorative process is oriented toward student and community well-being rather than toward meeting onerous procedural or investigative requirements.

How Would We Avoid Coercion or Using RJ to Avoid the Burden of the Investigatory Process?

Students are often understandably concerned about the implications of initiating an investigation and pursuing a formal complaint in the Title IX arena—many fear losing control of the process, their narrative, or the experience. Some are deeply concerned about the potential implications of an investigation for themselves or for the person they have reported. They might also be fearful about the confidentiality of the investigative process, especially if it involves witness interviews.

These are all valid fears and concerns, which can be addressed through robust options counseling and ongoing support. The answer is not simply to point individuals with these concerns to a restorative pathway. Rather, it is best to fully explore and explain the possibilities and the challenges of all available options and allow the reporting student to make a considered decision based on their hoped-for outcomes and which available processes will best support reaching them.

It is essential, both practically and philosophically, that engagement in a restorative process be free from coercion and voluntary to the greatest extent possible. If a reporting student wants disciplinary sanctions and a formal finding of responsibility, it is in their best interest to pursue an investigative path with as much awareness as possible about the possibilities and limitations of this approach. If, however, they are interested in getting their harm acknowledged by the person responsible, repairing social relationships, getting answers about their experience and how and why it came to pass, confronting the person who hurt them, and/or prioritizing meaningful accountability on the personal and interpersonal levels, then RJ options are likely the proper avenue for them. In this case, too, they should be well informed of the opportunities and pitfalls of this approach. It is important to remember that parties can change their mind about which pathway they would like to pursue throughout the process, up until the time they reach a final agreement and it is signed by all parties and the Title IX officer at the institution.

Avoiding coercion is also essential for responsible parties. This process must never be presented as "the easy way out"—while it is nonpunitive, it is not "easy," and it does not end after an RJ conference/meeting. It is a challenging process for those who have caused harm in its demands of deep reflection, vulnerability, and responsibility-taking. What it does do is provide an opportunity to engage in learning as well as personal and interpersonal healing, something that is not often available via the investigative pathway. It is difficult to ensure that there is no coercion involved when students are often mistrustful or pessimistic about their other options. That said, the solution is not to withhold the RJ options—instead, we are called to improve the diverse options that students might pursue.

What About Community Harms? Can These Be Addressed Through RJ?

When sexual violence occurs on campus, it often has impacts that extend far beyond the individuals directly involved. Friends and classmates often witness the impacts of the violence on their peers and can be caught up in the investigative process as well. Student groups receive allegations and are left without a clear understanding of what, if anything, they can do to take care of their communities. Professors and staff people are affected by changes in student behavior and patterns. These "secondary victims" can also be included in a restorative resolution process so that their perspectives, harms, and needs can be considered in the decision-making process.

Further, some harms occur that affect campus climate and students' feelings of safety. For example, a crude banner hung outside a fraternity house that implicates support for rape (i.e., one famous one a few years ago said "No Means Yes, Yes Means Anal"). This caused many students, particularly female students, to feel unsafe on campus. A restorative process could be used in these situations for harmed people to confront the individuals who engaged in this behavior, have those individuals relay an understanding of the harm caused by their actions, and set up for change in future behavior. Applying the restorative values and frameworks with fidelity in your community means identifying opportunities to support healing, accountability, and prevention work throughout the campus.

Legal Concerns

In addition to philosophical and process concerns, some may have specific legal questions related to using RJ for CSM. These include questions about due process, what to do about the concern of "false accusations," concurrent criminal process and discovery, and different requirements for public and private institutions.

What About Due Process?

Fundamentally, the purpose of a restorative intervention is not to gather evidence or make a determination of responsibility. Rather, this process allows individuals to do the more difficult (and ultimately more rewarding) work of taking meaningful accountability for their actions and to work collaboratively to address harms and promote healing.

As practitioners, it is our responsibility to make sure that participants understand the above facts and are aware of the full range of their options. Before practitioners ever conduct an intake meeting with the respondent, they are provided with a full accounting of the report against them. When conducting intake interviews with respondents, we engage with them honestly about their understanding of the events in question. If the respondent denies that the events happened as described or asserts that they had nothing to do with what happened, we never attempt to coerce a "confession" as we explore their experience.

If, on the other hand, the participants acknowledge that the general shape of the facts is accurate, or simply that they caused some kind of harm, we can proceed with the restorative process. From this point forward we focus on building shared understandings of their perspective, the other party's perspective, and the impact of their actions. In order to promote accountability and healing, we help the responsible party to identify the harms that they are responsible for, move through the stages of accountability, and prepare for encountering the person who they harmed. This preparation involves brainstorming possible restorative actions. The driving philosophy is to encourage meaningful reflection, challenge harmful thought patterns, and expand the responsible party's awareness from a place of respect and support. Throughout this process, we check in regularly about the voluntary nature of their involvement.

In an adversarial, adjudicative system, due process guarantees a notice of charges, an impartial judge, and a fair hearing. Federal Title IX guidance determines the requirements of what due process entails in cases of sexual misconduct. In today's legal environment there must be a formal complaint that spells out the reported harm. This would occur in both an adjudicative and RJ process because it happens before parties choose a pathway. Once this complaint is made and notice is given to the respondent, and all parties have formally agreed to a restorative resolution, the process can be effectively "diverted" from the investigative pathway. An RJ facilitator is equivalent to an impartial judge—their responsibility is to ensure harm is addressed in a safe manner throughout the process. The RJ conferences/ meetings, which include an agenda and are facilitated by a trained individual, are analogous to a hearing. The option for an investigative resolution with all of the rights outlined in federal Title IX guidance remains available until such a time as the complainant withdraws their complaint or the restorative process is concluded.

What About False Accusations?

First, it is important to reiterate the fact that, though the precise rate is difficult to quantify, false accusations of sexual violence are exceedingly rare. In a meta-analysis of false allegations in cases reported to police, the rate was about 5% (Ferguson & Malouff, 2016).

As covered in the question about due process earlier, it is essential that RJ processes be fully voluntary. Students who allege that they were falsely accused have every right to defend themselves and should not be pressured to participate in an RJ process.

We can and often do work from the assumption that both parties are sharing their experience of the truth—the truth of a harmed person's pain represents a real need for repair, and as long as the responsible party is willing to take on the obligations of addressing those needs, the process can be highly successful. The restorative process is about attempting to repair harm and build healthier communities—not about marking someone as a "harm-doer."

What About Criminal Processes and Discovery?

Responsible parties may be hesitant to participate in RJ if a case is also being, or may be pursued, in the criminal legal system. RJ processes cannot move forward without a reported party who is willing to take responsibility for the sexual harm done. The implication of this is that simply having participated in an RJ process could be used as evidence of guilt in a legal proceeding. There may be concerns that the discovery process in a legal proceeding could uncover additional evidence of guilt, such as written statements, notes from RJ conferences, signed documents admitting responsibility, apology letters, and accountability plans.

One solution could be to have a memorandum of understanding with the local jurisdiction regarding the use of RJ records in the discovery process. In the RESTORE program, there was a memorandum of understanding that indicated agreement between the program and the criminal legal system that a person's participation in RESTORE could not be used as evidence against them if their case reverted back to a criminal process. Written records in the program were the minimum needed to document the case and reparation plan so as to reduce the amount of potentially subpoenaed information.

Procedurally, note taking should be minimized to what is needed to ensure informed consent of RJ participants, document status of the RJ process, and monitor accountability. Notes should be robust enough to give confidence to survivor-victims that the process is being followed correctly, minimize discoverable information about both parties, and ensure that another staff member could pick up the case if the original RJ facilitator/conduct person leaves their position. Additionally, attention should be paid to include enough information that a retrospective audit of cases would be able to determine that the process was conducted correctly, in fairness, and with due process. For example, a simple checklist of process steps with completion dates and staff signatures could be used to help show the shepherding of the case from consent through completion of the accountability process. Qualitative notes can focus on the feelings of parties regarding the incident as well as the main points of any meetings with the parties. Doing so protects the safety of the parties and minimizes risk to practitioners. A written accountability plan can focus on behavior change of the reported party (e.g., attendance at behavioral education sessions or counseling) and an expected timeline of completion of the plan. There should be transparency with parties about what might or might not be discoverable and what the implications are likely to be.

What About the Different Requirements at Public Versus Private Institutions?

Title IX applies to institutions that receive any amount of federal funding (including work-study programs and federal student loans and grants). This is true regardless of whether the school is public, private, religious, or for-profit (though religious schools may apply for exemptions). What is common across institutions is that they all have their own honor codes or codes of conduct, which typically do cover sexual assault. Although schools that do not accept federal aid do not have to establish policies and practices as outlined in Title IX, this does not mean that they don't or can't address sexual assault via an accountability process. In fact, some may argue that exempt institutions have more freedom to develop and implement RJ programs for sexual harm because they do not have to comply with the ever-changing language in Title IX regarding "restorative justice," "mediation," and "informal resolution" that tend to shape the scope of RJ for campus sexual assault cases.

Closing

Through the thoughtful integration and application of restorative practices, we can provide effective and supportive recourse for students impacted by sexual harm. All of our students deserve the opportunity to thrive, and the restorative approach places student well-being at the center of the process. Adding a restorative option requires that practitioners address common concerns and myths about RJ, and we hope that the above reflections, and the detailed content in the rest of this volume, can support other practitioners and leaders in bringing RJ to campus sexual misconduct policies. Though the work can be difficult, we have also found it rewarding; restorative practices allow us to guide students through what is often the most difficult experience of their life and offer a pathway that centers healing, meaningful accountability, and individual restoration.

Acknowledgment

We extend thanks to prereaders Camila Pretel, Katie Mowrer, Hanan Ahmed, Colby Ball, Marcia Glickman, and Serene Harris.

References

Bizier, L. (2020). Maintaining the delicate balance between due process and protecting reporting students from retraumitization during cross examination: Title IX investigations in the wake of Trump administration's proposed regulations. *Roger Williams University Law Review, 25*(2). https://docs.rwu.edu/rwu_LR/vol25/iss2/3

Creative Interventions. (2012). *How to give a genuine apology.* Creative Interventions Toolkit: A practical guide to stop interpersonal violence. https://www.creative-interventions.org/toolkit/

Cruz, J. (2021). The constraints of fear and neutrality in Title IX administrators' responses to sexual violence. *The Journal of Higher Education, 92*(3), 363–384, https://doi.org/10.1080/00221546.2020.1809268

Ferguson, C. E., & Malouff, J. M. (2016). Assessing police classifications of sexual assault reports: A meta-analysis of false reporting rates. *Archives of Sexual Behavior, 45*(5), 1185–1193. https://doi.org/10.1007/s10508-015-0666-2

Koss, M. P. (2014). The RESTORE program of restorative justice for sex crimes: Vision, process, and outcomes. *Journal of Interpersonal Violence, 29*(9), 1623–1660. https://doi.org/10.1177/0886260513511537

Lorenz, K., Hayes, R., & Jacobsen, C. (2021, November 7). "Title IX isn't for you, it's for the university": Sexual violence survivors' experiences of institutional betrayal in Title IX investigations. *CrimRxiv.* https://doi.org/10.21428/cb6ab371.1959e20b

McGlynn, C., Westmarland, N., & Godden, N. (2012). "I just wanted him to hear me": Sexual violence and the possibilities of restorative justice. *Journal of Law and Society, 39*(2), 213–240. https://doi.org/10.1111/j.1467-6478.2012.00579.x

Mingus, Mia. (2019). The four parts of accountability and how to give a genuine apology. *Leaving Evidence Blog.* https://leavingevidence.wordpress.com/2019/12/18/how-to-give-a-good-apology-part-1-the-four-parts-of-accountability/

Nesbitt, S., & Carson, S. (2021). *The cost of reporting: Perpetrator retaliation, institutional betrayal, and student survivor pushout.* Know Your IX. https://www.knowyourix.org/wp-content/uploads/2021/03/Know-Your-IX-2021-Report-Final-Copy.pdf

RAINN (Rape, Abuse & Incest National Network). (2022, September). Perpetrators of sexual violence: Statistics. https://www.rainn.org/statistics/perpetrators-sexual-violence

Sered, D. (2019). *Until we reckon: Violence, mass incarceration, and a road to repair.* The New Press.

Swartout, K. M., Koss, M. P., White, J. W., Thompson, M. P., Abbey, A., & Bellis, A. L. (2015). Trajectory analysis of the campus serial rapist assumption. *JAMA Pediatrics, 169*(12), 1148–1154. https://jamanetwork.com/journals/jamapediatrics/fullarticle/2375127

The Violence Against Women Act (VAWA), Title IV of the Violent Crime Control and Law Enforcement Act, H.R. 3355. (1994)

Zehr, H. (2002). *The little book of restorative justice.* Good Books.

PART TWO

PROCESS AND INTERVENTION

4

BUILDING RESTORATIVE OPTIONS

Jessica D. Naidu and David R. Karp

Alicia and Derek[1] were in an intimate relationship, and during one sexual encounter Derek intentionally removed the condom without Alicia's consent or knowledge in an act called "stealthing." When Alicia realized what had happened, she was devastated.

She couldn't ignore what had happened, but Alicia, who is Black, said she "didn't want to see another Black man go through a criminal process." Alicia wanted to know if Derek cared and if he felt remorse. She needed him to admit that stealthing was sexual assault, understand how the experience left her feeling betrayed, and take responsibility for this harmful act.

Luckily, Alicia attended a university that offered an alternative to a formal and highly punitive hearing process. Instead of relying on a conduct administrator or board to determine Derek's responsibility and potential consequences, she could have a voice in how the case would be resolved. She chose an approach often referred to as a restorative conference, *which involves a facilitated face-to-face structured dialogue with restorative justice facilitators who are trained to handle cases of sexual harm.*—As told by Restorative Justice cofacilitators in an interview with the authors

estorative justice (RJ) is far from one-size-fits-all. In fact, many institutions offer a menu of options, allowing harmed parties to choose what type of restorative model suits their needs (see Table 4.1 for a comparison of models). Campuses have begun to offer a spectrum of restorative approaches, including conferences, shuttle facilitation, and circles for incidents of sexual harm, each offering its own method of achieving restorative outcomes. In each approach there are intentional facilitative design elements, such as scripts to follow for each model (see Appendix A), all of which allow for structured flexibility to tailor the experience to the participants' needs. Through each restorative model, a few elements are key: include support people, assess participant readiness, and don't rush the process.

> *"It's tough work. It's not easy," said Avery Arrington, an experienced RJ facilitator. "If you don't have time, then you don't really have a case. You have to be willing to put the time in—however long it takes."*
>
> —A. Arrington & A. Miele, personal communication, November 10, 2021

TABLE 4.1
Comparing the Models

Model	Circle	Conference	Shuttle Facilitation
Purpose	Widespread community harm, ripple harms, addressing climate/culture	Specific incident of harm, face-to-face communication	Specific incident of harm, no face-to-face interaction between person harmed and person responsible
Process	Circle process with talking piece	Structured and unstructured dialogue, use of a facilitator script	Indirect dialogue via facilitator who shuttles between parties
People to Include	Trained RJ facilitator and cofacilitator, person responsible, person harmed, impacted community members, other community stakeholders	Trained RJ facilitator and cofacilitator, person responsible, person harmed, support people for each, impacted community members	Trained RJ facilitator and cofacilitator, person responsible, person harmed
Examples	Rape chants, incidents involving groups and organizations, Incidents with several bystanders	1:1 incident of harm	Harmed party wants something restorative but does not want to be in the same room as the person responsible, when risk of revictimization is high
Roots	North American Indigenous peacemaking circles	Indigenous Maori conflict resolution, Australian policing	Shuttle diplomacy and mediation, preconference process

Note. RJ = restorative justice.

In this chapter, we describe the conference model as well as two others: shuttle facilitation and a restorative circle. An at-a-glance comparison of the models is pictured in Table 4.1.

Conferences

- Purpose: address a specific incident of harm, face-to-face communication
- People to include: a trained RJ facilitator and cofacilitator, person responsible, person harmed, (optional) support people for each

A Short History of Restorative Conferences

Conferences have two distinct histories, one from in the United States and another from New Zealand and Australia.

In 1978, a Mennonite Christian criminal justice reformer named Howard Zehr started the first contemporary RJ program in Elkhart, Indiana. Zehr was inspired by an informal restorative case facilitated by a Mennonite colleague in Canada a few years earlier and motivated by what Zehr (1990) defined as "covenant justice," the covenant between God and the Israelites: "To do justice is to make things right" (p. 137). This first program was organized by a simple model of bringing together victims and offenders into dialogue around "facts, feelings, and agreements" (Zehr, 1990, p. 161) and facilitated by a trained community volunteer. Into the 1980s, hundreds of victim–offender dialogue programs emerged across the United States and Europe (Umbreit & Armour, 2011).

A similar model independently emerged in New Zealand and Australia in the early 1990s. In 1989, landmark legislation was passed in response to concern about disproportionate representation of indigenous Maori youth in child welfare and youth justice cases. The legislation prioritized empowering families and being culturally responsive (MacRae & Zehr, 2004). A model emerged called *family group conferences* that would be tried first before referring to the courts. According to Moore and McDonald (1995),

> the phrase "family group" is a rough translation of the Maori *whanau*—the extended family, and the process itself derives from the traditional Maori practice of meeting on the *marae* [traditional communal gathering place] to seek a collective response to wrongdoing. (p. 4)

After learning about the New Zealand model, a police agency in Australia customized it for use in youth justice cases and created a facilitator script that now forms the basis of most restorative conference practices (Umbreit & Armour, 2011). Conferences are often distinguished from victim–offender dialogues and family group conferences by the use of a script, and all of them are distinguished from circle practices by the flow of the dialogue. Only in circle practices do participants use a talking piece and structure the flow of turn-taking by passing it from one person to the next around the circle. In contrast, victim–offender dialogues are typically unstructured but facilitated dialogues that focus on healing and mutual understanding. In restorative conferencing, the facilitator relies on the script to ask a series of questions to the person responsible; then a series of questions to the harmed parties; and then to others present, such as support persons, and finally repeating the pattern. Of all of the restorative practices, the conferencing model has accumulated the most empirical evidence evaluating its effectiveness, particularly with high participant satisfaction and reduced recidivism (Braithwaite, 2021).

About the Restorative Conference Process

A conference is an RJ model that facilitates a structured face-to-face dialogue between two or more people—typically the person harmed and the person responsible. Support people and other impacted community members can also join the process (Orcutt et al., 2020).

The following are some questions often included (Karp & Armour, 2019)

For the person responsible:

- What happened?
- What were you thinking at the time?
- What have you thought about since?
- Who has been impacted and how?
- What needs to happen to make things right (to the extent possible)?
- How can we rebuild trust?

For the harmed party:

- What happened from your perspective?
- What impact has this had on you?
- What has been the hardest thing about this?
- What do you need?
- What would you like to see the other person do to repair the harm they have caused you?

What many practitioners consider the most important part of the conference is what comes before the conference even begins. Facilitators spend the majority of their time engaged in individualized meetings, called *preconferencing*, to meet the following goals:

- Allow each party to share their story and feel heard.
- Unpack the needs of the person harmed. (Do they want support? To feel safe again? Peace of mind that the person responsible will not reoffend?)
- Assess whether the person responsible is ready to take accountability. (Do they understand the harm they have caused? Are they willing to take steps to repair harm and regain trust?)
- Evaluate willingness to engage restoratively. (Is the harmed party only looking for punishment? Is the person responsible simply trying to avoid punishment? Are there mental health concerns that would prevent parties from making informed choices? Have they been pressured to participate?)

As detailed in chapter 8, "Facilitating Repair and Restoration," facilitators need to tune into details, ensuring that everyone involved is participating voluntarily and assessing whether the process would cause further victimization. Although facilitators are not clinicians in a position to make a diagnosis, they should look for clear signs of mental illness that would inhibit effective participation. Another red flag would be if the person who caused harm is minimizing the impact or displacing responsibility. Each participant should be ready to approach the process with a restorative mindset, the belief that each of us is deserving of dignity and respect and capable of growth and change (Karp, 2019).

"The prework is so critical," Arrington said. "They both have to be in the right space" (A. Arrington & A. Miele, personal communication, November 10, 2021).

> *When Derek learned that Alicia had reported the assault and that she requested it be resolved using a restorative option, he agreed to participate. He recognized that he had hurt her, but he was not ready to call what he did sexual assault; that was a label he was not yet able to accept.*
>
> *When people are accused of sexual misconduct, our society (media, lawyers, family, friends) often encourages them to deny responsibility for it, and an RJ process helps them see value in accepting responsibility for their own personal growth and for people they have harmed. Initially, Derek was only able to accept partial responsibility. In this restorative framework, the journey began with separate preparatory meetings. Cofacilitators met with Derek at least four times over the course of 9 months to prepare for the restorative conference, providing counseling and education on stealthing so that he could start to grasp the impact. Over the same period, they also met with Alicia many times to help her with her own healing journey and to explore what she most wanted in the form of accountability.*

In addition to these meetings, the cofacilitators helped both students identify people who would commit to supporting them throughout the process. Factoring in identity and professional experience, cofacilitators intentionally recommended support people for Alicia and Derek to consider. With inclusive decision making being a central tenet of restorative practice, they wanted Alicia and Derek to have the opportunity to vet them as well, so they arranged 1:1 meetings for each to meet potential support people, get to know each of them, and decide whether it was a good fit. In this case, both found good matches. Alicia's support person was a woman of color and a clinician who could continue to counsel Alicia even after the process. Derek's support person worked with the university's Violence Prevention Victim Assistance program and helped to educate him about healthy relationships; communication during sex; and, specifically, stealthing.

Come conference time, there should be no surprises. Yet, even with months of preconference meetings, there are always surprises that require facilitative adaptability, discretion, and judgment. It is also a delicate balance of allowing for genuine emotion while preparing participants to hear the honesty as it comes through.

When Alicia and Derek sat down face to face for the first time since the incident, emotions were understandably high. "It was the opening sentence and [she] started spewing a monologue . . . there was a lot of rage," one cofacilitator said, adding that facilitators should not be afraid to pause the conference. "We took a moment, talked and regrouped."

An RJ conference begins with a discussion of the harm and the impact of the incident; then the facilitator guides the conversation to focus on the underlying needs of the harmed party. With the harm and needs at the center, the person responsible can take active accountability, committing to steps that begin repairing the harm to the extent possible. Desired outcomes vary widely depending on the participants, but some common examples include an apology, counseling, education and research, and engagement in activities to educate peers. Voluntary separation from the university, until the person harmed graduates, for example, is also a potential outcome. The parties discuss the possible outcomes and come to agreement about what best suits their needs.

For Alicia and Derek, the outcome included a no-contact order. Derek also agreed to continue working on himself through regular voluntary counseling.

Facilitators should follow up after the process to check in on and monitor the progress of the agreed-upon outcomes (Orcutt et al., 2020). Support people can also be tapped to continue the mentoring process. It is also common to agree on a contingency plan during the conference, so next steps are clear should the person responsible not comply with the agreements. Some institutions have policies that would revert the case through the traditional investigative conduct process and/or place the violation on the record of the person responsible.

Victim Offender Dialogue

We believe restorative conferences provide an excellent balance of structured communication to ensure safety and prompts that allow for authentic engagement. Some advanced conference facilitators have incorporated elements of the victim–offender dialogue model to enable deeper engagement and healing. This approach was developed in the 1980s as a humanistic approach to mediation by Mark Umbreit at the University of Minnesota School of Social Work (Umbreit & Armour, 2018). In this model, the facilitator works with the harmed party and the person who caused harm in great depth, carefully preparing them for face-to-face dialogue. Often, this predialogue work will include dozens of meetings over the course of many months or a year. It is also common for this approach to foster a healing dialogue, in which the participants have time and space to clarify their own stories, harms, and needs. Typically, they occur well after the case has been adjudicated, sometimes decades later. As such, they tend not to focus on developing a restorative action plan; instead, the dialogue itself is the end of the process. Advanced facilitators may draw on this methodology to create greater space for unscripted interaction.

Shuttle Facilitation

- Purpose: indirect communication that does not include face-to-face interaction between the person harmed and person responsible
- People to include: trained RJ facilitator and cofacilitator, person responsible, person harmed

A Short History of Shuttle Facilitation

Shuttle facilitation is an indirect communication model used between individuals when meeting face to face would be unsafe or unproductive. The model is also referred to by some practitioners as *shuttle negotiation* or *shuttle diplomacy*.

Shuttle diplomacy was the term coined in the 1970s when U.S. diplomats met with representatives separately while trying to negotiate a peace deal in the Middle East (Hoffman, 2011). Joanna Shapland (2007) called shuttle facilitation "indirect mediation." She evaluated two programs in England that offered both indirect (shuttle) and direct facilitation (conferences). These included both youth and adult criminal cases, including robbery, assault, burglary, theft, and fraud (Shapland et al., 2006). Of 180 cases, 134 were resolved with indirect facilitation:

> The "best thing" was, for . . . offenders, making the apology, making the other party feel better, and communicating with the other party. For victims, it was talking about the offence or the apology. . . . Almost all offenders interviewed apologised and most victims said they accepted the apology. There was a significant difference between direct and indirect mediation cases as to whether victims said in interviews with them that they accepted the apology, with the likelihood of accepting it greater in direct mediation. (Shapland et al., 2007, p. 32)

Although often compared to mediation, shuttle facilitation is distinct in that the goal is to foster communication between the parties (albeit indirectly) in order to lead to joint decision making.

When campuses offer restorative options, it is very helpful to distinguish between shuttle facilitation and conferencing so that potential participants understand that face to face is not a requirement. It is often the case that participants begin the process with reluctance about meeting face to face, but later, as trust develops, they end up choosing it.

About the Shuttle Facilitation Process

Had Alicia not wanted to meet face to face with Derek, shuttle facilitation may have been an alternative option.

Shuttle facilitation is a restorative model that does not include face-to-face dialogue. Instead, a facilitator works with participants individually and "shuttles" information back and forth until the parties come to resolution. As described in a chapter by Schrage and Hipolito in *Reframing Campus Conflict* (2020), shuttle facilitation or shuttle diplomacy is often used to deescalate conflict between student advocacy groups and campus administrators, particularly when the incidents are "deeply personal, multilayered, and extremely complex" (p. 228). Given the power dynamics and sensitivity inherent in cases of relationship violence and sexual harm, shuttle facilitation is also a useful tool in addressing gender-based misconduct. The indirect nature of shuttle facilitation can prevent further harm while still finding a path forward.

Shuttle facilitation can be thought of in two distinct ways. It can be a stand-alone process or one that is used as part of a face-to-face process. As a stand-alone process, it is similar to shuttle diplomacy, where the participants are never expected to meet face to face as part of the process (Brett et al., 1986).

At both the University of Michigan and Rutgers, early adopters of RJ for cases of sexual harm, shuttle facilitation is the most commonly chosen process when harmed parties have the option (Orcutt et al., 2020).

Shuttle facilitation is actually a core element of a face-to-face process as well. Before participants meet face to face, facilitators need to meet with the participants individually. In the context of a conference model, this is often called *preconferencing*, and practitioners have a set of tasks to accomplish during this phase of the process to ensure the meeting goes smoothly and reduce the risk of further harm being caused. The preconference includes (a) an explanation of the RJ process so participants can make fully informed decisions about whether to proceed; (b) gathering information about the incident that enables facilitators to determine if the participants are able to participate restoratively—such as the person who caused harm's willingness to take responsibility or a harmed party's willingness to seek restorative rather than punitive outcomes; and (c) the opportunity for participants to get to know the facilitator to build rapport and trust. Sometimes only one preconference meeting is necessary; however, it is more typical for there to be several meetings and for the facilitator to shuttle questions and answers between the participants. It may often happen that the participants find resolution during the preconference process and choose not to proceed with a face-to-face meeting. When RJ is narrowly defined as a face-to-face meeting such outcomes could be mistakenly perceived a a failure, that is, the facilitator was unable to get the participants to meet, when in fact it should be understood as a successful RJ process. In this sense, it is helpful to think of shuttle facilitation as a distinct process rather than simply preconference preparation.

Restorative Circles

- Purpose: mitigate widespread community harm, ripple harm, address climate/culture, but also sometimes use like restorative conferences to address specific incidents of harm
- People to include: trained RJ facilitator and cofacilitator, person(s) responsible, person(s) harmed, community members impacted

A Short History of Restorative Circles

Contemporary use of restorative circles is based on traditional circle practices of North American indigenous communities (Reed, 2021). In 1982, tribal judges established the Navajo Peacemaker Court to promote an a world-view where

> an offender is someone who "acts as if he has no relatives" and shows little regard for right relationships; the solution, according to traditional Navajo practice, is to "bring in the relatives" to teach that he or she is connected to and part of the community. (Boyes-Watson & Pranis, 2015, p. 13)

Also in 1982, Barry Stuart, a judge in the Yukon began using "circle sentencing" (Umbreit & Armour, 2011). In 1987, an Ojibwe community in Canada started the Hollow Water Community Holistic Circle Healing Programme to address pervasive sexual harm and intergenerational trauma (Ross, 1996).

Circle practices expanded beyond indigenous communities primarily as a result of the active work of Kay Pranis, a planner with the Minnesota Department of Corrections, who began a collaboration with Barry Stuart and a Carcross/Tagish First Nation Chief, Mark Wedge. They published a seminal book in 2003, *Peacemaking Circles* (Pranis et al., 2003), which was followed by Boyes-Watson and Pranis's (2015) guide to applying circles in schools, *Circle Forward*.

About the Circle Process

Imagine Derek did not harm just one individual, but instead was part of an athletic team that encouraged one another to stealth their partners. In this hypothetical scenario, a video surfaces that features several prominent student athletes stating unprotected sex feels better and encouraging each other to secretly remove condoms during sex. The video goes viral.

In this case, Derek isn't the only person responsible. He's one of a dozen students who participated in the harmful banter caught on video. Students across campus are outraged, demanding the institution hold the men accountable. Several women have sought counseling after the video triggered memories and retraumatization from past assaults. The local high school coach is concerned about sending his players to participate in summer camps with the collegiate athletes because parents in the community do not want their children exposed to such influences. The impact has spread far and wide.

An RJ circle shares some key elements with a conference but typically includes more participants that represent community-wide harm. The circle process is a structured dialogue with the community that has been harmed by the incident and its ripple effects, making it a useful tool to address not only specific incidents but also the underlying campus climate or culture (Orcutt et al., 2020). Depending on the number of participants and the issue, facilitators could hold numerous circles.

According to Pranis (2005), circle practices have a set of common elements, including the use of a talking piece that is passed from one person to the next around the circle to structure the flow of the dialogue and ensure equal opportunity for participation; opening and closing activities to help build trust and common commitment to a set of values; and a series of guiding questions that enable participants to share their perspective about the topic of the circle. Circle practices tend to be more inclusive than other RJ processes, meaning that they try to include more representation of the community rather than a more private dialogue, such as a facilitation between a harmed party and person responsible alone.

Community circles generally focus on larger social issues, such as sexism or rape culture, and include not only personal accountability but also efforts toward social change. In our scenario, not only would the individual athletes be accountable, but the community would be engaged in efforts to change the culture and prevent future harm.

In addition to addressing harm, circles can be used as an educational tool and preventative measure for various behaviors, including sexual misconduct. As described by McMahon and Karp (2020) in *Reframing Campus Conflict*, one application of a sexual misconduct circle facilitates a conversation among students about the continuum of inappropriate behavior (p. 317). After listening to a scenario involving sexual misconduct, the group discussed the points in the scenario they deemed inappropriate versus the points where the behavior violated the institution's policy. Students participating in the circle then watched "Tea Consent," a video that uses someone offering another person tea as a metaphor for consent (Blue Seat Studios, 2015). They discussed their reactions to the video and statistics about rape on college campuses while gaining a deeper understanding of setting and respecting boundaries and skillsets in interpersonal communication and healthy relationships (McMahon & Karp, 2020).

Note

1. *Alicia* and *Derek* are pseudonyms used to protect privacy. Their story is a real case study as told to us through interviews with the cofacilitators of their RJ conference.

References

Blue Seat Studios. (2015, May 12). *Tea consent* [Video]. YouTube. https://www.youtube.com/watch?v=oQbei5JGiT8&ab_channel=BlueSeatStudios

Boyes-Watson, C., & Pranis, K. (2015). *Circle forward: Building a restorative school community*. Living Justice Press.

Braithwaite, J. (2021). Street-level meta-strategies: Evidence on restorative justice and responsive regulation. *Annual Review of Law and Social Science, 17*, 205–225. https://doi.org/10.1146/annurev-lawsocsci-111720-013149

Brett, J. M., Drieghe, R., & Shapiro, D. L. (1986). Mediator style and mediation effectiveness. *Negotiation Journal, 2*(3), 277–285. https://doi.org/10.1007/BF00999113

Hoffman, D. A. (2011). Mediation and the art of shuttle diplomacy. *Negotiation Journal, 27*(3), 263–309. https://doi.org/10.1111/j.1571-9979.2011.00309.x

Karp, D. R. (2019). *The little book of restorative justice for colleges and universities: Repairing harm and rebuilding trust in response to student misconduct* (2nd ed.). Good Books.

MacRae, A., & Zehr, H. (2004). *Little book of family group conferences New Zealand Style: A hopeful approach when youth cause harm*. Good Books.

McMahon, S., & Karp, D. (2020). Building relational and critical thinking skills: The power of peer-led restorative justice circles among first-year college students. In J. M. Schrage & N. G. Giacomini, (Eds.), *Reframing campus conflict: Student conduct through the lens of inclusive excellence* (pp. 308–320). Stylus.

Moore, D. B., & McDonald, J. M. (1995). Achieving the "good community": A local police initiative and its wider ramifications. In K. M. Hazlehurst (Ed.), *Perceptions of justice: Issues in Indigenous and community empowerment* (pp. 143–173). Ashgate.

Orcutt, M., Petrowski, P. M., Karp, D. R., & Draper, J. (2020). Restorative justice approaches to the informal resolution of student sexual misconduct. *Journal of College and University Law, 42*(1), 1–76. https://digital.sandiego.edu/soles-faculty/15

Pranis, K. (2005). *The little book of circle processes*. Good Books.

Pranis, K., Stuart, B., & Wedge, M. (2003). *Peacemaking circles*. Living Justice Press.

Reed, T. (2021). A critical review of the Native American tradition of circle practices. In R. Throne (Ed.), *Indigenous research of land, self, and spirit* (pp. 132–152). IGI Global.

Ross, R. (1996). *Returning to the teachings: Exploring Aboriginal justice*. Penguin.

Schrage, J. M., & Hippolito, V. (2020). Negotiating peace on campus through shuttle diplomacy. In J. M. Schrage and N. G. Giacomini (Eds.), *Reframing campus conflict: Student conduct practice through the lens of inclusive excellence* (2nd ed.; pp. 228–240). Stylus.

Shapland, J., Atkinson, A., Atkinson, H., Chapman, B., Colledge, E., Dignan, J., Howes, M., Johnstone, J., Robinson, G., & Sorsby, A. (2006) *Restorative justice in practice: The second report from the evaluation of three schemes*. Centre for Criminological Research, University of Sheffield. https://restorativejustice.org.uk/sites/default/files/resources/files/Full%20report.pdf

Shapland, J., Atkinson, A., Atkinson, H., Chapman, B., Dignan, J., Howes, M., Johnstone, J., Robinson, G., & Sorsby, A. (2007) *Restorative justice: The views of victims and offenders.* Centre for Criminological Research, University of Sheffield. https://www.oijj.org/sites/default/files/documentos/documental_6425_en.pdf

Umbreit, M., & Armour, M. P. (2011). *Restorative justice dialogue.* Springer.

Umbreit, M., & Armour, M. P. (2018). *Violence, restorative justice, and forgiveness.* Jessica Kingsley.

Zehr, H. (1990). *Changing lenses.* Herald.

5

WHEN INFORMAL
IS FORMAL

Procedural Documents, Memoranda of
Understanding, Agreements, and Administrative
Case Management Considerations

Chelsea Jacoby and Joe Zichi

A s the coauthors, we want to introduce ourselves and provide context around the lenses we will be using in this chapter and how we are each situated in this space. Chelsea Jacoby has worked at The College of New Jersey (TCNJ) for 5 years, where she serves as Title IX coordinator and director of Title IX compliance and sexual misconduct. As Title IX coordinator and a leader on campus, she oversees the college's compliance with Title IX and other laws/regulations relating to discrimination and sex or gender-based violence. This includes receiving and monitoring all reports of sexual harassment/misconduct; implementing supportive measures; and facilitating resolution processes, including formal investigation/adjudication processes and those informal in nature and grounded in restorative practices.

Joe Zichi served as the associate director of the Office of Student Conflict Resolution at the University of Michigan—Ann Arbor (UMich) until May 2022, when he transitioned to another role at UMich, with a continued and expanded focus of collective impact on community well-being. As Office of Student Conflict Resolution associate director, Joe was responsible for determining appropriate sanctions and interventions when there is a finding of responsibility under the University of Michigan Sexual and Gender-Based Misconduct Policy (the UMich policy). Further, Joe supervised staff responsible for the Adaptable Resolution (AR) pathway under the UMich policy. Joe has been a practitioner of restorative practices for nearly 15 years and engaged with student sexual and gender-based misconduct cases for nearly a decade.

Both authors have been intricately engaged in developing student policies and procedures for sexual and gender-based misconduct on each of our campuses, and our institutions have been among the few to pioneer this work. This chapter will share practical knowledge and insight garnered over the years related to implementing informal resolution processes for cases of gender-based and sexual misconduct, in a tangible and practical way.

Incorporating informal resolution as a pathway to address gender-based and sexual misconduct provides an alternative approach to address Title IX obligations; this approach can be empowering to complainants, offering them voice and choice while allowing respondents to acknowledge and actively engage in repairing harm (Karp et al., 2016; Orcutt et al., 2020). Informal resolution processes at TCNJ and UMich embrace the restorative justice (RJ) philosophy outlined by Zehr (2015): inclusive decision making, active accountability, repairing harm, and rebuilding trust (Karp et al., 2016). Federal regulations are primarily focused on formal investigations and hearings yet do permit the use of informal means of resolution, leaving practitioners seeking guidance on how to implement informal approaches to achieve resolution. However, while adaptable by design, informal resolution is anything but informal.

Informal resolution practitioners have an obligation to their institution, complainants, and respondents, both in good faith and under federal law (i.e., Title IX of the Education Amendments of 1972 [Pub. L. 93-218], Violence Against Women Act, Jeanne Clery Disclosure of Campus Security Policy and Campus Crime Statistics Act of 1990) to formalize protocols, procedures, and case records to maintain the integrity of "informal" or AR processes and uphold due process. This chapter will highlight critical structures necessary to successfully maintain and carry out informal resolution processes.

While consistent in philosophy and spirit, our two campuses utilize different approaches, templates, and language to ultimately achieve the similar objectives. For simplicity, we strive to use consistent terminology throughout the chapter while fully recognizing that there may be large variations in vocabulary. For example, UMich informal resolution is referred to as *adaptable resolution*; TCNJ uses the term *alternative resolution*. The differences between our processes/approaches help to demonstrate that there is not a one-size-fits-all approach to informal resolution. This chapter will provide readers with essential templates (including examples from each of our institutions) when it comes to critical documents and forms used throughout an informal resolution process, best practices in administrative case management, and suggestions and points of consideration when creating memoranda of under-standing to preserve the integrity of informal resolution programs utilizing an RJ framework.

Critical Documents and Forms for Informal Resolution

Various types of correspondence, forms, and documents are required to be shared with the parties and utilized by the facilitator throughout the informal resolution process. Many of these are required to be sent to parties under federal regulations, while others serve to document different phases of the resolution process and efforts taken to ensure a fair and impartial process. Some specific examples include Formal Complaints, Notice of Allegations, Informal Resolution Intake Forms, and Resolution Agreement Templates.

Formal Complaint

Per the 2020 Title IX Final Rule (hereafter, *Final Rule*; officially titled the Nondiscrimination on the Basis of Sex in Education Programs or Activities Receiving Federal Financial Assistance, 34 C.F.R. § 106 [2020]), prior to an institution implementing a resolution process for allegations of sexual har-assment, a formal complaint must be filed and signed. A formal complaint, as defined by the U.S. Office for Civil Rights' Department of Education, is "a document filed by a complainant or signed by the Title IX Coordinator alleging sexual harassment against a respondent and requesting that the recipient investigate the allegation of sexual harassment" (Office for Civil Rights, 2020). The Department of Education did not set forth a particular format or structure that the formal complaint must take, so institutions have exercised their discretion to organize the template. Some institutions have incorporated formal complaints into their already-established case management systems, allowing complainants to submit a formal complaint electronically via a link accessible on their public-facing websites. Others have created standardized templates in Microsoft Word or PDF versions to be filled in and signed only after being granted access to it through their Title IX office. Institutions should utilize whatever method they feel works best for their campus while still meeting federal guidelines. A formal com-plaint form utilized at TCNJ for allegations of sexual harassment/miscon-duct can be found in Appendix A.

The formal complaint serves as the foundation on which the resolu-tion process is built. The formal complaint should include the information that will be essential to include within the Notice of Allegations (NOA) letter, specifically the nature/details regarding allegations in question, and an indication of what process the institution will be pursuing—either at the written/signed request of the complainant or determined by the Title IX Coordinator. Per federal regulations, the formal requirement must also apply to requests for use of informal resolutions. Once this formal complaint is officially signed, this prompts an NOA letter to be sent to both parties, which typically initiates the institution's designated timeline to resolve the case.

Notification of Allegations

Following the submission of the signed complaint, the institution must put the respondent "on notice," which requires that an NOA letter be sent to both parties. The Final Rule is prescriptive in what information must be included in this letter. The intent behind sending both parties comprehensive outreach is to adequately inform them of their rights, resources, and options (and is an example of due process protections). Because the NOA will typically be the first time the respondent is made aware of the allegations, they may be inundated with a substantial amount of information to process all at once—all of which may not even be relevant at that time, or at all. For example, the institution is required to include information regarding a formal grievance process (i.e., associated procedures, the standard of evidence to be used, the presumption of innocence), even when an informal resolution process has been requested and, on the opposite end, required to make the respondent aware of the availability of an informal resolution, even if the complainant has already indicated they are not interested or if the Title IX coordinator concludes informal resolution is inappropriate for the alleged behavior. These circumstances can unfortunately create unrealistic expectations for parties and potentially lead to confusion and distrust in the process. In addition to unpacking all that comes with being accused of sexual misconduct, the respondent may still be unsure and confused on how to best proceed, what options are realistically available, or the extent to which their education may be at risk, even after thoroughly reading through the NOA they receive. While the institution has provided the notice, and met its requirements under federal law, the parties may still not be in a position to effectively participate with only having received the NOA. This serves as a reminder that although institutions must send out this notice to both parties to comply with the obligations set forth under the law, the law itself sets the minimum for what is required, and there are ways institutions can go about both fulfilling their duties and engaging with members of their campus community in meaningful and helpful ways. Some schools schedule follow-up meetings with the parties as soon as possible, to help them understand the information shared, while other schools prefer to present these letters in person.

Variation exists in how institutions position their NOA letters to students. However, the imperative is for the institution to provide the robust information required by the Title IX Final Rule in a way that is user/student friendly and accessible. For example, in an effort to dose information to the respondent, the NOA letter at UMich makes it explicit that the respondent will be made aware of adaptable resolution viability at such time when it is known. Below are some further points for consideration in crafting an accessible and compliant notice of allegation.

Suggestions and Things to Consider

Clearly indicate what type of resolution process has been requested and which are available to decrease confusion. The following are two examples:

- UMich—"The Respondent will be made aware of adaptable resolution viability at such time when it is known."
- TCNJ—"In this particular case, the Reporter has signed a Formal Complaint requesting that the College utilize the Alternative Resolution Process to resolve this matter. As a result, a formal investigation into the alleged behavior has not been initiated through the Office of Title IX & Sexual Misconduct and no formal charges have been placed at this time. However, should circumstances change, and a Formal Grievance Process is pursued, you will receive formal notification of the investigation commencing and information regarding the associated alleged violation(s) and how to effectively participate in the process."

Organize the NOA into clearly defined sections (i.e., bolded and underlined headers to denote different, important topics). Sample structure might include:

- Details of allegations
- Resolution Processes (separate header for each process)
- Formal Grievance Process
- Informal Resolution Option
- Notice of Dismissal & Appeal Opportunity (if applicable)
- Scheduling of Intake Meeting
- Right to an Advisor
- Available Supportive Measures, Resources, & Reasonable Accommodations

Make intentional efforts to translate jargon into easily understandable language. It can also be helpful to utilize graphics and flowcharts to help explain processes rather than just plain text. To the extent feasible, maximize the inclusion of clickable hyperlinks to help deliver significant amounts of information without excessively lengthening the NOA. Additionally, it would be wise to consult with your institution's general counsel to determine their interpretation of the regulations. Items to discuss include the extent to which links can be utilized versus the expectation that text be dedicated in the allegation letter, or via PDF attachments.

The regulations require that all involved parties have access to the same information, and therefore, the NOA should provide an outline of both resolution pathways so that the parties can make an informed decision on how they would like to proceed. However, in recognizing how overwhelming and lengthy this outreach may be, it is encouraged that the respondent also be offered the opportunity to meet with appropriate staff for an intake meeting (similar to what would have already been offered to/taken place with the complainant) so that all of their rights, resources, options, and procedural expectations can be thoroughly reviewed and understood.

Informal Resolution Intake Process and Forms

Individual informal resolution intake meetings should be scheduled by the informal resolution coordinator/facilitator if the Title IX coordinator, complainant, and respondent consent to this resolution pathway. The primary objectives at this stage are (a) to explain the information resolution process in depth to the parties and (b) determine viability of the informal resolution pathway.

At UMich, during the separate intake meetings with the respondent and complainant the facilitator will review the AR Participation Agreement. Reviewing the Participation Agreement provides an opportunity for each party to understand the AR process, including their rights and responsibilities. Additionally, the Participation Agreement reiterates that AR is a voluntary process, that outcomes are not guaranteed, and that any party may decide to disengage at any time (with a referral back to the Title IX coordinator). The Participation Agreement does not dictate what the resolution pathway would specifically consist of, nor does it mandate a party's participation, but rather signing the agreement indicates a general understanding of the available rights, options, and a willingness to explore an informal resolution. Samples of how these agreements are laid out at each of our institutions can be found in Appendix A.

As is the case with all aspects of informal resolution, there is not a universal approach to crafting participation agreements. For example, at TCNJ, page 1 of the AR Agreement achieves the same goals as UMich's Participation Agreement, but the only difference is, because TCNJ has primarily facilitated informal resolution processes through shuttle diplomacy, the Participation Agreement and Resolution Agreement are commonly combined into one singular document that is ultimately signed by both parties prior to the initiation of the process, rather than parsing them out individually. With that said, should a complainant at TCNJ wish to proceed with a restorative circle, those agreements would be separated and the process would closely mirror that of UMich.

Both schools include a checklist approach to the intake meeting. For a facilitator, following the checklist model ensures consistency and that both regulatory and policy expectations have been discussed, understood, and affirmed by the individual parties (via initialing each bullet point). In the event that there is not an agreement with any aspect of the informal resolution process, the facilitator can refer the parties and the checklist back to the Title IX coordinator. For added flexibility, the checklist approach also allows for virtual meetings. Finally, the checklist format minimizes the need for facilitator case notes to be added to the electronic case file by referencing the checklist rather than writing a lengthy summary.

The use of a checklist should not negate the need for a live meeting. There are other critical goals of the informal resolution intake meeting, such as building rapport with each party, learning of desired outcomes, and determining the viability of engagement with each party (Orcutt et al., 2020). The informal resolution intake checklist is a valuable tool to facilitate this stage of the informal resolution process. Regardless of the approach, participation agreements should clearly articulate the scope of informal resolution and outline the rights and responsibilities of participating in informal resolution (Nondiscrimination on the Basis of Sex in Education Programs or Activities Receiving Federal Financial Assistance, 2020). Participation agreements help schools protect against coercion and are a key way to document willingness to move forward.

Informal Resolution Agreement

Common questions asked when implementing informal processes include What does an informal resolution process look like from start to finish? How is the informal resolution agreement created? What happens if the respondent doesn't agree with the options outlined in the agreement or doesn't wish to participate in the process at all? What if the respondent agrees to participate in the process, but then fails to comply with that agreement? Who gets to decide what accountability looks like, and how?

Because each case is so unique, as will be the approach utilized by each institution, it can be difficult to provide clear-cut answers to these questions. However, as institutions attempt to navigate informal resolution processes, it is important to continually consider how the spirit of RJ is upheld. An informal resolution process rooted in RJ is focused on harm acknowledgment and identification of possible paths to address that harm that is agreed upon by everyone involved in the process (Koss et al., 2014). Each case is going to be inherently different, and therefore the process to resolve the case, especially informally, will be unique—including the overall contents of an institution's resolution agreements.

Contents of the Resolution Agreement

While each institution's process is going to vary, there are common elements to a resolution agreement that commonly include the purpose of the resolution option; grounds and expectations for participation; exceptions for use; procedures regarding documentation and privacy; and in some cases, an accountability framework. Facilitators may find it beneficial to create a template for the agreement that ensures consistency and compliance can exist between cases, while still embracing the individualized aspects of the agreement and the overall intention behind restorative practices. When drafting the resolution agreement, whether utilizing a formalized template or not, facilitators should remember that each agreement will be individualized to meet the specific needs/harms experienced by the complainant. But in order to proceed, both the complainant and respondent must reach a consensus on each aspect of the informal resolution agreement. In the spirit of multipartiality, the facilitator should help the parties work toward a resolution that meets the complainant's needs. In a negotiated process the parties may not come to a point of total agreement, but they might be able to achieve a consensus on what they are willing to accept that works toward meeting their needs and addresses the identified harms.

As an example of a commonly sought element to a resolution agreement, the complainant may, perhaps, request that the respondent agree to never enter a particular academic building on campus so that the complainant can have peace of mind knowing they will not unintentionally encounter the respondent. However, it is important to explore the potential for unintended results, such as the effect of a de facto suspension if the respondent also has legitimate reason to frequent the academic building in question. In such a scenario, the facilitator should explore the interests behind the complainant's position and see if common ground can be achieved. In this case, rather than a complete prohibition, both parties may agree on specific times to enter the building or map out specific routes inside the building in an effort to minimize unintentional contact. By diving in to better understand the complainant's specific needs, especially as they relate to the harms experienced, it may be possible for the facilitator to work with the parties to identify specific parameters that allow for the complainant's interests to be honored without creating unduly burdensome and potentially unreasonable circumstances for the respondent.

One way to help parties understand the process and what is possible through these informal processes is to share redacted copies of other informal resolution agreements or sample language that might be used. This tends to be unfamiliar territory for most parties, and the provision of some sample language offers a form of scaffolding to facilitate the process and inspires parties to move forward.

Facilitators should be prepared for the parties to potentially express interest in incorporating terms into the resolution agreement that extend beyond the scope and jurisdiction of the institution, such as a lifelong no-contact directive. Remember, parties enter into informal resolution agreements facilitated by the institution for a variety of reasons, including peace of mind, accountability, closure, healing, and/or a multitude of others. Even after leaving the institution, a facilitated informal resolution agreement may be the tool necessary to share with law enforcement or an employer, in the event there is breach of the agreement or repeated or future concerns. As such, parties may ultimately end up requesting that the informal resolution agreement include measures that extend beyond the institution's accountability apparatus.

Accountability Frameworks

A common question is "What happens if the respondent does not comply with the details of the agreement?" One way to address this is through the addition of an accountability framework (or contingency plan) should the respondent not comply. This plan or accountability framework is the mechanism by which the parties agree the respondent will be held accountable should the informal resolution agreement not be completed in its entirety. For example, an accountability framework may include a provision that allows the institution to charge the respondent with noncompliance and receive punitive sanctions as a result, if found in violation. Alternatively, the parties may be uninterested in establishing an accountability framework. The facilitator should encourage the parties to think about what they believe is prudent in the event the respondent disregards any or all of the terms of the agreement. This can be a difficult phase of the conversation, as the parties may determine that future noncompliance is unlikely or if the consequences of noncompliance are disproportionately severe. Nevertheless, incorporating accountability measures is essential to the specific case and the larger vitality of the informal resolution process. Whatever the parties decide to include, the accountability framework (or lack thereof) should be built into the informal resolution agreement and agreed upon by both parties and the Title IX coordinator.

In Table 5.1, we offer two examples from UMich (co-created accountability framework) and TCNJ (standardized accountability framework) of how the accountability framework can be created/included within the resolution agreement.

The accountability framework at TCNJ is already established and presented to parties within the AR agreement. However, at UMich the approach is to assist the complainant and respondent in authoring an accountability framework together, which resembles the organic approach taken when drafting the overall agreement as well.

TABLE 5.1
Accountability Framework

UMich	TCNJ
No standardized language—it's crafted in collaboration with the parties.	Accountability framework is standardized for all cases.
"What does accountability look like for you should this agreement not be followed?" The Title IX coordinator will also review and approve agreed-to accountability mechanisms in determining whether the agreement meets our Title IX obligations and community needs.	"By signing below, I indicate that I understand the requirements that must be completed for this alternative resolution process (as part of college policy) to be satisfied, and I also agree to complete the activities set forth above. I understand and acknowledge that if I fail to complete the activities set forth above, I may be charged with Failure to Comply with a Directive of a College Official under the college policy. I further understand and acknowledge that any sanction listed under the college policy may be imposed if I am found responsible for Failure to Comply with a Directive of a College Official, and that the findings of that case will be shared with the reporting party."

Note. UMich = University of Michigan; TCNJ = The College of New Jersey.

Facilitators may need to remind the parties that the institution may only be able to hold participants to the components of the agreement so long as the respondent is a member of the campus community. We do not recommended that lifelong provisions inherently be prohibited from the informal resolution agreement, nor are they prohibited by regulation. Indeed, such provisions may meet the interests of parties, and therefore are appropriate for inclusion in an RJ framework. However, since the institution will not have a relationship with the respondent forever, it is advisable that in instances where parties, upon learning about the scope and life cycle of the informal resolution, remain committed to lifelong provisions, the facilitator and the written agreement should make it explicitly clear to the parties that such an inclusion is acceptable so long as both parties understand the limitations of the institution to uphold such an agreement (i.e., that is is contingent on the respondent's enrollment or employment at the institution). It is advisable, therefore, for facilitators to make such limitations known to the parties and explicitly incorporate language to codify this understanding. When informing the parties of these limitations, consider the following:

- How broad of a jurisdiction does the institution want to adopt in regard to elements within the agreement? Will this be indefinite? Dissolved upon leaving the institution?
- Who will be drafting some sample language regarding accountability frameworks to offer parties to review when drafting an agreement? Where will that resource live?
- If a template is used, who in an administrative capacity is responsible for creating and revising the document (as needed)?
- In what circumstances, if any, will the Title IX coordinator be willing to approve of an agreement that lacks any form of accountability framework? How will consistency, accountability, and equity be maintained?

In the end, informal resolution agreements may be the preferred method of resolution by all parties for a variety of reasons. And, while informal resolution agreements allow for a more nimble, tailored resolution for the parties, there are limitations that should be considered by the facilitator and communicated to the involved parties at the onset of the initial informal resolution process and reiterated with sufficient dosage throughout the process. In addition to crafting the agreement, facilitators must remember that both the end product and the steps that lead up to the finalization and ultimately the completion of the agreement must be documented.

Effective Documentation Through Administrative Case Management

Documentation is a vital safeguard to the integrity of the informal resolution process and, therefore, a vital component for facilitators' due diligence and risk management for the institution and the parties. Simultaneously, and by design, the informal resolution process is not the formal grievance process as prescribed by the Final Rule. Participants may have been motivated to pursue informal resolution, in part, to avoid the heavily regulated, prescriptive, and structured formal resolution process as outlined by the regulations. Therefore, facilitators must proceed with holding multiple truths in the balance: avoiding so many forms, protocols, and procedures in the informal resolution process so it does not have the spirit of the formal resolution process while tending to administrative case management necessities and due process requirements. For many facilitators this balance requires as much prowess as the facilitation itself. This section will strive to highlight best practices of administrative case management for informal resolution with respect to documenting case notes/files, the use/benefits of case management software, and being clear about parameters related to informal resolution agreements.

Less Is More: Case Notes

Administrators within Title IX and student conduct are typically highly skilled at writing detailed case notes, whose training commonly emphasizes that case notes should be written in the third person with the assumption that they will be seen by the president or submitted as evidence in court, while the students involved are standing over each shoulder while you type. Case notes should accurately account for a meeting, a hearing, an appeal, case closure, and/or any other event that may prove notable. An individual unfamiliar with the case should, upon reviewing all the case notes, have no further questions or need to speak with the facilitator of the case.

Informal resolutions are different by design and philosophy. Facilitators of informal processes will produce high-level case notes that confirm interactions or phases of process but do so without the intricate details to protect all parties involved, promote good faith participation, and preserve the integrity of the process and spirit of RJ.

A restorative process is intended to answer three questions: Who was harmed? How were they harmed? What needs to be done to make it as right as possible? (Karp, 2019; Zehr, 2015). While those questions seem simple on the surface, full exploration of all three is delicate, nonlinear, and comprehensive. When determining appropriate documentation methods to properly memorialize this exploration, it may be recommended that facilitators, especially those who tend to be particularly detail oriented, consider utilizing a summative format that captures the essentials of a case, rather than working to provide highly detailed case notes. Facilitators must balance a thorough account of all aspects of the informal resolution process with the possibility that records could be subpoenaed in legal proceedings (Coker, 2016; Nondiscrimination on the Basis of Sex in Education Programs or Activities Receiving Federal Financial Assistance, 2020). In truth, maintaining extensive case notes beyond administrative/procedural ones may have a deleterious effect on participation, and as a matter of transparency, participants should be notified of this possibility so they can make an informed choice on how to participate, if at all.

Fundamentally, case notes exist for three reasons: (a) demonstrate due process expectations have been followed at each phase of the resolution process; (b) memorialize critical developments or inflection points in the resolution process; and (c) catalog federal, state, and local reporting requirements. With these parameters in mind, facilitators should consider documenting major dates/events/milestones throughout the case that may be important to memorialize if/when they occur, including, but not limited to:

- initial intake and subsequent meetings
- submission/receipt of a signed formal complaint from the complainant
- informal resolution agreement signed by involved parties and Title IX coordinator
- withdrawal of formal complaint and/or dissolution of informal resolution process
- decision(s) made on behalf of the institution to decline the approval of the use of informal resolution, and associated rationale
- respondent noncompliance with established agreement
- upcoming action items, next steps, and meetings/facilitations
- confirmation of completion of the process

Suggestions and Things to Consider

Best practices and considerations for documenting these types of events include the following:

- Keep notes at a high level.
- Summarize the totality of meeting rather than documenting specific quotes from participants.

- Ensure case notes and summaries are written in an objective, rather than subjective, manner (avoid "I feel" or "I believe" statements).
- Document information/events as they occur and as the case evolves to ensure accuracy, reliability, and completeness.

To streamline the case management processes and documentation efforts, it's recommended that institutions consider utilizing a web-based platform, if they're not already doing so. As such, the next section will explore the ins and outs of administrative case management of informal resolutions and offer further context regarding available options and best practices.

Conclusion

The adoption of informal resolution as a pathway for sexual and gender-based misconduct represents an expansion of justice that offers an amplified voice for complainants and respondents. Informal resolution honors both the spirit of RJ and the comprehensive Title IX obligations all while dismantling rigid formalities required in formal procedures (Orcutt et al., 2020). Informal resolution facilitators strive to support impacted parties, cocreate resolution agreements that deliver high accountability, and provide support through informal processes and mutually agreed-upon interventions. This chapter was written with the intention to provide practitioners with insight and best practices related to informal resolution and demonstrate that there is not a one-size-fits-all approach to informal resolution. This is true from agreement to agreement and between institution to institution. Despite some noted differences, at both TCNJ and UMich, informal resolution processes seek to embrace the RJ philosophy through inclusive decision making, active accountability, repairing harm, and rebuilding trust (Karp et al., 2016). When negotiating these types of processes, facilitators have an obligation to their institution, complainants, and respondents, both in good faith and under federal law to formalize protocols, procedures, and case records to maintain the integrity of informal resolution processes and uphold due process. Informal resolution can be successful with established forms, protocols, and procedures that are documented and consistently applied. When it comes to creating these tools, do not feel obligated to reinvent the wheel; use examples provided in this chapter and tailor them to your institution. Facilitators must proceed with holding multiple truths in the balance: avoiding so many forms, protocols, and procedures in the informal resolution process so it does not have the spirit of the formal resolution process while tending to administrative case management necessities and due process requirements. Parties have chosen the informal process over the formal grievance process for a reason (or perhaps many), and there is no reason to conflate the two.

References

Coker, D. (2016). *Crime logic, campus sexual assault, and restorative justice*. *Texas Tech Law Review*, *149*(47), 149–210. https://papers.ssrn.com/sol3/papers.cfm?abstract_id=2932481

Education Amendments of 1972, § 506 and Titles VIII and IX. P.L. 92-318, 7 U.S.C. 301. https://www.govinfo.gov/content/pkg/COMPS-11127/uslm/COMPS-11127.xml

Jeanne Clery Disclosure of Campus Security Policy and Campus Crime Statistics Act of 1990, 20 U.S.C. §1092(f) (2018).

Karp, D. R. (2019). *The little book of restorative justice for colleges and universities: Repairing harm and rebuilding trust in response to student misconduct*. Good Books.

Karp, D. R., Shackford-Bradley, J., & Williamsen, K. M. (2016). *Campus PRISM: A report on promoting restorative initiatives for sexual misconduct on college campuses*. Skidmore College Project on Restorative Justice.

Koss, M. P., Wilgus, J. K., & Williamsen, K. M. (2014). Campus sexual misconduct: Restorative justice approaches to enhance compliance with Title IX guidance. *Trauma, Violence, & Abuse*, *15*(3), 242–257. https://doi.org/10.1177/1524838014521500

Nondiscrimination on the Basis of Sex in Education Programs or Activities Receiving Federal Financial Assistance, 34 C.F.R. § 106 (2020). https://www2.ed.gov/policy/rights/reg/ocr/edlite-34cfr106.html#S4

Office for Civil Rights. (2020, May 19). Rules and regulations. *Federal Register*, *85*(97), 30026–30579. Department of Education. https://www.govinfo.gov/content/pkg/FR-2020-05-19/pdf/2020-10512.pdf

Orcutt, M., Petrowski, P. M., Karp, D. R., & Draper, J. (2020). Restorative justice approaches to the informal resolution of student sexual misconduct. *Journal of College and University Law*, *45*(2), 1–76. https://digital.sandiego.edu/soles-faculty/15

Violence Against Women Reauthorization Act (VAWA); 42 U.S.C. § 136 (2022). https://www.govinfo.gov/app/details/USCODE-2021-title42/USCODE-2021-title42-chap136

Zehr, H. (2015). *The little book of restorative justice: Revised and updated*. Good Books.

6

SPECIALIZED INTERVENTIONS FOR ADDRESSING PROBLEMATIC SEXUAL BEHAVIOR

Joan Tabachnick and Jay Wilgus

Designing, implementing, and facilitating restorative practices for matters involving problematic sexual behavior involves many layers of practical, legal, cultural, organizational, and emotional complexity. The underlying pursuit, however, is quite clear: addressing and repairing, to the greatest extent possible, the harm created as a result of problematic sexual behavior. Various chapters in this volume speak directly toward that issue and offer thoughtful guidance on how the work is accomplished. This chapter is intended to complement others by focusing on the person who caused harm. But rather than asking how a restorative process can address and repair existing harm, as is the focus elsewhere in this volume, this chapter explores what can be done to prevent a student who caused sexual harm from engaging in similar behavior in the future. These questions are asked within the context of our overall goal of reducing or eliminating sexual and gender-based violence from college campuses.

Drawing from various lines of research in public health and criminology, including specific studies applicable to adult and adolescents who have committed a sexual offense, this chapter focuses on specialized interventions, including assessment mechanisms, designed for individuals who engage in problematic sexual behavior and ways in which those interventions can be made part of restorative processes—as a preparatory mechanism, as a feature of restorative agreements, and as part of reintegration processes. We begin with a quick note about the importance of language and how our framing of an issue—or, in this case, our description of the student who caused harm—can limit the possibilities and shape the outcome. We then transition to an overview of what we know about individuals who engage in problematic sexual behavior and the existing evidence-based or research-informed interventions designed to reduce the likelihood of an individual engaging in similar behavior in the future. We conclude by exploring how these interventions can be integrated into campus practice in a way that supports the overarching principles of RJ.

Language and Terminology

Throughout this chapter, and in our work with individuals who engage in problematic sexual behavior, we try to be consistent in using "person-first" language. This concept began in the public health sphere by reminding practitioners that neither people nor patients are defined by the disease they acquired or their underlying condition. It's equally important in the victim advocacy community that recognizes that adults, adolescents, and children who have been sexually harassed, sexually abused, or sexually assaulted are more than the labels "victim" or "survivor" and more than what happened to them. We echo this trend and encourage similar language when referring to students or other individuals who cause sexual harm. If, after all, we hope to prevent problematic behavior from persisting, then "why are we labeling people by the very behaviors we want them to change?" (Willis, 2018). In addition to casting dispositional properties onto individuals for behavior that *may* be limited, dynamic, or situational in nature, static terms like *sex offender, creep, predator, perp, perpetrator*, or even *rapist* actually offer little information about what that person actually did, their understanding of what they did, their motivations, their ability to control or change their behaviors, or the risk they pose to the community. Further, static terms like these provide no information about whether the individual successfully completed a treatment program, whether their developmental or cognitive abilities permit understanding the harm caused or why the behavior was problematic, what support they have for avoiding these behaviors in the future, whether they continued their behavior in any way, or whether they have been living offense free since the incident (Tabachnick & Prescott, 2022).

In this chapter, we use the phrase "students who engage in problematic sexual behavior" to encourage person-first language and to reflect a growing consensus in the criminal justice system that acknowledges that children, adolescents, and young adults respond well to interventions and need not be limited by static labels tied to prior behavior. We use the term *problematic sexual behavior* (*PSB*) to include the broad spectrum of behaviors regulated by existing Title IX regulations and more commonly referred to as *sexual harassment, sexual misconduct,* or *sexual and gender-based violence.* We use this terminology to acknowledge that a student's behavior is not necessarily a reflection of their underlying disposition or a permanent feature of their character (Chaffin et al., 2006; Kenney, 2020). We occasionally use the term *respondent* when discussing a student who may be, has been, or once was reported to campus authorities for a potential violation of campus policy applicable to sexual or gender-based misconduct. In so doing, we acknowledge it as inconsistent with our desire for person-first language and yet more convenient or precise in some instances.

What We Know About Students Who Engage in PSB

Contrary to some dominant myths, most students who engage in PSB understand the impact of what they have done and, especially with a well-matched intervention, will not repeat those behaviors. Although one campus study suggests that a few students who rape do so repeatedly and are responsible for the majority of sexual assault on campus (Lisak & Miller, 2002), more recent research (Swartout et al., 2015) described three developmental pathways of those who cause this type sexual harm: (a) those who repeat their behaviors, (b) those who stop before entering college, and (c) those who perpetrate once and then stop. This notion of "persisters" and "desisters" suggests that at least some of what campuses define as sexual misconduct is perpetrated by a wider range of individuals than many have come to believe, and it provides insight into the importance and utility of specialized interventions for students who are receptive to change. It also mirrors the studies of adolescents in the criminal justice system that indicate that most adolescents will stop their PSBs with a well-matched intervention (Caldwell, 2016; Lussier, 2015).

We share more about those interventions later in this chapter and now simply emphasize that attempts to characterize the population of students who engage in PSB in singular terms (e.g., this is how they all act, this is what they all do) tend to limit the conversation to a one-size-fits-all approach, while discounting the variations in behavior and the heterogeneity of students who engage in PSB. For that reason, statements such as "It is always about power and control" or "This is how all campus rapists will act" should be a red flag that the full complexity of this issue and the multitude of factors to consider are not being reflected in the conversation. If, after all, the goal is to create an effective intervention for the student who has violated a campus policy, one must invest the time to fully understand the student who caused harm, including their intentions; motivations; tactics; cognitive ability; developmental stage; the context of those behaviors; and, of course, the specifics of their harmful behaviors.

Before diving into these items more deeply, it is important to clearly state that understanding students or other individuals who cause harm does not discount, diminish, or lessen the very real impact on victims of sexual violence. As outlined in Figure 6.1, we must always prioritize victims and survivors in our response to PSB. Understanding those who cause harm, however, may help with creating a safer community, correcting the behaviors, and establishing responses that link most closely to increasing safety in the future.

Presentations of Problematic Sexual Behavior

Figure 6.1 provides a visual representation of the various ways in which PSB presents on campus and highlights the layering of individuals and communities impacted by such behavior. Organized as distinct "buckets," the graphic also highlights the importance of understanding a student respondent in the context of both the student who is harmed (complainant or survivor) and their surrounding community. Just as one cannot examine the experiences of the student who experienced harm without understanding the context around the student, their history, and the specific situation, one cannot look at a student who caused harm (respondent) without this larger context. Within the existing regulatory framework, institutions must provide remedies designed to restore or preserve equal access to the recipient's education program or activity. Part of that effort includes holding a student respondent accountable for their behavior. This chapter suggests that in some cases, it may be necessary to provide longer term remedies for the student respondent or the student complainant while continuing to preserve and/or restore their access to educational programs or activities. Figure 6.1 also points out the importance of the community and institutions role in preventing and responding to sexual misconduct. Although the grievance process appropriately focuses on the individuals involved, the responses at each bucket should also include ways in which the community and the institution may have supported, condoned, permitted, or encouraged the harmful behavior.

Although it is beyond the scope of this chapter to address the way in which research-informed strategies might be employed at each stage, we offer the full continuum here to encourage further inquiry about the perpetration-focused opportunities in each bucket and the way in which institutional goals may vary across time points, along with the most appropriate interventions.

Figure 6.1. Presentations of problematic sexual behavior.

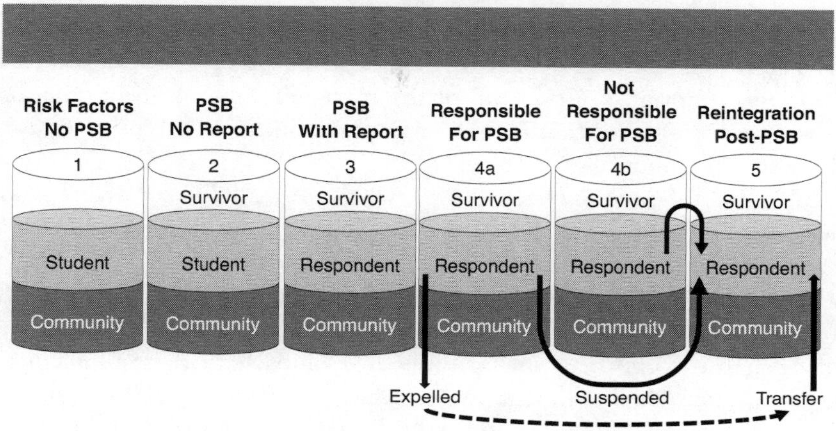

Bucket 1 in Figure 6.1 refers to circumstances in which a student on campus presents risk factors for engaging in PSB but has not yet engaged in such behavior. Bucket 2 refers to situations in which some form of PSB has occurred on campus but that has not been reported to the institution. Bucket 3 represents instances in which a report regarding PSB has been made to the institution, yet before an investigation or adjudication has been completed, when institutions must consider (a) what supportive measures might be necessary and (b) whether it's necessary to conduct an individualized "risk and safety analysis" as dictated by existing regulation when the institution is considering a student's emergency removal. Bucket 4 refers to instances in which an accused student has accepted responsibility or been found responsible for the reported PSB following an adjudication process (in Bucket 4a) or found not responsible for the behavior (in Bucket 4b). As indicated by the arrows, students in this stage may transition from one bucket to the next. And as indicated by the arrow proceeding from Bucket 4b to Bucket 5, students who are found not responsible for the reported PSB often still find themselves trying to reintegrate into various communities and may benefit from support provided by the institution. Bucket 5, on the far right, draws attention to the stage at which the student found responsible for PSB is reintegrating back into their campus community following a period of suspension or into a new campus community following transfer to a separate institution (or found not responsible, but requesting additional support).

A great deal could be written about specialized interventions at each bucket, but the primary focus of this chapter is on Buckets 4a and 5 and ways in which specialized interventions applicable at those stages can be integrated into restorative processes.

A Continuum of Healthy and Problematic Behavior More Than Just Behaviors

As Figure 6.2 illustrates, there is a wide range of sexual behaviors that campuses confront. On one end of the spectrum are those behaviors that might be described as healthy, safe, and consensual. On the other end are those that are problematic or illegal (Johnson, 2009).

Within the latter two categories, there are a multitude of behaviors involving physical contact, noncontact offenses, voyeurism, exploitation, and more. In fact, a 2014 examination by Koss et al. (2014) identified at least 42 different behaviors that could be considered a violation of Title IX. These behaviors present different levels of concern for the institution and create unique forms of harm for individuals impacted by the problematic and illegal behaviors. Although it is possible to talk about each at length, it's most important at this point to acknowledge the wide variety of behaviors because they're engaged in by a wide variety of students for a wide variety of reasons. For this chapter, *PSB* will be used to describe both problematic and illegal sexual behaviors.

Heterogeneity of Students Who Engage in PSB

To develop the most effective sanction and set the stage for the most effective intervention, the institution must recognize the broad heterogeneity of this population. Most institutions will recognize the wide range of PSBs as well as the impact of those behaviors on the student harmed, as most institutions make their decisions based upon these two factors. However, this decision-making approach is quite limiting. If the student is allowed to remain on campus or transfers to another campus, an effective intervention must recognize a number of other factors as well. An effective intervention ultimately means a safer campus for everyone, including the student harmed and the student who caused harm.

The additional factors to consider are briefly explained below and include a student's varying levels of cognitive understanding as well as their development stage, intentions, and motivations, as well as the tactics they

Figure 6.2. A continuum of behavior.

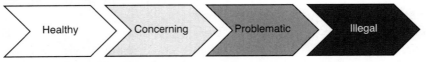

Note. From *Understanding Children's Sexual Behaviors: What's Natural and Healthy* (p. 13), by T. C. Johnson, 2009, NEARI Press. Copyright 2009. Adapted with permission.

used. This more complex approach to developing well-matched interventions is based upon research indicating that there are multiple factors to be considered that either encourage or discourage an individual's decisions (Malamuth et al., 2021; U.S. Department of Justice, 2017). In addition, when considering how to prevent future harm, the institution should explore the environment in which the student lives (e.g., housing, social groups), which will have a significant impact on individual behavior decisions. Although accountability for causing harm lies with the individual student, the responsibility for preventing future harm will be most successful if a wider community is engaged to protect everyone involved.

As mentioned earlier, understanding the many individual and environmental factors affecting perpetration does not lessen the impact on the student who was harmed. It can, however, help inform the decision-making capacity of campus administrators or restorative practitioners and the community's overall ability to develop an effective intervention or sanction for each student.

Intentions

Given this multifactor approach, one of the considerations (in addition to behavior) for developing an effective intervention is to explore the intention of the student causing harm (see Figure 6.3). For example, was the act done as a malicious act, was the student drunk themselves, or was this a student who did not understand the concept of consent? Equally important to think about are the cognitive ability and developmental stage of the student. For example, if a student is found responsible for stalking, or accepts responsibility for such behavior, was the behavior malicious in nature, or is the student unable to appreciate the impact of their actions or understand how a soft but not concrete response to their questions may actually mean "no" (e.g., a student saying "I can't" to a request for breakfast does not give permission to ask for lunch the next day and dinner the following night).

Motivations

In the early days of the sexual and domestic violence victim advocacy movement, many would say that the motivation is "always about power and

Figure 6.3. Intentions.

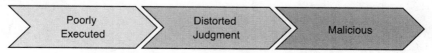

control" (Domestic Abuse Intervention Programs (n.d.). Certainly, that is true for some students, but the full picture is likely much more complex for many. For other students, the motivation may be about proving they are a part of a group on campus, for a sense of closeness when they are far from home, or, as Jennifer Hirsch and Shamus Khan (2020) described in their book *Sexual Citizens: A Landmark Study of Sex, Power, and Assault on Campus*, it may be about a student's "project" while they are a college student to have sex. The motivation may also be influenced by the expectations a student may have that stem from their family, community, or culture. As students from a variety of cultures are gathered on a single campus, values, communication styles, language, family expectations, cultural expectations, machismo, and many other factors will affect a student's expectations and motivations on important decisions such as how a student navigates a mutual understanding of consent. Understanding the motivation of a student will directly impact the decision about an effective intervention for that individual student (see Figure 6.4).

Figure 6.4. Motivations.

Tactics

Finally, it is important to understand the tactic that was used by the student (see Figure 6.5). Was there physical force or significant coercion used to force another student? When making an assessment or deciding on the appropriate intervention or sanction, it is also helpful to know if the act was planned and premeditated or, at the other end of the continuum of tactics, was it more situational, not planned, and culminated from a series of factors on the part of the student who caused the harm which ultimately resulted in harm for another student?

All of these factors should be considered when designing an intervention or a sanction that would be most effective in changing the PSB of the student upon their return to campus.

Figure 6.5. Tactics.

Interventions Likely to Help Reduce the Risk of Reoffense

With this baseline regarding students who engage in PSB, this section explores what is known about the specialized interventions most likely to help reduce the risk of reoffense. These interventions most often flow from a specialized assessment and are designed to meet a student's unique risks, needs, and protective factors, while accounting for the student's responsivity to various interventions. More often than not, institutions make decisions with sameness in mind and confuse this consistency with effectiveness. By doing so, institutions may unwittingly overlook critically important differences in a student's specific risks, needs, and protective factors. For example, research with adult and adolescent sex offenders clearly demonstrates that denial is not linked to recidivism (Harkins et al., 2010, 2015; Nunes et al., 2007). Nevertheless, many in this work may focus on the fact that a student did not, or has not yet taken, full responsibility for their behavior and assign a greater level of concern to that student than may be warranted following a specialized assessment. In making such an assignment, the institution may feel they "need to send a message" to others that this PSB is not acceptable and inadvertently set a standard that does not flexibly account for individual needs or circumstances, or the reality that a student may initially (or even continually) deny the accusation prior to coming to the realization that the PSB does not necessarily reflect their fundamental character.

As described below, what leads to campus and broader community safety is a focus on dynamic factors that make sexual violence more likely (criminogenic needs) and the use of interventions that target and change those factors. Interventions that focus only on consistency with others who engaged in similar PSBs (single-factor decisions) or those intent on sending a clear message to the broader community about the seriousness with which an institution takes specific matters do not have a basis in research regarding their impact on a student's likelihood to engage in future PSB. Research with young adult and adolescents convicted of a sex offense has repeatedly shown that an effective response is based upon a specialized assessment, followed by well-matched interventions. Two specific types of interventions are addressed below: (a) those involving psychoeducational approaches (in instances involving individuals for whom a knowledge deficit needs to be addressed) and (b) therapeutic interventions (for individuals requiring greater attention from a trained clinician).

Specialized Assessment

A specialized assessment is the foundation for a research-informed approach to reduce risk and a student's likelihood to engage in further PSB. It can also serve as the foundation for all intervention and sanctioning decisions, including the type of intervention needed; recommendations for intervention priorities; and insights into a range of decisions, from housing to removal. A specialized assessment is based upon research to evaluate an individual's risks, needs, and protective factors as well as the environment in which they live. Based upon this assessment, a campus can then provide an intervention or sanction that specifically targets the factors (criminogenic needs) that make sexual violence more probable, while supporting and leveraging the protective factors that make PSB less likely in the future.

At the root of these assessments and the interventions that flow from an assessment is the risk–needs–responsivity model. This model provides the evidence-based framework that supports this individualized approach to assessment and treatment (Andrews & Bonta, 2010). The *risk* principle focuses on factors in the student and their environment associated with PSBs. The *needs* principle focuses on factors that can be changed and which directly contribute to PSB, such as the student's use of alcohol or association with students with attitudes that do not deter PSB. The *responsivity* principle holds that interventions must be developed in a way that the student can respond to them fully. This includes consideration of learning style, presence of mental health conditions requiring attention before treatment can begin, and the effects of trauma.

Key to a successful assessment is therefore the opportunity to look at the "whole student," their risk and protective factors, co-occurring issues, and the student's immediate environment. Students can be profoundly affected by the environment surrounding them, so considering the environment is key to a safe and successful outcome (Hirsch & Khan, 2020). Also key is access to a clinician or a specially trained psychoeducational facilitator who specializes in addressing PSB and who has access to various assessment tools to help with recommendations for a well-matched intervention. Information from an assessment can include, but need not be limited to:

1. What risks does the student pose (e.g., other allegations)?
2. Are there associated risks, such as alcohol and/or drug abuse?
3. Is the student involved in prosocial activities (safety factors)?
4. What is the student's cognitive understanding and developmental stage?
5. Is the student motivated to change?

Following an assessment of this type, institutions are better situated to make decisions about interventions that best fit the student found responsible, the student who was harmed, and the broader community.

What Works: A Well-Matched Intervention

How institutions decide which sanctions would be most appropriate varies considerably from one campus to another and even within each campus. According to one survey (Wilgus et al., 2014), most participants said they consult the range of options available under their campus policy and select the best option. Many of these relied on the decisions of past cases or written guidelines. The problem with this approach is that very few institutions examined whether their past sanctions or written guidelines were effective, and none of them said they based decisions on available research.

To update campus practices in a way that relies on the best available evidence or research, it may be necessary to shift away from what has been done in the past and rely instead on new tools, resources, research, and expertise. Once a specialized assessment has been completed, a campus can then encourage or mandate an intervention that is well matched to the student. As detailed in Table 6.1, the two intervention approaches

TABLE 6.1
The Differences in Psychoeducation and Psychotherapy Approaches

	Psychoeducation	*Psychotherapy*
Goal	Increase knowledge, self-awareness, and prosocial life skills to help modify future behavioral responses and enhance quality of life, including within intimate relationships	Facilitate positive behavioral change by targeting and mitigating risk-relevant thoughts, feelings, and behaviors associated with sexual misconduct and promoting respectful, prosocial intimate relationships
Method	Didactics and planned curriculum	Use of therapeutic relationship and specific clinical techniques within a principled framework
Delivery	Trained facilitator; no licensure requirement	Licensed mental health provider
Effectiveness	Support for specific outcomes	Strong support for various outcomes
Cost	Cost-effective, particularly when administered in a group	Varies, depending on insurance; diagnosis may be required

Note. Adapted from *Two Programs, Two Approaches: Psychotherapy vs. Psychoeducation* (pp. 18–19), by R. Prentky, M. Koss, R. Lamade, E. Lopez, J. Wilgus, and S. Righthand, 2017. Copyright 2017 by Klancy Street, LLC.

that are becoming more commonly used in the campus environment fall into two general categories: (a) psychoeducation and (b) psychotherapy (Lamade et al., 2018).

Psychoeducational approaches are, generally speaking, used for students who have been identified through an assessment with one or more knowledge deficits as the primary cause for a student's behavior. By providing education about specific items (e.g., consent, boundaries, social skills, policies governing sexual behavior), institutions aim to address the deficit and thereby prevent a student from engaging in similar PSB in the future. This approach is more commonly used with PSB that presents less concern for institutions and in which the student presents with fewer risks and needs, or increased protective factors. A psychoeducational approach focuses on factors related to PSB but also provides education about basic social skills necessary for healthy, safe, and consenting sexual behavior. This approach is based upon the assumption that the traditional-age college students are developmentally similar to adolescents (emerging adults), readily influenced by peers, and can change their behaviors and responses through either individual study with a facilitator or facilitated groups.

A *psychotherapy approach*, in contrast, can address a range of more serious sexually problematic behaviors involving contact, forced contact and penetration, or multiple cases of PSB. Psychotherapy needs to be offered by a licensed mental health professional with experience working with PSBs for this emerging adult population. If this expertise is not currently on campus, it may be found with local treatment providers who can be located through the Association of the Treatment of Sexual Abusers (https://www.atsa.com) or the Safer Society Foundation (https://www.ssfi.org). In addition to what is offered through education, a psychotherapy approach will focus on facilitating positive behavioral change by targeting and mitigating risk relevant thoughts, feelings, and behaviors associated with PSB and promoting respectful, prosocial intimate relationships. The core modality of the most effective psychotherapeutic approaches is cognitive behavior therapy (CBT), a research-informed approach that focuses on changing a student's understanding about sexuality, intimacy, and relationships as well as their behaviors.

Over the past few years, a number of models have emerged in the campus environment for integrating psychoeducational and/or psychotherapy-based interventions. Some institutions have established a relationship with a local provider and offer referrals for students who either have been identified or found responsible for PSB on campus. And at times, a referral for a student has come forward to ask for help with questions about their own approach to sexual behaviors. In these cases, a campus may have a memorandum of understanding with the local service provider in much the same way that a campus may have a memorandum of understanding with a local rape crisis center. A second approach is a campus-based program that has been developed on the campus to address various behaviors. This has typically been a psychoeducational program developed through the Title IX office or a supporting unit, like student conduct or the campus counseling center. These programs, to a greater or lesser extent, may be based upon research and what is known about working with adolescents and young adults with PSB. Thus far, none of these programs have been evaluated for their effectiveness, but few have documented further PSBs (that are reported) in the students who have participated. A third approach utilized on some campuses is STARRSA (Science-based Treatment Accountability and Risk Reduction for Sexual Assault), a research-informed initiative funded through the U.S. Department of Justice, Office of Sex Offender Sentencing, Monitoring, Apprehending, Registering, and Tracking (SMART) spelled out as requested (Lamade et al., 2017). Developed specifically for the traditional college-age population, STARRSA recognizes the unique features of this population and provides two distinct standardized programs for use by institutions of higher education. The standardized programs utilize assessment mechanisms to individualize the programs to the risks, needs, and responsivity of each student. The Active Psychoeducation program is intended for students with fewer criminogenic needs and can be facilitated by a nonclinical facilitator. The CBT program is intended for students with greater needs and must be facilitated by a trained clinician (Prentky & Koss, 2018). Both programs include a Contributing Factors Checklist that can be used by Title IX personnel and related student conduct professionals to guide their sanctioning decisions and assessment instruments for use by facilitators of the Active Psychoeducation program or clinicians utilizing the CBT program. Although not widely utilized, the program offers a promising set of research-informed tools and programs developed by clinicians with significant experience managing PSB in criminally adjudicated populations and whose techniques have been adapted in the STARRSA programs for use on campus.

In concluding this section, it is important to note the relative paucity of campuses utilizing specialized interventions like those noted above. Readers are encouraged to think about the possibilities presented here as promising practices, rather than "standard practice" being employed by institutions nationwide.

Methods for Integrating Specialized Interventions Into Campus Practice

Despite the lack of widespread adoption, specialized interventions have attracted attention from many restorative practitioners because the objectives are consistent with RJ and with the common desire among harmed parties for responsible parties to learn from their harmful behavior and not repeat it in the future. Specialized interventions and RJ both seek meaningful and effective responses to PSB that recognize human fallibility, our capacity for change, and our ability to make appropriate amends. Both also recognize that individualization is often at the heart of creating effective responses given the variability in impact experienced by students harmed by PSB and the heterogeneity of those who cause harm. Although the integration of specialized interventions into campus practice remains relatively rare, the practice is growing, and various opportunities exist for further incorporation. This section briefly explores how specialized interventions can be utilized in three specific contexts which are likely to be of the greatest interest to restorative practitioners: (a) specialized interventions as a prerequisite to a restorative process, (b) specialized interventions as an outcome of a restorative process, and (c) specialized interventions as part of a student's reintegration into a campus community.

Specialized Intervention as a Prerequisite to a Restorative Process

A primary consideration of any restorative process is making sure the parties are appropriately prepared and that the process is reasonably likely to address and repair the harm caused without creating secondary trauma. This concern is particularly acute in matters involving PSB where the harm is often so personal and profound and where the person who experienced harm is often, if not always, seeking assurance that the individual who caused harm "gets it" and will not cause harm of a similar nature in the future. One way to ensure both are true following an initial acceptance of responsibility by the student who caused harm is to require a specialized assessment prior to the process itself and completion of any recommended intervention(s), whether rooted in psychoeducation or psychotherapy. This approach has various benefits, including providing the facilitator with increased confidence in the appropriateness of the matter for an RJ-based approach and providing additional assurance to the harmed party that the student who caused harm is actively and meaningfully engaged in addressing the behavior.

The Office of Student Conflict Resolution (OSCR) at the University of Michigan began utilizing this approach as a prerequisite to a respondent's participation in an informal resolution process for Title IX matters. Under this approach, the OSCR helps the student prepare to participate in a restorative process by requiring them to complete the aforementioned STARRSA Active Psychoeducation program, which includes a baseline knowledge assessment intended to address knowledge-based deficits that may have contributed to the PSB and which, if left unaddressed, may increase the student's likelihood of engaging in similar behavior in the future. This research-informed approach provides OSCR staff members with increased confidence in the appropriateness of the restorative process while also providing the student who caused harm with increased understanding of how their behavior impacted the student harmed.

Specialized Intervention as an Outcome of a Restorative Process

Specialized interventions can also be used as a feature of restorative agreements produced as an outcome of an informal resolution process. Such measures can be incorporated voluntarily into agreements on a case-by-case basis or embedded as a feature of all informal resolution agreements. The College of New Jersey utilizes the latter approach in their informal resolution processes and requires students to complete a specialized educational workshop called *Salient Analysis of Interpersonal Dynamics*, which was developed by The College of New Jersey staff. Other institutions and other matters may benefit from a direct referral to a specialized clinician who is accustomed to treating individuals who have engaged in PSB. Regardless of approach, the goal remains the same, that is, incorporating research-informed interventions into the restorative agreement as a way of reducing the risk of reoffense and as a way of more fully addressing the PSB.

Specialized Interventions Upon Reintegration

Last, specialized interventions may be useful when students are reintegrating into their campus community following a period of separation or upon transfer to a new institution with a notation in their transcript. In both instances the institution may have an interest in having a specialized assessment completed to help gauge a student's current risk, needs, and protective factors. Institutions may also have an interest in having the student complete (unless completed previously) a specialized psychoeducation or psychotherapy program. This may be particularly true when an institution to which a student is transferring has concerns regarding the student's behavior at a prior institution and wants some additional assurance that the behavior will not persist. To further enhance their effectiveness, these interventions might also be incorporated into other restorative processes intended to support an individual's reintegration into various communities, like the circles of support and accountability, which have been utilized to help reduce the risk of reoffense among high-risk sex offenders (Wilson & McWhinnie, 2010).

Although implementation models that incorporate specialized assessment, treatment or psychoeducational interventions remain relatively rare, there is clear overlap in purpose as institutions and restorative practitioners seek effective responses to PSB.

Conclusion

To those unfamiliar with specialized assessment, treatment, and psychoeducation approaches to PSB, the options outlined above might feel overwhelming. This chapter introduced language that may be new to readers; research that may challenge some of what readers previously thought they knew about individuals who engage in PSB; and options that may feel difficult to implement, particularly on campuses with few resources, those in rural areas without easy access to specialized providers, or those where retributive models remain embedded in campus culture. If that's the case for you, allow us to offer a succinct summary. The most effective interventions for students who engage in PSB are based upon the understanding that no two students or situations are exactly the same. In tailoring a response to each student, it is essential to individualize the approach and account for a student's unique risks, needs, and protective factors (as well as their responsivity to specific interventions). One way this can be done is through the use of a specialized assessment. From this assessment, a campus can then consider the intervention that is best matched to that individual. This may include a research-informed psychoeducational or CBT-based psychotherapy approach to meet that particular student's needs. Rooted in the risk–needs–responsivity model, these approaches, when matched to the student needs, have the greatest likelihood of preventing the recurrence of PSB and, therefore, future harm.

This chapter outlined various ways in which specialized interventions might be integrated into campus practice, including as a prerequisite to restorative processes, as a feature of restorative agreements, and as a function of reintegration processes. Although there remains much more to discuss, explore, and study in this area, and although these approaches remain far from commonplace in higher education, they're critically important to understand as institutions work to reduce or eliminate sexual and gender-based violence from college campuses.

References

Andrews, D. A., & Bonta, J. (2010). *The psychology of criminal conduct,* (5th ed.). Anderson.

Caldwell, M. F. (2016). Quantifying the decline in juvenile sexual recidivism rates. *Psychology, Public Policy, and Law, 22*(4), 414. https://doi.org/10.1037/law0000094

Chaffin, M., Berliner, L., Block, R., Friedrich, W. N., Garza Louis, D., Lyon, T. D., Page, J., Prescott, D., & Silovsky, J. F. (2006). *Report of the task force on children with sexual behavior problems.* Association for the Treatment of Sexual Abusers. https://www.atsa.com/pdfs/Report-TFCSBP.pdf

Domestic Abuse Intervention Programs. (n.d.). *Wheel information center.* https://www.theduluthmodel.org/wheels/

Hirsch, J. S., & Khan, S. (2020). *Sexual citizens: A landmark study of sex, power, and assault on campus.* W.W. Norton.

Harkins, L., Beech, A. R., & Goodwill, A. M. (2010). Examining the influence of denial, motivation, and risk on sexual recidivism. *Sexual Abuse, 22*(1), 78–94. https://doi.org/10.1177/1079063209358106

Harkins, L., Howard, P., Barnett, G., Wakeling, H., & Miles, C. (2015). Relationships between denial, risk, and recidivism in sexual offenders. *Archives of Sexual Behavior, 44*(1), 157–166. https://doi.org/10.1007/s10508-014-0333-z

Johnson, T. C. (2009). *Understanding children's sexual behaviors: What's natural and healthy.* NEARI Press.

Kenney, J. W. (2020). *Problematic sexual behavior in schools: How to spot it and what to do about it.* Rowman & Littlefield.

Koss, M., Wilgus, J., & Williamsen, K. (2014). Campus sexual misconduct: Restorative justice approaches to enhance compliance with Title IX guidance. *Trauma, Violence, & Abuse, 15*(3), 242–257. https://doi.org/10.1177/1524838014521500

Lamade, R., Lopez, E., Koss, M. P., Prentky, R. & Brereton, A. (2018). Developing and implementing a treatment intervention for college students found responsible for sexual misconduct. *Journal of Aggression, Conflict and Peace Research, 10*(2), 134–144. https://doi.org/10.1108/JACPR-06-2017-0301

Lisak, D., & Miller, P. M. (2002). Repeat rape and multiple offending among undetected rapists. *Violence and Victims, 17,* 73–83. https://doi.org/10.1891/vivi.17.1.73.33638

Lussier, P., McCuish, E., & Corrado, R. R. (2015). The adolescence–adulthood transition and desistance from crime: Examining the underlying structure of desistance. *Journal of Developmental and Life-Course Criminology, 1*(2), 87–117. https://doi.org/10.1007/s40865-015-0007-0

Malamuth, N. M., Lamade, R. V., Koss, M. P., Lopez, E., Seaman, C., & Prentky, R. (2021). Factors predictive of sexual violence: Testing the four pillars of the confluence model in a large diverse sample of college men. *Aggressive Behavior, 47*(4), 405–420. https://doi.org/10.1002/ab.21960

Nunes, K. L., Hanson, R. K., Firestone, P., Moulden, H. M., Greenberg, D. M., & Bradford, J. M. (2007). Denial predicts recidivism for some sexual offenders. *Sexual Abuse, 19*(2), 91–105. https://doi.org/10.1177/107906320701900202

Prentky, R., Koss, M., Lamade, R., Lopez., E., Wilgus, J., & Righthand, S. (2017). *Two programs, two approaches: Psychotherapy vs. psychoeducation* [Brochure]. Klancy Street, LLC.

Prentky, R., & Koss M. (2018). *STARRSA active psychoeducation (AP) manual.* Office of Justice Programs' National Criminal Justice Reference Service. https://www.ojp.gov/pdffiles1/smart/grants/304700.pdf

Swartout, K. M., Koss, M. P., White, J. W., Thompson, M. P., Abbey, A., & Bellis, A. L. (2015). Trajectory analysis of the campus serial rapist assumption. *JAMA Pediatrics, 169*(12), 1148–1154. https://doi.org/10.1001/jamapediatrics.2015.0707

Tabachnick, J., & Prescott, D. (2022). What we can learn about effective prevention from the treatment of individuals convicted of sex crimes. In L. Orchowski & A. Berkowitz (Eds.), *Engaging boys and men in sexual assault prevention: Theory, research, and practice* (pp. 437–456). Academic Press. https://doi.org/10.1016/B978-0-12-819202-3.00001-8

U.S. Department of Justice. (2017). *Sex offender management assessment and planning initiative.* https://smart.ojp.gov/somapi/initiative-home

Wilgus, J., Rider-Milkovich, H., & Vander Velde, S. (2014). *National Survey of Sanctioning Practices for Student Sexual Misconduct at Institutions of Higher Education.* University of Michigan Office of Student Conflict Resolution and Sexual Assault Prevention and Awareness Center, The Center for Effective Public Policy's Center for Sex Offender Management, and the Association for Student Conduct Administration. https://www2.ed.gov/policy/highered/reg/hearulemaking/2012/vawa-sanctioningpractices.pdf

Wilgus, J., & Tabachnick, J. (2019). Incorporating what is known about respondents and their perspectives into a thoughtful adjudication process. In C. M. Renzetti & D. R. Follingstad, (Eds.), *Adjudicating campus sexual misconduct,* (pp. 159–180). Cognella.

Willis, G. M. (2018). Why call someone by what we don't want them to be? The ethics of labeling in forensic/correctional psychology. *Psychology, Crime & Law, 24*(7), 727–743. https://doi.org/10.1080/1068316X.2017.1421640

Wilson, R. J., & McWhinnie, A. J. (2010). Circles of support and accountability: An innovative approach to community-based risk management for high-risk sexual offenders. In M. Herzog-Evans (Ed.), *Transnational criminology manual* (pp. 241–260). Wolf Legal Publishing.

PART THREE

FACILITATION FOCUS

7

EMBODYING A RESTORATIVE APPROACH

Attending to the Complexities of Restorative Justice for Campus Sexual Misconduct

Sheila M. McMahon and Desirée Anderson

It has been 35 years since Mary P. Koss et al.'s landmark study of sexual violence on college campuses (referred to here as *campus sexual misconduct* [CSM]). Yet, prevalence rates of CSM remain largely unchanged (Koss et al., 1987, 2022). Restorative justice (RJ) has been suggested and used as a novel tool, philosophy, and approach to address CSM to create a new pathway for change. As there is not a singular definition of RJ, there are tensions in how we engage with these practices to explore the ways in which our approaches are compatible with our existing structures. For the purposes of this chapter, *RJ for CSM* includes a range of practices (e.g., RJ conferencing, circles, victim impact statements) that center on the needs of the harmed party, provide accountability for responsible parties, and invite the impacted members of the community to lend both support and accountability to the process.

As more and more institutions of higher education view RJ as a powerful and beneficial resource for creating change in communities, it can also be co-opted and misused. RJ as a tool is not immune from personal biases and institutional betrayal. As practitioners look to incorporate RJ into the scope of their work, we invite them to expand their concept of what it means to embody a restorative approach. To embody restorative work requires acknowledging that while RJ processes can be more holistic than traditional campus responses to CSM, they do not by themselves correct for the failures and limitations of formal CSM adjudication processes. A restorative approach requires that practitioners attend to long-standing structural and historical harms that have plagued higher education. These include issues of racism; misogyny; homophobia; and in some cases, a campus environment that overlooks inappropriate sexual behaviors by long-standing and powerful members of the community (consider, e.g., a recent case at Harvard; Brodsky, 2022).

Thus, the invitation of this chapter is for readers to get curious about what it means to heal CSM as a community; to imagine an approach to CSM that names historical and structural harms, witnesses the impact of CSM on community members, and creates opportunities for individual *and* community accountability with regard to CSM (and other forms of harm) on your campus. This requires immense courage because it entails each of us to be willing to listen, to allow RJ participants to lead the conversation about outcomes, and to take responsibility for our part in creating the campus culture as it is currently experienced by those who are most marginalized, including those impacted directly by CSM. This chapter will look at embodying RJ at three levels. First, attending to self: How do RJ facilitators incorporate restorative practices into their daily lives? Living restoratively means that individual facilitators engage in self-awareness and self-accountability practices regularly. Second, attending to people: (a) what understandings must one have about power differentials to truly engage in restorative justice? (b) How do you coach people to think about themselves as equal participants in these processes? and (c) What equitable work has to be done to create equality? Finally, this chapter addresses attending to systems: How does one engage within systems that are inherently hierarchical ("power over" structures) and find ways to make them compatible with RJ ("power with" processes)? What measures, steps, and procedures are required to maintain the integrity of RJ, especially when engaging with sensitive topics such as CSM? This chapter will allow current or potential facilitators to ask questions of themselves to understand what additional work must be done to fully embody a restorative approach.

Attending to Self

We have observed in ourselves and other colleagues that sometimes the focus for facilitators is so fixed on the parties involved in an incident of harm that we may forget to begin with ourselves. In this section, we will discuss aspects of attending to one's own experience, including questions about self-awareness, safety, creating the conditions for respectful interactions with others, and attending to our own power and privilege. We hope the following reflections and questions will support facilitators in seeking the necessary support so that they may thrive as they accompany RJ participants in doing so as well.

Self-Awareness

The role of the facilitator and the skills they bring with them are essential to establishing rapport, helping participants in perspective-taking, and creating the conditions for the process. The conditions necessary for restorative dialogue to take place include the safety of the environment, respectful interactions, and positive energy (Umbreit et al., 2007). When stepping into the role of facilitator and beginning to engage with RJ, two things should be at the forefront of your mind: (a) "What are my triggers?" (self-awareness) and (b) "What are the power differentials at play?" (self-accountability)? A restorative approach assumes that behaviors are a form of communication. What we communicate and how we communicate are based on our lived experiences, so it is imperative that as you engage in a restorative approach, you understand your own behaviors and ways of communicating.

Establishing Safety

Trauma-informed care has been established as a best practice for working with survivors of trauma, including sexual violence (McMahon et al., 2019; Substance Abuse and Mental Health Services Administration, 2014). The Substance Abuse and Mental Health Services Administration (2014) described *trauma-informed care* as care that is based on the following principles: "1. Safety 2. Trustworthiness and Transparency 3. Peer Support 4. Collaboration and Mutuality 5. Empowerment, Voice and Choice 6. Cultural, Historical, and Gender Issues" (p. 10). Because these principles may seem like common sense, it is easy to overlook the importance of establishing safety, which begins with the RJ facilitator's mindset and physical presence. Research on interpersonal neurobiology has affirmed that individuals in a help-seeking role are profoundly impacted by the caregiver's presence and response (Yap, 2018). In the context of RJ for CSM processes, the RJ facilitator is the practitioner who creates the conditions that affirm the fundamental safety and well-being of all parties. In order to ensure safety for others, we must first feel secure within our own bodies. It may be helpful to consider what things will trigger painful emotions and distract a facilitator from engaging genuinely and authentically. When thinking about our triggers, it is important to understand how we are creating safety for ourselves and others. To that end, an example of a typical behavior that results from facilitators feeling unsafe or ungrounded is the tendency to interpret the information shared by participants through the haze of our own discomfort. To remedy this issue, moving into self-inquiry is recommended.

Ask yourself these questions:

- How do the stories they tell connect to my lived experiences, and how am I processing their stories?
- Am I leaning too much into one person's story because I can relate? Am I shutting down because I can relate?
- Are the biases I have toward one experience impacting my ability to be able to behave and listen compassionately?
- Am I able to hear and tell the story of each participant without imposing my "truth" and views?

In addition to being mindful of the kinds of things that may trigger uncomfortable feelings, such as anger or shame, RJ facilitators ought to be aware of their own trauma history and how that impacts their role in any RJ process. Haines (2019) defined *trauma* as "an experience, series of experiences, and/or impacts from social conditions, that break or betray our inherent need for safety, belonging, and dignity" (p. 74). Traumatic experiences understandably overwhelm our capacities to cope and, unfortunately, may remain with us as automatic responses to a perceived threat. When a facilitator is guiding a process, words or behaviors by participants that may be interpreted as threatening can cause a facilitator to suddenly feel "stuck" in a memory or sensations from their past traumatic event(s).

One of the common antidotes to managing triggers and past trauma is through the concept of "self-care." While self-care is often promoted as a material response to spiritual or structural harms, Laura van der Noot Lipsky (TEDx Washington Corrections Center for Women, 2015) pointed out that true self-care is taking time to attend to our own needs as a matter of ethics. If we do not care for ourselves, we risk doing harm to those whom we intend to support or guide.

In addition to ongoing therapy, rest, and mentoring or supportive dialogue with colleagues, there are now many effective body-based interventions that we can learn that support facilitators to stay in the present moment during an RJ process. Some RJ facilitators may benefit from practicing body-centered healing practices such as trauma-informed yoga and taking time before facilitating a circle to practice belly breathing, humming, chanting, or other physical movement that helps ground their body in the safety of the present moment (Menakem, 2017; van der Kolk et al., 2014).

Respectful Interactions and Positive Energy

When most practitioners and scholars speak of *respectful interactions*, they are most often referring to respecting the process and the participants themselves: "Without some base level of respect for participants and for the process itself, the likelihood of achieving positive outcomes is slim, facilitators will determine that participants are not yet ready to meet, and even safety will be questioned" (Umbreit et al., 2007, p. 31). Taking it a step further, respecting the participants requires facilitators to also respect different lived experiences as well as be understanding of cultural nuances that inform how individuals understand the situation. RJ facilitators should hold themselves accountable to attending to those nuances by being mindful of their own biases, understanding of culture, and recognizing how those differences create power differentials. Through this, RJ facilitators can create and maintain respect between participants and between the facilitator and the participants. Taken as a whole, when participants feel connected through the shared understanding of the process, and the acknowledgment of their lived experiences can create a positive energy. The positive energy may support participants to share more openly, which is especially important when discussing issues such as power-based violence.

Self-Accountability and Power

Facilitators should attend to power dynamics in the RJ process, beginning with the self. Self-accountability begins with awareness of one's own values first, and then the choices we make in relation to other people and the RJ process itself. In order to engage as a responsible steward of an RJ process, especially for CSM, the development and nurturance of a critical consciousness is required. Garcia et al. (2009) defined *critical consciousness* as "the ability to recognize and challenge oppressive and dehumanizing political, economic, and social systems" (p. 19). When we are aware of our own power and positionality as RJ facilitators for CSM, we are better prepared to model multipartiality in our restorative processes.

Multipartiality and Critical Consciousness

One of the most difficult but essential aspects of the role of the facilitator is the ability to maintain a *multipartial stance*, the recognition that identity-based power dynamics are present in all human interactions (Koss et al., 2014) and that the facilitator will attend to these dynamics while holding space for all of the parties involved in the process. This means holding space for survivors who may be fearful of not being believed. It also means holding space for responsible parties who may be reluctant to step into accountability, often due to fears of reprisal. It also means that facilitators need to attend to systemic, structural, and historical harms. Without a thorough appraisal of the structural harms, both the ubiquity of CSM and the denial of the humanity of survivors who are not cisgender, heterosexual female students remain uninterrogated. The historical racialized, gendered tropes of perpetrators and victims of sexual assault in our society that permeate campus culture can lead to the co-optation of RJ for CSM processes. Applying the lens of critical consciousness is a key antidote to this trap. While a thorough dive into multipartiality and critical consciousness is beyond the scope of this chapter, we encourage RJ facilitators to seek out further reading and training with scholars–practitioners whose work illuminates the ways in which our individual conditioned responses are often rooted in racism, sexism, homophobia, transphobia, ableism, and other forms of discrimination (some suggested further reading includes Anderson, 2018; Turner, 2020; Vaandering, 2010).

Cultural Humility and Competence

Developing a sense of *cultural humility* and a critical lens will be a vital part of becoming an effective facilitator. Cultural humility affirms that it is not possible to learn every aspect of any culture, including one's own, but it is important to develop a baseline level of cultural competence. Facilitators should adopt a growth mindset that creates opportunities to receive critical feedback from participants and cofacilitators. To that end, before engaging with restorative practices, facilitators should engross themselves in self-reflection and self-critique. In restorative processes, all of the participants and the facilitator may speak from different cultural lenses—and, as a result, misunderstandings among all the participants become a reality (Umbreit et al., 2000). These differences underscore the need for cultural competence. Developing cultural competence requires both understanding and being aware of generalizations that exist in different cultures but also not making assumptions about behavior because of those generalizations. This means that as the facilitator, you have to be willing and able to "study" the cultures that will be represented in your process. This is essential for creating respectful interactions and positive energy.

Embodying a restorative approach at the individual level (attending to self) requires more than knowing the restorative questions and the script by heart. It means understanding and recognizing your limitations and striving toward improving your self-awareness so as to not be hindered by biases and lack of cultural understanding.

Here are some questions to ask yourself:

1. In what ways do I demonstrate lifelong learning, understanding that gaining insight into a person's culture is an ongoing process?
2. How will I engage in critical self-reflection, such as examining unconscious bias to determine how attitudes, perceptions, and values might impact my approach to restorative work with others?
3. What do I know about my own culture, and how does that understanding of my cultural influences impact my ability to empathize with individuals who have different cultural experiences?
4. In what ways have I practiced differentiating participants' relationships with their culture from overgeneralized beliefs and stereotypes?
5. To what extent am I capable of showing compassion and holding space for others, which requires listening without judgment?
6. How do I foster respectful relationships by recognizing and mitigating power imbalances that are often inherent in provider/client dynamics?
7. What skills are necessary to demonstrate awareness of others' cultures and communities and systemic issues to be able to help participants understand each other's worldviews and lived experiences?
8. In what ways do I communicate that I understand that culture is not limited to values, norms, language, place of origin, race, and ethnicity? (Cultural elements may also include class, sexual orientation, gender identity, disability, immigration status, generation, or other identities and variables affecting an individual's reality.)

Attending to People

Moving at the speed of trust (brown, 2017; Piepzna-Samarasinha & Fukui, 2020), a concept described by transformative justice and disability justice activists, provides a way of thinking about restorative work as an unfolding process that rests on building relationships rather than on a preset checklist of action items. Attending to people's needs at the interpersonal level is about establishing trust. As we just discussed in attending to self, as you learn more about yourself, you will be able to better communicate and work with participants. Greater self-awareness on your part supports your ability to sympathize and empathize with participants' lived experiences. In turn, your effective communication makes it more likely that they will trust you and the process. So how do you build that trust? Like any good facilitation, a skilled facilitator needs to be able to practice active listening, listen through a multipartial lens, and create an environment comfortable for sharing. Restorative facilitation is no different; however, there is an increased focus on the ability to coach participants.

Coaching is a process that continually returns decision-making power to the participants, who are empowered to state their needs and make agreements based on those needs (not on the preferences of the facilitator, friends, or well-meaning administrators). Creating shared restorative expectations at the outset of the process (e.g., ground rules of engagement) creates a container of support and safety. In the context of restorative conferencing processes, ground rules are essential to the process because they provide support for accountability based on acknowledging harms and meeting needs. These are the ground rules that conference participants have created for themselves. They are not agreeing to a set of rules that someone else has dictated for them. This gives power and agency to the participants. It is again another paradigm shift that is required when engaging in restorative processes in comparison to traditional models of justice. Through the decision-making process, participants are able to step into ownership of the process, resulting in meaningful engagement. If participants are hindered from meaningful participation, it means they are unable to be fully involved in the interactive process of repairing harm, and any chance of reforming societal inequality is severely hindered (Braithwaite, 2006). Coaching is a crucial part of restorative work. Coaching is especially important during the preparation phase.

It can never be stated enough how *important preparation is to addressing issues of harm* through a restorative process. Often referred to as *preconferencing*, this preparation includes individual meetings with parties involved to explain the process, assess readiness, and allow parties to have a voice in a safer environment. Preconferencing is designed to allow participants to share comfortably and to hear the perspectives of others in a contained way (because those others are not present). In turn, this one-on-one time with the facilitator provides participants with the opportunity to practice perspective-taking. This does *not* mean ignoring participants' feelings but rather supporting them in being able to hear one another without freezing up or closing themselves off to the transformation that unfolds in a restorative process.

Trauma-Responsive Facilitation

In order to effectively coach RJ participants, facilitators need various skills. Given the possibility of trauma histories among the harmed party, responsible party, community members, and even facilitators themselves, extensive preparation of participants is needed. One study of RJ for CSM found that the most well-equipped facilitators had extensive experience in circle keeping and understanding the dynamics of sexual harm. As well, they were also highly skilled in empathetic communication approaches that support self-regulation and help to create a holding space for other people's strong emotions. These include nonviolent communication, intergroup dialogue, training in unconscious bias or implicit bias training (e.g., Implicit Association Test [IAT]), social justice mediation, self-compassion, healing and energy work, and mindfulness meditation (McMahon et al., 2022; Neff, 2009). These types of training may become critical in RJ processes for CSM because of the likelihood that multiple parties in the process will have experienced some form of sexualized victimization prior to the incident that is being addressed through the present moment process (Cusack et al., 2021). As well, facilitators need support from colleagues and peers to ensure that their own personal trauma histories do not disrupt or decenter the needs of the parties in the process.

As stated in in the discussion of attending to self, the facilitator's sense of safety lays the groundwork for a process that creates a sense of well-being for participants; the purposeful and ongoing attention to the participants' sense of safety is critical to moving the RJ process forward. This may include actions such as inviting the participant to select the seating arrangement for the conversation, asking what the individual might need to make them feel that their privacy is protected in the conversation and moving forward, and taking time to check in about their well-being before diving into the preconferencing RJ questions.

Since RJ is not a fact-finding process but rather a meaning-making process, it may be helpful to explicitly state that the purpose of the preconferencing process is to understand the impact, harms, and needs of the parties. Detailed timelines about the events that led to the harm are not always necessary to understanding impact and conveying empathy to the participant, but they may be important or critical, and as the facilitator it could be helpful to look to cofacilitators or the participants to drive appropriateness. Using the typical restorative questioning with individuals who have experienced sexual harm may not be appropriate. For example, restorative questions for people who have been harmed typically begin with the question, "What happened?" While it may be tempting to rely on this question, it can be interpreted as fact-finding, which raises safety concerns about whether one will be believed. Table 7.1 illustrates the differences between traditional preconferencing questions and restorative questions

TABLE 7.1
Typical Restorative Justice Preconferencing Questions

Typical RJ Preconferencing Questions for Harmed Parties	*Suggested Revised RJ Preconferencing Questions for CSM Survivors*
What happened?	Please let me know what stands out to you from the incident that occurred (this could include sounds, smells, repetitive thoughts, etc.) that you think are important for me to understand as we begin this process.
What impact has this incident had on you?	What impact has this incident had on you?
What has been the hardest thing about this?	What has been the hardest thing about this? (Facilitator summarizes the hardest things and describes them through the lens of "harms.")
Is there anything that you can do to help meet your needs?	As a result of the harm you've experienced (restate harms to seek clarification and confirmation), what are some of your resulting needs or goals?
What could the other person do to repair the harm?	What do you think the responsible party could do to repair the harms and address the needs (goals) you have identified?

Note. RJ = restorative justice; CSM = campus sexual misconduct.

for CSM, and before getting to these questions we suggest adding the following:

1. How are you feeling now in terms of your level of safety? How are you feeling physically? Emotionally? (Varlack-Butler, 2022)
2. What is your support system like now? Do you feel you have enough support to move forward in this process? (If not, this could be an opportunity to present referrals to campus resources.)
3. Now, we're going to shift our attention to the incident(s) that have impacted you. I am going to ask a series of questions so that I better understand your experience and what might help you to move forward in your healing process. Please let me know if you would like me to rephrase anything I ask, if you need to take a break at any time, and/or if I misunderstand you at any time. I really appreciate your willingness to talk with me and want to make sure I understand your needs.

Critical Consciousness

Cunneen and Goldson (2015) argued that structural divisions in regard to race, class, gender, and so on may inadvertently exclude individuals from restorative practices "because they are without a community or without the right community" (p. 147). Thus, RJ facilitators will want to consider whether there is a supportive community for each of the participants and whether that community can be called in for support as well as to repair harms to those supportive community members and people not included in the restorative process for a variety of reasons. When engaging in restorative practices, especially in cases of CSM, it is important to remember that there is often not an ideal "victim" and an unnamed "offender" engaging in predatory behavior but rather people with complex relationships (Hirsch & Khan, 2020).

Accountability and Power

In the same way that it is important for facilitators to consider power differentials as they work with participants, it is equally as important that facilitators work with participants to help them understand those differentials. Power imbalances created by differing social identities exist, consciously or unconsciously, within all forms of communication in one way or another. Therefore, within restorative practices, such as circles and reparative panels, the differing positionalities of participants can have a negative effect on their willingness and ability to authentically participate (Furnell, 2017, p. 9). As facilitators, when we are listening for harms and needs, inflamed structural harms are often not thought about because participants themselves may not name them or know how to articulate them. You as the facilitator may need to ask open-ended questions that support the exploration of these kinds of harms.

Embodying a restorative approach while attending to people means thinking and coaching participants beyond a binary in understanding and care.

Here are some questions to ask yourself:

1. How can I, as the facilitator, be mindful of existing power imbalances between participants and create an environment where all parties feel comfortable sharing authentically and listening intently?
2. How do we move away beyond the victim–perpetrator mindset to creating a process that honors the complexity of human life?
3. What are times when I have caused/experienced (sexualized or other) harm in my life? How can remembering this help me guide an inclusive RJ process?

Attending to Systems

As previously noted, critical consciousness is the ability to recognize, reflect, and act to address systems of power and oppression. Within the context of CSM, the complex structural and historical tendencies to blame victims, minimize the seriousness of these harms, and narrowly define who can be a "victim" or a "perpetrator" are present with us even as we seek to restore well-being and prevent future harm. Given these complex dynamics within higher education, restorative justice is sometimes operationalized in a way that can ignore the role of institutionalized economic, social, and political inequalities that create the conditions for harm to occur (Conners, 2003). Institutions should engage with restorative justice through an equity lens. If there is no vigilance with regard to dynamics such as racism, sexism, homophobia, transphobia, and stigma regarding mental health, these dynamics are reinscribed in processes that are labeled restorative (McMahon et al., 2019; Todić et al., 2020; Vaandering, 2010; Varlack-Butler, 2022).

Power Focus

As discussed in when attending to people was addressed, institutions must consider the way their policies, procedures, and practices may contribute to historical and structural harms as well as the ways that they unintentionally privilege some in their communities because they have the "right" community. This requires designing a restorative response system that resists both unnecessary gatekeeping and unnecessary net-widening for RJ processes that address CSM. In essence, *gatekeeping* entails denying individuals who are in need of a restorative process the opportunity to participate because they have been deemed "unworthy" of redemption or "not a good fit" for the restorative process. "Net widening" involves using RJ when another, less invasive intervention would have been effective. To navigate the pull of these two proverbial poles requires applying an intersectional lens that opens up insights into the power dynamics inherent in institutions' of higher educations policies, practices, and interpersonal interactions around issues of sexual assault on campus.

Listening deeply to campus community members whose voices and experiences are marginalized is a critical step on the journey to building a more restorative campus, one that has strong community safety nets for preventing and addressing CSM.

Policy Focus

To effectively address CSM, institutions have to be willing to rethink their ideas of justice and be able to share with their community how a restorative approach benefits the whole campus. This includes policy changes to support RJ for CSM. Institutions such as the University of Michigan, Rutgers University, and The College of New Jersey have made space in their policies for restorative justice–informed processes for sexual misconduct. These institutions' approaches can serve as springboards for other schools that want to create space within policies for RJ to become an option in instances of CSM. Some early adopters of RJ for CSM recognized that a relational approach to policy creation not only mirrors restorative processes but also helps to prevent future instances of litigation by thinking together with campus and community partners about the implications of restorative options prior to implementation. For example, McMahon et al. (2022) found that by engaging early with the local district attorney's office, one campus was able to design their RJ policies in anticipation of possible conflicts with law enforcement, building trust and allaying fears about trying out restorative approaches for some cases of CSM. Additionally, consider what remedies institutions can put into place to provide an increased sense of safety and security during these processes. One measure to put in place to aid in an increased sense of safety is to ask, what other avenues the institution has, or can put into place, to allow parties to communicate beyond face to face? Face to face may not always be the best process, so facilitators and institutions may wish to create policies and opportunities for indirect communication, such as impact statements, video messaging, and so on.

Prevention Focus

For restorative justice to be truly effective and impactful it cannot only be used as a reactive measure. As Schlosser and Sedlacek (2001) explained, administrators are often working in a reactive rather than proactive manner toward solutions designed to provide a quick resolution, one that places "emphasis . . . more on 'putting out the fire' than working toward preventing future 'fires'" (p. 25). Because any singular incident of CSM could be seen as a manifestation of what is perceived as acceptable in that community, engaging in proactive restorative efforts, such as community building circles, and circles focused on being an active bystander or other specific issues, helps to underscore the value of community and creates an environment in which to share community expectations and norms.

Prevention-focused institutions should have RJ processes that push participants and the institution to consider the relationships the involved parties have beyond the incident itself and what relationships the participants have with the campus community, their peer groups, society as a whole. This helps participants to think more broadly about root causes of CSM-related issues and can help participants to better understand each other's perspectives. While this starts to get into transformative justice territory, it is important to think about the ways that RJ is not simply a reactive measure but a preventative tool. RJ practitioners should consider how we can think more broadly about community responsibility in our efforts to address CSM in our restorative processes. Institutions should also consider what messages are being communicated to and within our campus communities that make the persistence of CSM so prevalent and how RJ could be used to build better community accountability.

Changing the ethos of a community through the use of restorative approaches will take more than simply enacting some practices of restorative justice; you will need to include the means to explore the values, attitudes, and expectations of the school or campus community by "focus[ing] on the idea of the group, a collective understanding of how things are done" (Munn et al., 2000, p. 49) to create opportunities to alter campus climate and culture (Anderson, 2018).

In designing your institutional RJ plan, consider your aims and goals. Where do we set the bar for what is achievable? Is it harm reduction? Is it more than that? These and the questions below are just the start in thinking about how we attend to institutions as we engage in practices to further embody RJ.

Here are some questions to ask yourself:

1. What are my resources on or off campuses to help educate me as I prepare to facilitate this case?
2. What additional training might we require as facilitators that the institution already offers or can invest in? Consider issues of neurodiversity, same-sex partnerships, and race and racism.
3. What assumptions/biases might I have about the people in the process?
4. What policies, practices, or procedures exist that may be disproportionately impacting some populations of students?
5. What community members, educators, or other campus partners might I need to engage to be able to prepare best for this?
6. Is my institution willing to engage in ethos changing? Will the administration commit to not only reactionary restorative processes but also proactive processes, such as community-building circles?
7. Can my institution commit the resources to market and provide an educational understanding of what RJ is and the necessary shift in thinking?
8. How do we tell the narrative of RJ?

Closing

Embodying a restorative approach in addressing CSM requires taking a step back and determining how much learning you are willing to commit. Individuals have to be willing to develop a level of self-awareness and dedicate some time to understanding their own and others' cultures to be able to create the best environment for sharing, relationship repairing, and respectful interactions. Also, a critical and intersectional approach to sexualized violence provides support for designing a restorative process that attends to the power dynamics present in the process. Finally, making time to attend to our own histories of trauma and harm can be scary, but as facilitators we can only take participants as far as we ourselves have gone.

Doing and embodying all these steps can be cumbersome and exhausting as you begin to hold the lived experiences of others in your body. Being authentic, attending to expectations, and supporting others is a complex process that requires a lot of support from key stakeholders to succeed. Lack of buy-in or overexertion may result in compassion fatigue, so it is essential that you find methods of self-care and people with whom to share the burden of empathy.

References

Anderson, D. (2018). *The use of campus-based restorative justice practices to address incidents of bias: Facilitators' experiences* [Unpublished doctoral dissertation]. University of New Orleans. https://scholarworks.uno.edu/td/2442

Braithwaite, J. (2006). *Crime, shame and reintegration.* Cambridge University Press.

Brodsky, A. (2022, February 18). Why did Harvard faculty close ranks to defend an alleged abuser? *Al Jazeera.* https://www.aljazeera.com/opinions/2022/2/18/why-did-harvard-faculty-close-ranks-to-defend-an-alleged-abuser

brown, a. m. (2017). *Emergent strategy.* AK Press.

Conners, R. (2003). How restorative is restorative justice? In M. D. Free, Jr. (Ed.), *Racial issues in criminal justice: The case of African Americans* (pp. 255–268). Criminal Justice Press.

Cunneen, C., & Goldson, B. (2015). Restorative justice? A critical analysis. In Goldson, B. and Muncie, J. (Eds.) *Youth, crime and justice* (2nd ed., pp. 137–156). SAGE.

Cusack, S. E., Bourdon, J. L., Bountress, K., Saunders, T. R., Kendler, K. S., Dick, D. M., & Amstadter, A. B. (2021). Prospective predictors of sexual revictimization among college students. *Journal of Interpersonal Violence, 36*(17–18), 8494–8518. https://doi.org/10.1177/10778012221145294

Furnell, M. (2017). *Is restorative justice doing enough to address the power imbalances caused by systems of privilege and oppression?* [Unpublished master's thesis]. School for International Training. https://digitalcollections.sit.edu/capstones/3010

Garcia, M., Kosutic, I., McDowell, T., & Anderson, S. A. (2009). Raising critical consciousness in family therapy supervision. *Journal of Feminist Family Therapy*, *21*(1), 18–38. https://doi.org/10.1080/08952830802683673

Haines, S. K. (2019). *The politics of trauma: Somatics, healing, and social justice.* North Atlantic Books.

Hirsch, J. S., & Khan, S. (2020). *Sexual citizens: A landmark study of sex, power, and assault on campus.* W.W. Norton.

Koss, M. P., Gidycz, C. A., & Wisniewski, N. (1987). The scope of rape: Incidence and prevalence of sexual aggression and victimization in a national sample of higher education students. *Journal of Consulting and Clinical Psychology*, *55*(2), 162–170. https://doi.org/10.1037/0022-006X.55.2.162

Koss, M. P., Wilgus, J. K., & Williamsen, K. M. (2014). Campus sexual misconduct: Restorative justice approaches to enhance compliance with Title IX guidance. *Trauma, Violence, & Abuse*, *15*(3), 242–257. https://doi.org/10.1177/1524838014521500

Koss, M. P., Swartout, K. M., Lopez, E. C., Lamade, R. V., Anderson, E. J., Brennan, C. L., & Prentky, R. A. (2022). The scope of rape victimization and perpetration among national samples of college students across 30 years. *Journal of Interpersonal Violence*, *37*(1–2), NP25–NP47. https://doi.org/10.1177/08862605211050103

McMahon, S. M., Karp, D. R., & Mulhern, H. (2019). Addressing individual and community needs in the aftermath of campus sexual misconduct: Restorative justice as a way forward in the re-entry process. *Journal of Sexual Aggression*, *25*(1), 49–59. https://doi.org/10.1080/13552600.2018.1507488

McMahon, S. M., Williamsen, K. M., Mitchell, H. B., & Kleven, A. (2022). Initial reports from early adopters of restorative justice for reported cases of campus sexual misconduct: A qualitative study. *Violence Against Women*. https://doi.org/10.1177/10778012221108419

Menakem, R. (2017). *My grandmother's hands: Racialized trauma and the pathway to mending our hearts and bodies.* Penguin UK.

Munn, P., Cullen, M. A., & Lloyd, G. (2000). *Alternatives to exclusion from school.* Sage.

Neff, K. D. (2009). The role of self-compassion in development: A healthier way to relate to oneself. *Human Development*, *52*(4), 211–214. https://doi.org/10.1159/000215071

Piepzna-Samarasinha, L. L., & Fukui, E. (2020, April 10). *Moving at the speed of trust: Disability justice and transformative justice.* [Video]. YouTube. https://youtu.be/TwWdv_uBGNY

Schlosser, L. Z., & Sedlacek, W. E. (2001). Hate on campus: A model for evaluating, understanding, and handling critical incidents. *About Campus*, *6*, 25–27.

Substance Abuse and Mental Health Services Administration. (2014, July). *SAMHSA's concept of trauma and guidance for a trauma-informed approach.* https://ncsacw.acf.hhs.gov/userfiles/files/SAMHSA_Trauma.pdf

TEDx Washington Corrections Center for Women. (2015, April 23). Laura van der Noot Lipsky: *Beyond the cliff* [Video]. YouTube. https://youtu.be/uOzDGrcvmus

Todić, J., Cubbin, C., Armour, M., Rountree, M., & González, T. (2020). Reframing whole school restorative justice as a structural population health intervention. *Health & Place, 62*, 102289. https://doi.org/10.1016/j.healthplace.2020.102289

Turner, J. (2020). Creating safety for ourselves In E. C. Valandra & R. Yazzie (Eds.), *Colorizing restorative justice: Voicing our realities* (pp. 291–324). Living Justice Press.

Umbreit, M. S., Coates, R. B., & Roberts, A. W. (2000). The impact of victim–offender mediation: A cross-national perspective. *Mediation Quarterly, 17*(3), 215–229. https://doi.org/10.1002/crq.3900170303

Umbreit, M. S., Coates, R. B., & Vos, B. (2007). Restorative justice dialogue: A multi-dimensional, evidence-based practice theory. *Contemporary Justice Review, 10*(1), 23–41. https://doi.org/10.1080/10282580601157521

Vaandering, D. (2010). The significance of critical theory for restorative justice in education. *The Review of Education, Pedagogy, and Cultural Studies, 32*(2), 145–176. https://doi.org/10.1080/10714411003799165

van der Kolk, B. A., Stone, L., West, J., Rhodes, A., Emerson, D., Suvak, M., & Spinazzola, J. (2014). Yoga as an adjunctive treatment for posttraumatic stress disorder: A randomized controlled trial. *The Journal of Clinical Psychiatry, 75*(6), 22573. https://doi.org/10.4088/JCP.13m08561

Varlack-Butler, L. T. (2022, March 1). *Reframing restorative approaches to harm: Responding restoratively.* https://respondingrestoratively.com/with-a-restorative-heart-1/f/reframing-restorative-approaches-to-harm

Yap, R. (2018). Implicitly regulating the stress of oppression: Re-establishing safety in intercultural practice. *Smith College Studies in Social Work, 88*(1), 4–19. https://doi.org/10.1080/00377317.2018.1403247

8

FACILITATING REPAIR
AND RESTORATION

Guiding Restorative Practices With Those Who
Have Experienced and Caused Sexual Harms

Carrie Landrum

*Land and Practices Acknowlegement: Acknowledgment and deep appre-
ciation are extended to the many indigenous wisdom keepers (globally,
historically, and currently) who have practiced and shared their restorative
ways since time immemorial. Special acknowledgement and gratitude are
offered to the Anishinaabeg, and in particular the Council of Three Fires
Niswi-mishkodewinan confederacy of Ojibwe, Odawa, and Potawatomi
tribes, early stewards and caretakers of the land this text was written on in
Michigan (a name derived from the Anishinaabemowin/Ojibwe word for
"Great Lake"—Mishigami; The Decolonial Atlas, 2015).*

*The Three Fires Confederacy ceded land to the University of Michigan
in 1817 to support education. Anishinaabeg have been practicing peacemaking and restorative ways since long before we had those terms, and they continue to teach others these practices. Through these words of acknowledgment
reverencing the Anishinaabeg, their contemporary and ancestral ties to the
land, their historical and ongoing contributions to education and peacemaking, and their place as a progenitor of restorative practices are respected and
reaffirmed.*

W*á'tkwanonhweráton Sewakwékon*. This Kanyen'kè:ha (Mohawk)
phrase communicates greetings, love, and respect. These words,
taught to me by filmmaker and educator Kahstoserakwathe Paulette
Moore, are a common greeting used in a restorative community we frequent.

I begin with indigenous words and values to honor the indigenous origins of restorative practices. I also begin with these words as they reflect a restorative approach: one grounded in love and respect. The Rev. Dr. Martin Luther King, Jr., taught: "Power at its best is love implementing the demands of justice, and justice at its best is love correcting everything that stands against love" (King, 1968, p. 38). Restorative justice (RJ) facilitators will do well to ground their justice efforts in love.

Howard Zehr (2002), known for popularizing and defining RJ, sums it up as *respect*:

> If I had to put restorative justice into one word, I would choose respect: respect for all, even those who are different from us, even those who seem to be our enemies. Respect reminds us of our interconnectedness but also of our differences. Respect insists that we balance concern for all parties. If we pursue justice as respect, we will do justice restoratively. If we do not respect others, we will not do justice restoratively, no matter how earnestly we adopt the principles. The value of respect underlies restorative justice principles and must guide and shape their application (p. 36).

Working restoratively with those who've experienced harm and who've caused harm requires that we always treat them with dignity and respect. How can we teach students to respect others if we don't actively respect them during the process? A restorative facilitator must embody a restorative approach and engage in a trauma-informed, culturally competent, multi-partial way with respect. Supporting students in addressing sexual harms is sacred work that demands great care and thoughtfulness. Ideally, restorative facilitators embody the agape love that the Rev. Dr. King (1957) preached about: "The Greek language comes out with another word for love. It is the word *agape*. . . . Agape is something of the understanding, creative, redemptive goodwill for all men. It is a love that seeks nothing in return" (para. 17). If we pursue justice as respect with agape, we harness the potential to transform lives and communities.

What follows are some of my reflections on working restoratively with students who've experienced and caused sexual harms, drawing from 15 years of experience facilitating restorative practices at the University of Michigan and elsewhere. Beginning in 2011, I helped build and refine one of the first university programs to offer restorative practices to students who experienced sexual harms while honoring our federal Title IX obligations to respond promptly and effectively to eliminate sexual violence, prevent its recurrence, and address its effects. Following are some of my takeaways from years of facilitating restorative practices that have addressed and contributed to the repair of campus sexual harms: thoughts on the facilitator role; principles, and practices employed by restorative facilitators; and specific tips on working with students who've experienced and caused sexual harms. I conclude with the importance of attending to facilitator support and sustenance.

Facilitator Role

While information on the role of a restorative justice facilitator is readily available in myriad places, I wish to draw attention here to the specific additional roles that university employees bear when facilitating restorative practices. In the following section, I highlight the imperative to serve responsibly, particularly when supporting those impacted by sexual misconduct, and bearing in mind the additional responsibilities conferred when facilitating restoratively as educators or campus administrators. I also include thoughts on being multipartial and attentive to power dynamics.

Facilitating and Serving Responsibly

There are some key considerations to heed when working with those who've experienced or caused sexual harms. First, a restorative facilitator must recognize and appreciate the great responsibility and duty they carry: a duty and responsibility to ensure that no additional harm is caused through engaging in the restorative process—not just harm from other parties, but also by the facilitator and the process itself. We must additionally appreciate the tremendous responsibility inherent in supporting someone navigating what may possibly be (or follow) the most difficult or challenging experience of their life to date (which can be true for those who caused harm as well as for those who experienced harm). In many ways, it is sacred work to hold others' traumas, and should be appreciated as such.

Many books, articles, and websites discuss the roles and responsibilities of a restorative practitioner. The Alberta Restorative Justice Association offers an invaluable road map in their guide, *Serving Crime Victims Through Restorative Justice: A Resource Guide for Leaders and Practitioners* (Bargen et al., 2018). My goal here is to build on the existing foundation by highlighting the extra care required when working restoratively with those who've experienced or caused sexual harms in the context of a campus community. That a practitioner doing such work needs training and/or background in working with those who've experienced trauma and/or sexual harms should be evident.

Serving as Educators

Facilitators of restorative practice within an educational setting have an additional role beyond that in other settings. We serve as educators and teachers within our facilitation role. Doing so helps meet the number-one justice need articulated by the harmed students I've met with: "I just want them to understand the harm they caused and that what they did was wrong, so that it doesn't happen again." For students unaware of how they caused harm, campus facilitators play an important role in their learning. To create space for learning, it is imperative to ensure the learner feels safe, respected, and supported in their learning. For a student who caused harm to be willing to go on a learning and accountability journey, they need to feel respected and heard, and they must experience a certain level of trust and safety. Campus facilitators serve as key teachers and guides for those who caused harm. They also play a role in supporting the learning and growth of those who were harmed by letting them know that what happened wasn't their fault; by connecting them to support resources; by interrupting false narratives, myths, or stereotypes; and by affirming them where possible as they harness their courage and strength.

Serving as Thoughtful Administrators Attentive to Power Dynamics

A restorative facilitator who is also a campus administrator is an agent of justice as well as an agent of the institution. We need to be clear on what the bounds of confidentiality are that we can or cannot offer. We also need to be clear in letting participants know (in an informative, nonthreatening way) what may happen should they exit a voluntary restorative process prior to its conclusion. It is common practice for restorative facilitators to let potential participants know what the role of the facilitator is and is not. It is important for campus practitioners to recognize the compounded power and authority we have in facilitating the process as well as serving as a campus administrator. Acute awareness and attention to the power dynamics this creates is essential. One time I was in a third or fourth meeting with a respondent who had been extremely reticent to share with me. During the meeting, they remarked: "I just realized you are not the attorney for the complainant." I was shocked and confounded to learn that they'd had this misconception (and for so long), and yet it is my responsibility to ensure that all participants are crystal clear on what my role is and is not. As restorative processes are still unfamiliar to most, and campus facilitators may likely be seen as (or indeed serve as) campus disciplinarians or attorneys, and especially as many respondents are actively experiencing trauma responses when we meet with them (and may be less capable of processing complex information), it is important for campus facilitators to clarify again and again what our role is (and isn't) in an unfamiliar process.

Power dynamics are already immense between students and administrators. When we add to these social identities that confer privilege and power or marginalization, the power imbalances widen even further. In the previous example, the student respondent I was working with was an international student with marginalized racial, ethnic, religious, and sexual identities. The student felt that the claims against them were based in bias rooted in racism and harmful narratives around their religious identity. The graduate student surfaced this in our meeting and shared articles illustrating their point to counter dominant harmful narratives in our society. All students may not be able or equipped to self-advocate in this way, or have the time and wherewithal to educate their facilitators. It is our responsibility as restorative facilitators to be culturally competent; receptive to alternate narratives; aware of power dynamics; and attentive to biases in ourselves and others, whether unconscious or otherwise. I recommend *Colorizing Restorative Justice* (Valandra, 2020) and the Right Use of Power Institute (2023) as two aids in these areas.

Being Multipartial

Finally, while there are many additional facets to serving in the role of an RJ facilitator that are covered in other places, the importance of being multipartial, particularly when working with those accused of having caused sexual harms, is vital. Many facilitators (and investigators) are trained to be impartial and neutral. Paulo Freire (1985), founder of critical pedagogy, wrote in *The Politics of Education*: "Washing one's hands of the conflict between the powerful and the powerless means to side with the powerful, not to be neutral" (p. 122). Nobel Peace Prize winner and internationally renowned advocate of RJ, Archbishop Emeritus Desmond Tutu, said:

> If you are neutral in situations of injustice, you have chosen the side of the oppressor. If an elephant has its foot on the tail of a mouse and you say that you are neutral, the mouse will not appreciate your neutrality. (Oxford Reference, 2017, para. 1)

These wisdom teachers evince a need to move beyond neutrality. Being impartial by definition is being partial to no one; being multipartial or polypartial is the opposite—being partial to many or all. I learned the concept of multipartiality from Leah Wing and Deepika Marya, who teach facilitators how to account for privilege and power dynamics in their facilitation. I learned that being a truly multipartial facilitator requires being equitably partial to all sides while necessarily attending to (and disrupting) dynamics of privilege and power, while also explicitly inviting personal narratives related to social identities (Wing & Marya, 2008).

Being multipartial in situations of campus sexual harm means that if a young white woman asserts that she felt "intimidated" and "threatened" by a Black male student, we can simultaneously hold and care for the truth of her experience of feeling threatened while also problematizing a harmful racist narrative and long-standing stereotype perpetuated in U.S. culture that socializes white women (and others) to fear Black men. Being a multipartial, restorative facilitator of sexual harms also means that we extend equitable amounts of respect, care, and even empathy to those who are accused of having caused harm, while balancing support and accountability (more on this balance of support and accountability follows).

Principles, Practices, and Presence

Facilitating restorative practices with students who've experienced and caused sexual harms requires thoughtful attention to the process of facilitation itself. Maintaining mindful attention on the process and act of facilitating, even more so than on any outcomes, is helpful when facilitating repair and restoration. Attending to the quality of facilitator presence; seeking to meet needs; balancing accountability and support; and fostering agency, choice, and voice at all times are helpful practices and principles to actualize when facilitating restorative processes.

Listening With Presence

The skill set, mindset, and heartset required for this work is multitudinous. Skills and mindsets can be taught, but having the right heartset—like exuding compassion and empathy while you hold space for others—is more a way of being than utilizing a specific skill set. A report on Canada's first victim–offender dialogue program (a precursor to restorative conferencing) noted: "For both victims and offenders, it was vital that they were being not only listened to but heard. This attribute did not come across simply as a professional technique, but as one human being caring about another" (Bargen et al., 2018, p. 79). As the Alberta RJ practitioner's guide notes:

> Skills are also a focus of many restorative justice training workshops. Yet . . . restorative justice participants value qualities in practitioners that are more primary than "skills." These qualities can be thought of collectively as a facilitator's "presence." Most simply, facilitator "presence" refers to a state of being mentally quiet and attuned to another person. Presence begins with attentiveness, open-mindedness, caring and striving for acceptance of the person and their story. (Bargen et al., 2018, pp. 79–80)

The guide suggests that as practitioners we can develop presence by actively aspiring toward personal capacities such as steadiness, emotional regulation, self-awareness, unconditional positive regard and compassion, deep respect, and radical curiosity; "a desire to understand the participant on their terms rather than the expectations or mental 'maps' we have drawn for them; challenging our preconceptions about others and inviting them to challenge our conclusions" (Bargen et al., 2018, p. 80).

I agree with the guide's conclusion that "It may be that the facilitator's presence is more fundamental than any specific skills. Certainly, such a capacity seems to be a key ingredient in how listening and communication skills will 'land' with participants" (Bargen et al., 2018, p. 80). Renowned writer, activist, and facilitator adrienne maree brown (2021) offered:

> How you are, how you show up, invites a quality of presence from participants. If you want to change what *is* possible in the room, change what *you believe* is possible. Change how present you are, increase your rigor, focus your energy. Invite participants to have the same power to transform themselves to transform what is possible in the room. (p. 17)

While the facilitator is responsible for the restorative process, and therefore for each meeting, it would be wrong to assume that a facilitator must then lead every meeting or accomplish a specific list of things in each meeting. Whereas many campus administrators, like investigators, have a very specific task list for meetings and often conduct them in a very linear way, we know that healing is not linear, and therefore a restorative meeting need not be. As my colleague and adaptable resolution facilitator Ramonda Kindle notes:

> When students have chosen that moment to share their story with you, as a facilitator, you should handle your dialogue with them with care. I find it helpful to hold space for students and allow them to define how we will spend our time together. Some students may want to use that space to process their experiences, thoughts, and feelings and may seek permission to do so. Thus, it is essential to set aside the need to ask questions and allow them to navigate the space and time as they see fit. When the students can define the space, you are meeting their needs and allowing them the opportunity to determine how they wish to develop their healing process. (Personal communication, June 3, 2022)

Striving to Meet Needs

The primary principle I employ in meetings with students is that of *being in service* and meeting needs. I essentially begin every meeting with "How can

I help you?" I then let them drive the meeting from there. If they want to ask me specific questions, or tell their story, or hear more about RJ, I want to meet their needs. RJ, after all, is fundamentally about meeting needs. Howard Zehr (2002) explained "For restorative justice, then, justice begins with a concern for victims and their needs" (p. 22). I operate from this principle in every restorative meeting I hold.

Balancing Accountability and Support

The other principle I keep as my compass is that of working *with* students (not *to* them or *for* them), balancing support and accountability. This is engaging restoratively, as the Restorative Window of Support and Accountability in Figure 8.1 illustrates.

The Restorative Window of Support and Accountability demonstrates that working restoratively requires balancing a high amount of accountability with a high amount of support. When working with students who've caused harm, it could be easy to focus on accountability and righting wrongs. This is, after all, a primary goal of restorative practices: repairing harm. However, especially when working with students—who are in a growing and learning phase of life—it is crucial for a restorative facilitator

Figure 8.1. Restorative window of support and accountability.

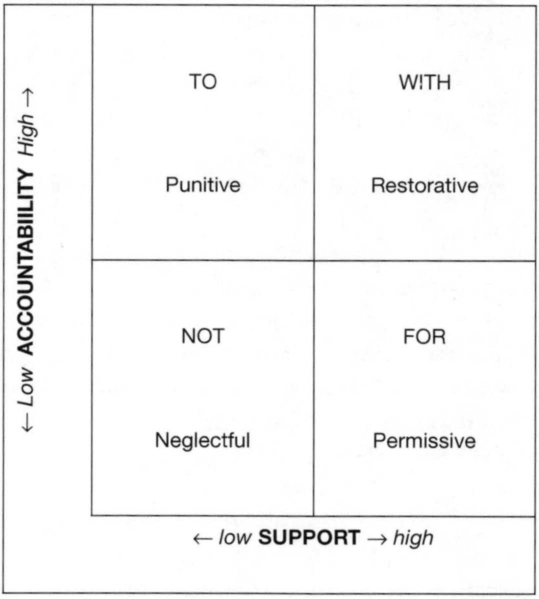

Note. Based on the social discipline window adapted by Ted Wachtel in Defining Restorative, IIRP, 2016.

to provide an appropriate amount of support. In some situations, we may be meeting with a young student to discuss what happened in their very first sexual encounter. In many cases, we are working with young people whose brains are literally still growing and developing. When I meet with someone accused of causing harm, it is essential to the success of a restorative process that I treat them with dignity and respect (without assumptions), that I am genuinely curious about them as a person and work to build trust and rapport with them, that I attempt to meet their needs in our meetings, and that I take the time to invite and listen to their story (allowing them to begin their story wherever it makes sense for them to begin it). This is working *with* students, and balancing support and accountability. I have had many students who caused harm effusively thank me for listening to them, telling me "You are the first person to actually listen to me."

Fostering Agency, Choice, and Voice

The primary practice I employ in my work as a restorative facilitator addressing sexual harms is to continuously offer opportunities for voice as well as agency and choice whenever and wherever possible. In the trainings I lead I'm often asked "How do you convince potential participants to try RJ?" The answer is: I don't. Despite my passion and enthusiasm for restorative processes, I recognize and appreciate that it's not for everyone, and I do my best work when I don't have a personal stake or investment in a particular outcome. Survivors of sexual harms have usually experienced coercion and/ or their agency or choice taken away from them; for me to be coercive or pushy about absolutely anything when I'm working with them would be inappropriate and potentially retraumatizing. It is my intentional goal to engage restoratively by constantly finding ways to offer agency, choice, and voice back to people who were harmed.

The ways that I offer agency and choice when I'm working with survivors of sexual harms (or anyone) begin with the very first invitation to them. An email invitation to the process doesn't assume they will want to meet with me or that they will agree to participate, and it offers choices in dates, times, and format. If we're meeting in person, I ask them their preference on having the door open or closed (recognizing that their personal and psychological safety may depend on it one way or the other). When identifying the space for our meeting or a restorative process, I offer choices on the location, date and time, room or platform, setup, seating arrangements, speaking order, support people, prep time, debrief time, and so on. *Everything* about a restorative process, as well as potential outcomes, should work to meet the needs of harmed parties to the extent possible. This is being restorative.

Many understand this when it comes to agreements or outcomes, and yet it applies to absolutely every part of the process itself as well.

Some administrators or facilitators may mistakenly believe it's their job to get participants to reach a resolution agreement or to get the matter resolved. While current Title IX obligations require U.S. campuses who receive federal funding to address misconduct and remedy its effects, a restorative process doesn't inherently require a written agreement, and an agreement itself is not the goal—repairing harm is the goal (which can happen without necessarily entering into a resolution agreement). Restorative best practices (as well as current U.S. Title IX regulations) require that participants be allowed to end or exit a restorative process at any time. To push anyone to enter into an agreement is again to replicate coercive power dynamics that we seek to remedy and prevent. Additionally, the role of a facilitator is by definition one who facilitates, aids, or helps someone or something—they don't do things *for* others. Restorative facilitators need not work harder than the participants involved to find solutions—what is needed and possible for repair or restoration is up to the participants involved. Facilitators work *with* (and not *for*) restorative process participants to discover what that might be.

Working With Students Who've Experienced Sexual Harms

A restorative process must center the needs of the person or people who experienced harm. There is much knowledge available on how best to support and work with survivors of sexual harm. Restorative facilitators will do well to explore and internalize this knowledge. The notable research of Judith Herman, M.D., Lifetime Achievement Award recipient from the International Society for Traumatic Stress Studies, revealed survivors' most acute justice needs as acknowledgement, validation, and vindication (Bargen et al., 2018, p. 35). A restorative facilitator can provide some of this themselves. Indeed, Herman found that, to survivors, "Their most important object was to gain validation from the community" (Bargen et al., 2018, p. 35).

Support Healing and Agency

In working with college students, I've found that I can be supportive to survivors even if the person who caused them harm didn't engage in the process. In one of the few cases I've had that didn't result in a resolution agreement, I was aware (because I'd asked) that the young student I was meeting with had very little support—she hadn't told her parents or many friends about her experience, and she had not met with survivor advocates despite my repeated encouragement that she do so. It seemed apparent to me that she was struggling with her experiences. When it became clear to me that I would need to close her case due to lack of engagement by the other person involved, I didn't email her and in effect say: "Sorry; I'm closing your case and you're out of options here." I didn't want to do something *to* her, I wanted to engage *with* her, restoratively. I engaged her in this decision-making and framed it in a way to highlight her choices. Her email reply to me said:

> As much as I wish this process would've resulted in a resolution, it doesn't seem like the respondent is willing to engage with it. I agree closing this case might be best for now.
>
> Thank you for all your help during this. I can't express how important you've been to me and my healing process. You gave me so much strength and reassurance when I didn't even realize I needed it.

I highlight this to show that we can find ways to illuminate choices and invite agency even when options are being eliminated or a process is ending. More importantly, I can't emphasize enough that even if there is no accountability-taking by the person who caused the harm, restorative facilitators can aid students in their healing and restoration journey.

One primary difference in facilitating restorative responses to sexual harms versus other harms is the incredibly intimate and personal nature of the harm. Many people who experience sexual harms feel a great deal of shame (even though what happened wasn't their fault) in addition to a wide range of emotions around what happened, and they may not want to talk about their experience—especially with someone they've just met. Typical restorative questions ask "What happened?" When I meet with survivors of sexual harm for a restorative meeting, however, I don't ask this. I seek to meet their needs, as mentioned previously. If they want to share what happened, I will certainly listen as a compassionate witness. But I don't ask. Given our curiosity as humans to know what happened, and the responsibility of investigators to determine what happened, and our responsibility as restorative facilitators to repair harm, it may be counterintuitive to realize we don't actually need to know exactly what happened in order to facilitate repair and restoration. Restorative facilitators may likely need to understand the *impact* of what happened in order to help meet needs and facilitate ways that the harm can be repaired, but we don't actually need to know the details of what happened. I have definitely had cases where I didn't know what happened, or I was privy to only the fewest and faintest vignettes related to what happened.

More Agency, Choice, and Voice

In one memorable case I met numerous times with a student who'd experienced harm, and she didn't share with me what happened, even when I reported to her that the person who'd caused her harm claimed to not have any memory of what harm he had caused, and that in order for him to learn from this process it would be helpful for him to gain that understanding. When it became apparent to her that the restorative process would require him to gain additional clarity, I offered her choice in how she would like her experience communicated: would she like to tell me (verbally) for me to then tell him; would she like to tell him directly or indirectly (verbally) in a live, in-person meeting or a recorded audio or video format; or would she like to write it down for me to share with him? Ultimately, she chose to write a letter to him that she shared with me via email. Again, I provided a choice: Was she comfortable with me giving him a copy of the letter, or would she prefer he read it in my presence and not retain a copy of it? Again and again, I offered voice, choice, and agency in how she proceeded.

Supporting agency, choice, and voice is essentially my mantra when working with survivors of harm (and others). I orient myself as one who serves. How can I meet their needs? Whether it's providing weekly updates even when there are no updates to report—because silence from the facilitator can contribute to anxiety—or it's conversely recognizing the potential impact of my name in someone's inbox—as my name and role can trigger an unwelcome reminder of a harmful experience—and thus intentionally emailing less frequently or emailing a survivor advocate my updates instead, I strive in as many ways as possible to meet needs and satisfy preferences. An empowering experience with a person in a position of power (i.e., a campus administrator) can, in a small or even large way, provide a healing balm to someone who has had their agency and bodily autonomy violated. Adding empathy and grounded, compassionate presence into this balm can greatly enhance its healing potential.

A graduate student survivor I supported through a lengthy, complex, and multipronged adaptable and restorative process shares a snapshot of her experience:

> The Adaptable Resolution process firstly asks what us as claimants need to heal from our experiences. Each process is tailored to our individual requests and needs so as to ensure our safety. As a part of my process, I was able to request tailored respondent education, restorative justice circles, and formal departmental notifications of the respondent's behavior to ensure accountability and prevention from further harm. By placing our needs and requests at the center of the process, this ensures that our voices are

heard. And while we are not responsible for respondent's behaviors or willingness to change, we can ensure accountability and prevent future harm through this process. We give ourselves the power to change the narrative and write the story of our own healing and empowerment. By tailoring a process that meets our specific needs, we have the tools to reclaim our space and safety at [the university].

While this process can be long and taxing, it was far more transformative for me. My journey through the Adaptable Resolution process allowed me to stand in my story and assert accountability for the respondent's behavior. This has been incredibly healing, as I no longer carry the shame and fear that defined me as a victim. I have taken back the power that was once stolen from me. I feel empowered on this journey and emboldened to stand tall as a survivor. And for that, I will always be grateful to this process.

Working With Students Who've Caused Sexual Harms

While my facilitation strengths include being a fairly nonjudgmental and compassionate person, and I've honed my restorative facilitation chops to not be overly, consciously biased generally against those who cause harm (being acutely aware of the trauma, socialization, and ignorance behind much harm), I noticed as I was doing this work that I wasn't providing as much space for respondents (those named as causing harm) to share what was on their hearts and minds as I was providing for those who identified as having experienced harm. I did offer space to respondents, of course, and I got defensive once when a respondent told me that I hadn't given him space to tell his story. I knew I had invited him to do so after extensive rapport building, and the assertion threw me as patently inaccurate. I realized upon self-reflection, however, that the quality of my *presence* hadn't given him quality space to tell his story. I hadn't been sufficiently attentive, caring, or open to hearing or receiving his story. It was an important lesson on the work I needed to do to be more fully restorative and multipartial.

Restorative facilitators need to be equitably invested in hearing the stories of those who caused harm as those who experienced harm. Those who experienced harm have often (but not always) already told their stories to supportive allies and advocates before they meet with campus administrators, and typically a fair amount of time and reflection have passed since their experience of harm until the moment they meet with a restorative facilitator. For those who've caused harm, the restorative facilitator may commonly be the first and only person they've shared their story with about the situation, and they may likely not have had much, if any, reflection on what happened. The moment a respondent is notified by a campus administrator that they've been accused of engaging in sexual misconduct may very well be (a) the first time they actually became aware that they'd caused harm and (b) a catalyst for traumatic stress or grief.

Peter Levine, famed trauma expert, recognized the distinction between stress and traumatic stress, noting that "traumatic stress occurs when our ability to respond to threat is overwhelmed" (p. 49). When recognizing traumatic stress or grief and loss in those we work with, "The loss may be actual or perceived and is the absence of something that was valued. An actual loss is recognized and verified by others while others cannot verify a perceived loss. Both are real to the individual who has experienced the loss" (Oates & Maani-Fogelman, 2022, para. 1). When a student is notified that they are a respondent in a campus sexual misconduct process, they tend to experience actual and perceived losses from fear of being kicked out of school, to being socially isolated, to being criminally liable, to losing their own self-concept and identity as a good person, to losing their family's love and respect. The time between getting a campus notification related to this perceived loss and meeting with a campus administrator is usually pretty minimal and brief, so respondents typically haven't had a lot of time or necessarily people to process this traumatic grief and loss with. It is very possible that when meeting with a respondent they've told absolutely no one that they are going through a campus sexual misconduct process, and therefore they lack support entirely. (This is one of the reasons why providing support resources to student respondents, in addition to survivors of harm, is so important.)

As mentioned earlier, restorative facilitation requires being equitably multipartial with all students, and sometimes this may require providing more space for a respondent to process through their feelings and experiences than for those who experienced the harm. Elisabeth Kübler-Ross famously identified the stages of grief as denial, anger, bargaining, depression, and acceptance (1969, pp. 37–132). In my experience, respondents frequently show up with denial, anger, and/or defensiveness first, often accompanied by confusion. This response can be an unconscious protection against feeling shame. Respondents may employ defense tactics in order to avoid feeling shame, to avoid confronting the possibility that they actually hurt another person, and in order to feel safe. Sometimes this shows up as respondents blaming or attacking the person who's named them as having caused harm, and sometimes it shows up as attacking the facilitator or the institution. Allowing respondents space to go through their stages of grief and loss can help to build trust (with the facilitator and the process) and can ultimately culminate in acceptance.

I remember a memorable exchange I had with a graduate student respondent once. While he'd accepted responsibility for some of the harm he'd caused, he didn't agree with everything that had been reported, and he was upset with his classmates for not calling him out and letting him know that his behavior was harmful and unacceptable before they chose to report their concerns to the university. In our first few meetings I did a lot of space-holding as he processed through a wide range of feelings, including anger, shame, bitterness, and resentment (in his own words). At one point, he said to me something along the lines of "I just want to make my class-mates suffer like they made me (suffer)." On its face, he was talking about wanting to cause harm to his classmates. Not only is this the opposite of restorative, it could have been quite alarming if I'd taken him at his word and considered it a serious threat. I could have shut down the meeting and our explorations of a restorative process right then. Rather than react to his statement, however, I received his words quietly and calmly, and responded with silence. He filled the silence by saying "This is where you're supposed to say: 'you can't do that!'" But I knew that he knew it, and I didn't need to tell him so. (I had already discussed personal values with this student and knew he held strong Christian values.) The student simply needed time and space to process through his hurt feelings regarding his classmates. He would not be ready to repair harm to them until he worked through his own feelings of victimization first. I gave him space to do that and built trust with him while I did. He ultimately did repair harm to his classmates by participating in an RJ circle with them where he genuinely apologized, expressed remorse, and took accountability through words and actions.

We won't usually be able to help a respondent move from denial and defense to empathy and repair in a single meeting. However, we can invite them on the journey. Once we've established trust and mutual respect and we've met them where they're at, we are better situated to help students understand other perspectives and experiences. Respondents may likely need to feel heard and affirmed first, before they can begin to perspective-shift or have empathy for others. To support this building of empathy we can plant seeds of understanding and empathy, even if the respondent isn't quite ready to see or hold such things. If we nurture these seeds by coming alongside a respondent and supporting their autonomy and intrinsic motivation, we may be surprised at the change we witness. To cultivate growth, seeds need to be planted as well as repeatedly nourished.

I worked with another respondent once who shared his experience so that I could share it with others:

> In my final year of graduate school, I participated as a respondent in the University's adaptable resolution process. I was surprised to be invited to engage in the process—I didn't even think I had met the classmate who

had accused me of sexual assault. But I had. I had [sexually assaulted] her at a party while blackout drunk, and then continued on in my academic career in blissful ignorance while she was left to cope with that traumatic experience alone.

My classmate initiated the adaptable resolution process. In retrospect, I think that her decision to choose that path was brave and kind. At first, when I was invited to participate in the program, I was scared and confused. I expected lectures, shame, and perhaps punishment. Instead, the process was an eye-opening and learning experience for me as my classmate explained to me the trauma that I had caused her and sought to hold me accountable for my actions. Our coordinator worked with both me and my classmate to determine what I could do to make amends, repair harm, and grow to not repeat my behavior, all the while prioritizing healing and accountability rather than punishment. . . .

I am immensely grateful that I had the opportunity to take part in the adaptable resolution process—not just in place of a more punitive process, but also in place of simply not confronting my problems at all. Thanks to my experience, I feel that I have a better relationship with women, more fully consider my effect on those around me, and live a healthier lifestyle than I would have had I not had the opportunity to participate. I sincerely hope that the process was equally valuable to my classmate.

This student's narrative illustrates that RJ, in addition to providing an opportunity for repair and restoration to someone who experienced harm, can also be an opportunity that benefits the person who caused the harm, too. It can be a transformative experience beneficial to everyone involved. That's the beauty and the magic.

Facilitator Support and Sustenance

I've shared some reflections on how to support those who've experienced and caused harm. One additional and essential element to this work is supporting *yourself* if you're involved in holding others' traumas, and if you're not personally facilitating this work, but you support it, then *intentionally supporting* the facilitators of restorative processes. This work can absolutely lead to compassion fatigue and burnout. It all can be a lot to hold. It is vital that restorative approaches to campus sexual misconduct include restoration of the facilitators in restorative work.

Some misunderstand *restorative practices* to be about restoring relationships. Survivors commonly do not want to restore relationships where there was one, and many times there wasn't a relationship to begin with. When I think about restorative practices, I think about restoring justice, restoring wholeness, and restoring balance. When harm has occurred between people there is an imbalance that needs to be restored; wrongs need to be righted, wholeness restored. One of the many indigenous progenitors of restorative practices is the Hawaiian practice of *Ho'oponopono*. While translating this succinctly is challenging (the definition of *pono* in the Hawaiian dictionary takes almost half a page), *pono* means to be (or make) right or correct, balanced, in harmony, to be well; *ho'o* in front of it adds an action element, to do or be (Leialoha, 2020). *Ho'oponopono* is the art of restoring balance. Justice is also about restoring balance; the symbol of justice is the scale of balance.

Facilitators of RJ hold many people's traumas and harms, spend significant energy facilitating and holding space for deep healing and transformation, and within higher education settings do this in an institutional context that is not typically supportive or conducive to this work, which lies very much outside dominant paradigms and hierarchical systems. It can be taxing and lonely work in many ways, particularly in institutional settings. If an institution is going to support restorative practices, then it also needs to support restorative facilitators. How? By asking about and meeting needs, of course. And finding ways to restore balance.

For those who will be facilitating repair and restoration of harms it is important to ensure that there is ongoing adequate facilitator support and sustenance. RJ doesn't just look to those at the center of the harm and stop there. RJ expresses a more expansive and communal concern by focusing first on the needs of those directly harmed and the needs and responsibilities of those causing harm, and from there it continues on to explore the needs of all other affected persons and communities (Davis, 2019). Through its fullest extension and expression, this naturally includes the facilitators of the process. Per famed activist, civil rights trial attorney, and RJ practitioner Fania Davis (2019), "Attention to the entire collective distinguishes restorative justice as a communal, holistic, and balanced justice" (p. 26).

References

Bargen, C., Edwards, A., Harman, M., Haslett, J., Lyons, A. (2018). *Serving crime victims through restorative justice: A resource guide for leaders and practitioners.* Alberta Restorative Justice Association. www.arja.ca/_files/ugd/adb2db_0aa56d ae8ae149808afac83b6869546d.pdf

brown, a. m. (2021). *Holding change: The way of emergent strategy facilitation and mediation.* AK Press.

Davis, F. E. (2019). *The little book of race and restorative justice.* Good Books.

Freire, P. (1985). *The politics of education: Culture, power, and liberation.* Greenwood Publishing Group.

King, M. L., Jr. (1957, November 17). *Loving your enemies.* The Martin Luther King, Jr. Research and Education Institute, Stanford University. https://kinginstitute .stanford.edu/king-papers/documents/loving-your-enemies-sermon-delivered-dexter-avenue-baptist-church

King, M. L., Jr. (1967). *Where do we go from here?* Martin Luther King, Jr. Beacon Press.

Kübler-Ross, E. (1969). *On death and dying.* Scribner.

Leialoha. (2020). *Ho'oponopono: To make things right and balanced.* Naturally Aloha. https://naturallyaloha.com/hooponopono-to-make-things-right-and-balanced/

Levine, P. (1997). *Waking the tiger: Healing trauma.* North Atlantic Books.

Oates, J. R., & Maani-Fogelman, P. A. (2022). *Nursing grief and loss.* StatPearls.

Oxford Reference. (2017). Desmond Tutu. *Oxford essential quotations* (5th ed.). Oxford University Press.

Right Use of Power Institute. (2023). *About.* https://rightuseofpower.org/about/

The Decolonial Atlas. (2015, April 14). *The Great Lakes: An Ojibwe perspective.* https://decolonialatlas.wordpress.com/2015/04/14/the-great-lakes-in-ojibwe-v2/

Valandra, E. C. W. W. H. (Ed.). (2020). *Colorizing restorative justice: Voicing our realities.* Living Justice Press.

Wachtel, T. (2016). *Defining restorative.* International Institute for Restorative Practices. https://www.iirp.edu/images/pdf/Defining-Restorative_Nov-2016.pdf

Wing, L. & Marya, D. (2008, April 30). *Social justice mediation training.* Social Justice Mediation Institute.

Zehr, H. (2002). *The little book of restorative justice.* Good Books.

9

HEALING THROUGH
SUPPORTED DIALOGUE

A Reflection and Three Case Studies

Toni McMurphy

Case Study 1: My First Supported Dialogue:
Jessica and Corey (Pseudonyms)

When the 2011 Dear Colleague Letter served as our guidance, a student, Jessica, walked into my office and stated, "I don't want to ruin his life. I don't want to interfere with his education. I do want him to understand that what he did was not OK with me. I want him to witness my harm. I want him to stop bad-mouthing me to our friends and our supervisor at work. I don't feel safe meeting with him alone. I need your help! Will you please meet with us to support me in telling him what I need to say?" How could I say no?

When I met with Corey he fully accepted responsibility for kissing Jessica against her will when she broke up with him again in their on again–off again relationship that had spanned several months. He had begun to cry when she told him her decision was final, and when she offered a hug to console him he misinterpreted her action as being ambivalent about her decision and began to kiss her. He did not stop kissing her when she resisted. When she stood up and asked him to leave, he complied, but she still felt violated and she wanted to find a way to let him know she wanted clear boundaries going forward without needing a no-contact directive in place.

The three of us met. and I witnessed a healing conversation that resulted in both of them being able to continue having overlapping friends, be in the same classes, and continue working in the same place, with Jessica trusting that Corey would respect the boundaries she put in place.

Lesson Learned: Focus on the needs of those who have been harmed. Be willing to chart new territory.

152

Over the next several years, I facilitated dozens of cases and developed a process that supports parties who choose to engage in a restorative dialogue in their quest for healing. I have witnessed many breakthroughs and extraordinary moments of remorse, active accountability, growth, learning, empowerment, inspiration, and healing. I have even witnessed students harvest something good out of what has been painful and difficult.

Practitioner Reflection: A Focus on Healing

My unwavering commitment as a restorative practitioner is to maximize the opportunity to move toward healing in every case of sexual harm. Designing a customized response for each situation has resulted in healing for both complainants and respondents and, in many cases those most deeply connected to them, including their partners, families, and close friends. As a survivor myself, I am all too familiar with the ripples of harm created by sexual harm and the need for healing. Every human being is unique. The same event can impact humans in different ways based upon their identities, lived experiences, past trauma, personalities, and worldview. Why would we think that using the same approach when responding to sexual harm would work equally well across the diverse landscape of humanity? Designing a customized response to sexual harm is the most effective way I've found to replace ripples of harm with ripples of healing.

I have discovered that when I create the conditions for authentic and restorative engagement and support both parties in preparing to participate with a mutual goal of healing, extraordinary conversations become possible. The space that we can cocreate through clear intention, preparation, vulnerability, honesty, and genuine caring feels sacred and results in the parties feeling safe enough to be brave. Individuals can say what needs to be said to have more peace and closure. Survivors have the freedom to pose questions that have kept them up at night and offer peace and clarity where there have been angst and confusion. Respondents can bear witness to the harm they caused and offer a genuinely empathic response, which facilitates healing for both parties.

I am deeply grateful to every human I've had the privilege to walk with in a healing process following sexual harm. This includes complainants and respondents. I will refer to anyone I reference using pseudonyms to protect their anonymity while sharing specific examples and quotes that I hope will elucidate what is possible in a facilitated restorative dialogue.

Facilitating Restorative Dialogues

The vast majority of cases I've worked on have resulted in the parties choosing to engage in a supported restorative dialogue. If they could have resolved it on their own, they would have. Often, the complainant is yearning for a safe space to convey whatever they want or need to say to complete the past and to chart a path forward. Often, one or both parties recognize that there are things they want to say, share, or ask the other party that paves the way for healing. Not everyone begins choosing this path when I lay out the options available during the intake process, but once we begin exploring what they are hoping for and what healing looks and feels like to them, even survivors who begin by saying that meeting with the respondent doesn't appeal to them sometimes realize their healing would be enhanced through a restorative dialogue with the respondent.

One survivor, Lauren, a graduate student in medical school, stated very clearly in our first meeting that she never wanted any contact with the respondent, Sumit, again. She was suffering from anxiety and depression after he had stalked her and assaulted her in the weeks after she terminated a brief romantic relationship with him. I *always* trust the survivor to know best what represents healing for them and understand and respect their choice. With Lauren, we began the process planning for a more traditional approach in working toward a resolution agreement, including remedies like respecting boundaries in the workplace because they both worked in the same research lab, how to reduce the number of meetings they both attended, and an agreement that he would never initiate contact with her or come near her home again.

As Lauren began journaling about the healing, she began to imagine how it would feel to hear Sumit accept responsibility for his behavior and acknowledge that what happened was not consensual and had deeply impacted her well-being. As we began our third session, she announced, "I now realize my healing involves Sumit acknowledging that he violated me and all the ways his behavior has impacted me, my sleep, my peace of mind, and my ability to focus on my research."

When I reached out to Sumit to ask him if he would be willing to participate in a restorative dialogue with Lauren, he was initially ambivalent, but as I described the process and what she was hoping for he recognized there was significant alignment with his own desire for healing and closure. And it would open up the space he wanted and needed to apologize, which was restricted in the no-contact directive put in place when she filed her formal complaint.

In the time that followed, Lauren and I collaborated on a customized design for a healing process that acknowledged the full history of her relationship with Sumit: her serving as his mentor, a friendship, preparing meals together, a brief romantic relationship that she terminated, him attempting to convince her to give him another chance, and then him plowing over multiple "no"s to intercourse after a consensual massage one night. I worked independently with Lauren and Sumit to help them prepare for the restorative dialogue. They imagined what it would be like when we convened, how they would feel in those first few moments, what they were hoping for, how I could best support both of them, what topics we would discuss, and how to say a final goodbye, because Lauren was clear that she didn't want any more contact with Sumit following the restorative dialogue. During Sumit's preparation he came to understand the finality of Lauren's wishes to not have him in her life and work, and he explored other options so he could continue his research elsewhere.

When the three of us came together virtually, we intentionally cocreated a space that was vast enough to hold everything they experienced, for Sumit to sincerely apologize, to harvest lessons learned for both of them, for Lauren to forgive him, and to say goodbye. In the supported dialogue, they spoke about what they had appreciated and respected about each other. They unpacked cultural differences as he was an international student. They actually laughed as they reminisced about how difficult it was to find ingredients for some of the Indian meals he prepared for her in the small conservative town where they lived and worked. They talked about how their friendship had evolved into a romantic relationship, Lauren's upset about blending professional and personal relationships, and her decision to end the romance.

In the course of dialogue, Lauren chose to acknowledge the good she saw in Sumit and some of their history together before she pivoted to the utter betrayal she felt when he didn't respect her boundaries. In fact, she was able to convey to him that the positive interactions they had shared was why she felt so deeply betrayed. She talked at length about the impact of finding him waiting for her in front of her apartment when she came home late one night, finding notes he left on her car, about not being able to go into the lab for more than 2 months because even seeing him retraumatized her. She talked about how difficult it was to be in the same Zoom meetings, and how she always felt like he was staring right at her. All three of us wept.

Mutually acknowledging the totality of their history and the impact of Sumit's behavior on Lauren's well-being freed both of them up to heal and move on with their lives. Having witnessed their process, I firmly believe that the full extent of the healing they achieved may not have been possible if they had glossed over some aspects of their shared history. It's not that Lauren had to do this *with* Sumit, but in doing so they both felt heard and understood and were able to move forward. Not all parties have such a rich history, however; often, survivors who choose an informal resolution process do so because they don't want to "ruin the respondent's life and academic career." Often, factors like a shared history, overlapping friend groups, or personal values drive the desire to not cause harm when responding to harm.

In my experience, survivors who want harsher consequences tend to opt for a traditional investigation and hearing.

I have learned that most survivors who choose to engage in a restorative dialogue want the respondent to understand the impact of the sexual harm and have benefited from the respondent holding space for them and witnessing the many ripples of harm in their lives. Survivors have spoken about ripples like self-loathing; hating their bodies; wondering if they were somehow at fault; not being able to be present to their current partners in sexual encounters; or, in one case I worked on, acting out and escaping harmful memories by flooding them with new memories being generated by becoming promiscuous.

One such survivor, Chelsea, wanted to feel "in charge of her body," so she initiated sexual encounters with others throughout college after she felt like someone violated her body and choice when she was a freshman. Some survivors choose to prepare detailed letters of impact to be incorporated into the restorative dialogue. Others don't want to rehash the details. Some survivors have asked that the respondent read their letter of impact to them as part of the supported dialogue and then offer an empathic response. Hannah, a survivor, said that she trusted that "her words got in" when she heard the respondent, TJ, read aloud the letter she had written. John, a respondent, broke down in tears when reading aloud the portion of Sarah's letter of impact describing her many sleepless nights, nightmares, inability to study, and self-loathing.

Finally, every survivor I have worked with wants the respondent to harvest meaningful lessons learned from the healing process, whether it's the definition of enthusiastic consent, that saying yes to one thing or one time doesn't mean yes to everything and every time, and that alcohol consumption can interfere with one's ability to give consent. What gives peace of mind to most survivors is trusting that the respondent will never impose sexual harm on anyone again. Not all respondents or cases have the potential to achieve these outcomes for survivors, and a guiding principle in restorative processes is to never cause additional harm when responding to harm. As restorative practitioners, we must carefully assess the fit, willingness, and capacity of the parties involved to engage in a restorative dialogue. A thorough intake process that establishes rapport, uncovers hopes, concerns and needs, and assesses fit is essential. This is the outline and script for the intake process I developed.

Sample Intake Process

In this section I provide an example of an intake process with both the the survivor and respondent. In intake sessions I try to get to know both individuals, learning about what is important to them and what they would like to get out of this process. I adjust each of these sessions to the needs of the participants; more than one session may be required for each individual.

Meeting With the Survivor—(Example)
Before we speak about your complaint, let's spend some time getting to know each other—human to human. What would you share about yourself to help me get to know you beyond this situation? Would you prefer to go first, or would you like for me to go first?

My role: I am a facilitator, not an investigator. The North Star for me is your healing. As we explore your hopes for the process, I will ask you to work with me in designing a process that will best meet your needs. Most survivors find this empowering—especially after feeling violated. We will explore options, and I will follow your lead. I will also answer any questions you have. Please know that it's important to me that you work with someone you feel comfortable with. I've asked the Title IX officer to reach out and ask you if you want to proceed with me as your facilitator in the next day or two.

What we speak about is important to me, and I want to remember the details. The notes I take are for my eyes only. I will not share them with the institution or the other party. If at some point you want to refer to my notes (from our meeting) as we engage in designing your healing process, I am happy to share them with you.

Questions for the Survivor
Hopes

- Why did you choose informal resolution? What are you hoping for?
- What are you hoping to walk away from the informal resolution process thinking or feeling?
- What does healing look like? What would give you more peace? How will you measure success?

Content

- How much detail do you want to provide regarding the Title IX complaint? Some survivors want to share the details. Others prefer not to. It's completely up to you. If you do want to share, is today a good time, or would you rather talk about this at a different time?
- How do you want me to refer to the respondent—by name or by the title of "respondent"?

If/when appropriate, incorporate the following questions:

- What happened? What were you thinking at the time?
- What have you thought about since?
- What are all the ways this situation has impacted you? Who else has been impacted? In what ways?
- Out of everything that has happened, what has been most difficult for you?
- What needs do you have at this point?
- What are you hoping to include in the resolution agreement?
- Which things feel negotiable? Which things don't feel negotiable?
- Tell me about your support system. It's important that you have a support system and engage in self-care throughout this process. What do you have planned for the rest of the day?
- Do you want or need a support person to walk with you in this process? If so, who comes to mind?

Options (explore and attempt to help them explore options that help them achieve what they are hoping for):

- Some survivors want to focus on the terms of an agreement by using a shuttle approach. I would meet with both parties individually to talk about needs and share information back and forth in an attempt to reach a resolution agreement that you would both sign and would be approved by the Title IX Officer.
- Others prefer to work toward *a facilitated restorative dialogue*, where you would ultimately come together for a supported virtual or in-person dialogue to focus on meeting your needs. There would be individual preparation for such a meeting. Typical elements include the respondent witnessing and acknowledging your harm and talking about how to put things as right as possible given what happened and how you were affected. In some cases, we reach even higher to identify ways to harvest something good out of what has been painful and difficult; however, timing is important, and we don't start there.
- And, there are options in the middle, *like impact letters, written apologies, videos, using surrogates*, and so on. Preferences can also evolve. Only you know what will best contribute to your healing. Do you have a sense of what approach you are leaning toward at this point? And feel free to take time to reflect and decide.

Logistics

- How do you prefer to communicate in between meetings? Email, text? (Provide my cell phone number.)
- When are the best times for you to meet? Days of the week, time of day?
- Are there any times in the upcoming weeks when it will be difficult for you to focus/meet (exams, big papers due, etc.)?
- Let's schedule our next meeting. Between now and then I will be meeting with the respondent to let them know what you are hoping for and to describe the process and answer any questions they have.

Meeting With the Respondent—(Example)

Before we speak about your complaint, let's spend some time getting to know each other—human to human. What would you share about yourself to help me get to know you beyond this situation? Would you prefer to go first or would you like for me to go first?

My role: I am a facilitator, not an investigator. The North Star for me is healing. We start with the needs of the complainant but will also factor in your needs too. As we explore your hopes for the process, I will be asking what matters most to you. I have already met with the complainant and know that they are hoping for. . . . What are your thoughts about their hopes?

Please know that it's important to me that you work with someone you feel comfortable with. I've asked the Title IX officer to reach out and ask you if you want to proceed with me as your facilitator in the next day or two.

Questions for the Respondent
Hopes

- Why did you agree to participate in an informal resolution process? What are you hoping for?
- What are you hoping to walk away from the informal resolution process thinking or feeling?
- What does healing look like? What would give you more peace? How will you measure success?

Content

- I asked the complainant about how much detail they wanted to provide regarding their Title IX complaint? Their choice is to . . . What are your thoughts?

- Tell me about your support system. It's important that you have a support system and engage in self-care throughout this process.
- Do you want or need a support person? If so, who comes to mind?

Options (share what you've learned from the survivor):

- Some survivors want to focus on the terms of an agreement by using *a shuttle approach*. This means I would meet with both parties individually to talk about their needs and share information back and forth in an attempt to reach a resolution agreement that you would both sign and would be approved by the Title IX officer.
- Others prefer to work toward *a facilitated conversation or dialogue* where you would ultimately come together in a facilitated virtual dialogue to focus on healing and closure. There would be individual preparation for such a meeting. Typical elements include the respondent witnessing and acknowledging the harm the complainant experienced and talking about how to put things as right as possible, given what happened. In some cases, we reach even higher to identify ways to harvest something good out of what has been painful and difficult; however, timing is important, and we don't start there.
- And, there are options in the middle, *like impact letters, written apologies, videos, surrogates*, and so on. Preferences can also evolve. Only the complainant knows what will best contribute to their healing. And, of course, you have a choice regarding your participation. What are your thoughts about what I've shared about what the complainant is seeking at this point?

Logistics

- How do you prefer to communicate in between meetings? Email, text? (Provide my cell phone number.)
- When are the best times for you to meet? Days of the week, time of day?
- Are there any times in the upcoming weeks when it will be difficult for you to focus/meet (exams, big papers, etc.)?
- Let's schedule our next meeting. Between now and then I will be meeting with the complainant to let them know what you are hoping for and to discuss next steps.

Assessing Readiness for a Restorative Process
There are also questions I must consider as the facilitator when assessing fit and readiness for a restorative dialogue:

- Has the respondent accepted responsibility for the harm?
- Is there sufficient overlap in what both parties are hoping for?

- Are they both willing to engage authentically *and* restoratively?
- What can I do to best create the conditions for authentic and restorative engagement if/when they choose to come together for a supported dialogue?
- How can we cocreate a response to the sexual harm that occurred without causing additional harm in the process?
- What will give the survivor agency after they lost it as a result of the sexual harm they experienced? How might a restorative process empower them in a way that contributes to their healing?
- What needs to happen for the respondent to prevent them from imposing future sexual harm on anyone?
- What needs to be witnessed, discussed, or decided when they come together for a supported dialogue?
- How can I best support both parties in meeting as many needs as possible?
- What process will best support learning, growth, and healing for the survivor and the respondent?
- What will put things as right as possible, given what happened?
- How might we harvest something positive out of what has been painful and difficult?
- Are there ways to expand that to include positive impacts for others?

When the parties choose to engage in a restorative dialogue, it is incumbent upon us as facilitators to create the conditions for authentic and restorative engagement and support the parties individually in their preparation to come together. Regardless of whether they choose to engage in a supported dialogue or not, I hold myself accountable to design a healing process that will best meet their needs.

Multipartiality Matters

Creating the conditions for authentic and restorative engagement is contingent upon both parties trusting that I want what is best for them—individually and collectively. Bringing a multipartial lens to the process means having radical empathy for everyone involved. I hold myself accountable for looking through the eyes of both parties and, to the best of my ability, imagine what they are thinking and feeling, given what I know about them, so we can achieve the best possible outcome.

An essential element of any restorative dialogue is the willingness of the respondent to show up fully and engage authentically and restoratively in supporting the complainant in their quest for healing. This represents a portion of how they can make amends for the harm they caused. Respondents are often navigating fear, guilt, shame, and blame, all of which threaten authentic engagement and accepting responsibility for the harm they caused. They often don't talk with others about what happened or share that a complaint was filed against them. They rarely choose a support person to join them in the process.

Respondents also need and deserve meaningful support so that they can show up to meet the needs of survivors, who, by the nature of their role in cases of sexual harm, typically and more easily access the essential support they need and deserve. This in no way means that I dilute my commitment to center the needs of the survivor in the healing process. I support the respondent *because* I am centering the needs of the survivor.

Case Study 2—Ground-Breaking Case: Kara and Zack

A case I worked on recently opened up new possibilities. I witnessed two students engage in a healing process that expanded the focus to not only what happened between them but also included healing previous sexual harm that the complainant had experienced before this incident. Both students learned about themselves and genuinely supported each other in learning how to navigate boundaries, engage in clear communication, and understand what enthusiastic consent means in a sexual encounter.

Background: Kara became a social media phenomenon on campus. Male students would follow her around like the paparazzi, snapping photos of her working out at the gym and at parties and then post the photos with the caption, "Who wants to f____ Kara?" While she acknowledged that some small part of her enjoyed some of the attention, she was distraught and felt like she had become the campus conquest.

While at a fraternity party one night, she began drinking and dancing. Zack suggested they go upstairs and do some shots. She believed she was accompanying him to the kitchen, but they wound up in his room. They began kissing, but she did not want to go further. He was insistent and slipped his hand up her shorts and assaulted her. He then got up to go to the bathroom and she began frantically texting several friends to come and find her. As she rushed to leave, the event became very public, and some of their peers began posting about it on social media.

When Kara met with the Title IX coordinator, she knew she did not want to participate in an investigation and hearing. She became curious about the alternative resolution option. When I met with her, she said that an investigation would never meet her needs, but she was curious about the alternative resolution process. She went on to say it would be that or nothing at all. I generally meet with the complainant first, but Kara was in the midst of taking exams, and Zack was nervous and really wanted to learn more about the process, so I scheduled the intake with him with the understanding that I hadn't yet met with Kara and wouldn't be able to speak to her needs at that point. I told him I would be happy to describe the process and answer any questions he had.

Zack was tentative and visibly nervous in the first few minutes of our conversation. I always begin by asking people to tell me a little about themselves as a human before talking about the situation that resulted in a Title IX complaint. Zack told me about how close he was to his family and that his mom was in the hospital and quite ill. I was struck by how quickly he accepted responsibility for what happened with Kara. He concluded our first meeting by saying, "I want to do whatever I can to support her healing."

When I met with Kara, she told me about how public the situation was due to social media. She said she knew that Zack had a crush on her and she described what happened when they went up to his room. She described it as "no big deal, really . . . " and said, "It is nothing compared to other experiences I've had." Kara had a long history of sexual harm. I felt incredibly sad. She added that the only reason she was taking any action is that a female student came into her room, drunk, shortly after the situation was posted on social media and thanked her for taking action. Kara said she felt a responsibility to hold Zack accountable because of the historical harm of all female students. Because healing serves as my North Star as a practitioner, I asked Kara, "What if we could find a way to heal some of your previous sexual harm while working through the situation with Zack?" She asked, "How would that work?" I responded by saying, "I don't know, but I believe it's possible if you are open to exploring ways we could accomplish this." Who Kara and Zack were as human beings—their honesty, curiosity, compassion, caring, and willingness to reflect and engage authentically—made them ideal candidates for this exploration.

Kara engaged with me in unpacking themes from previous encounters, how she came to learn that no didn't mean no because it had never been respected by men in her life. She came to understand her pattern of dissociation as a coping mechanism. She journaled extensively and began choosing entries that she wanted to read to Zack so he would understand more about the woman he had harmed and how she got to be the way she was, and why it was so important to her that he learn more about enthusiastic consent and never be responsible for imposing sexual harm again. As she reflected, she gained clarity about the similarities and differences between her past encounters and what she experienced with Zack. She recounted her experience of being kissed by dozens of students on campus when she really only wanted to be kissed by two of them.

Kara had also connected with someone on campus who taught her about enthusiastic consent. Part of her didn't fault Zack for not knowing what he didn't know because, as she said in the dialogue, "Most people don't understand this until they are with someone who actually does it." Zack had been researching enthusiastic consent and asked Kara, "Doesn't it seem awkward when a partner keeps asking the same question over and over?" She responded by saying, "Yes, a little bit the first couple of times, but there are different ways to check in, like, 'Is this OK? How does this feel? Do you want to . . . ?'" She added, "I feel so respected when he communicates with me as we go." She added, "It's kind of hot."

Kara shared that she felt uncomfortable, almost guilty sometimes when she rejected someone, and she didn't like hurting peoples' feelings. She said, "I've never been rejected by anyone, but I can imagine it hurts." When asked "What has it been like for you when a girl rejects you?", Zack said, "I don't want that, but I understand. I only want to be with someone who wants to be with me." Given the willingness of both Kara and Zack to authentically engage in a healing process, I worked closely with Kara to design their healing process, checking in with Zack along the way, to support him on his exploration of enthusiastic consent and prepare him to engage meaningfully when the three of us came together for the restorative dialogue. Their hard work resulted in all three of us emerging transformed.

Agenda for Virtual Restorative Dialogue: Kara and Zack

Logistics:

- Kara enters first
- Check-in: How are you feeling? Do you still want to move forward?
- Zack is in the waiting room until I admit him.

"Build the Container": Opening the Restorative Dialogue

- Warm Welcome
- Customized Reading (shared here)

Opening Reading

> We gather based on the courage and willingness of Kara and Zack, who have chosen an alternative path over a formal investigation, in hopes of moving toward healing and closure. We gather to learn, grow, do better, and prevent harm from happening again.
>
> We come with a willingness to explore, listen, ask and respond to questions, and chart a path forward that addresses the harm and works for everyone involved.
>
> We will seek to better understand what happened, acknowledge any and all harms, and put things as right as possible between them.

We acknowledge that there is a difference between intent and impact, *and* it is essential to acknowledge the impact of our actions on another human being, whether we intended harm or not.

We acknowledge that we all carry wounds and we have all caused scars. Our choices and actions impact others. It is important to be intentional in preventing harm and responding to harm when it happens.

Finally, we commit to engaging in ways that foster healing versus causing additional harm in our conversation and actions.

I would like for each of you to acknowledge that no one else is present or witnessing and that you are not using any devices to record this session.

We will take a break at some point, if necessary. If either of you need a break at any point or want privacy to talk with your support person, please let me know.

Mindfulness Moment

- As we prepare for the restorative dialogue, let's take a few deep breaths together. Notice what you are hoping for from our time together. Notice what strength, value, or quality you want to lead with in our time together.

Expectations (Offered by the Facilitator and Contributed by Participants)

- Engage authentically *and* restoratively
- One person speaks at a time
- Encourage questions—interactive along the way
- WAIT—Why Am I Talking? Why Aren't I Talking?
- Anyone can pass
- Confidentiality: Honor the learning and leave the stories
- No recording or off-camera witnesses
- Kara added: "Are you OK with me asking you questions? I want to hear how certain things were from your perspective."

Both parties respond to the following prompts (in the order identified):

- Why did you choose this process versus the traditional investigation and hearing? (Kara, then Zack.)
- And what strength, value, or quality will you lead with? (Kara, then Zack.)
- How might you inadvertently hinder the best possible outcome? And how will you hold yourself accountable? (Zack, then Kara.)

Kara answers the following prompts:

- "What I most want you to know/understand . . ."
- "The impact on me was . . ."
- "Most recent experience with you . . ."
- "Similarities and differences between this and my other experiences. . ."

Opportunity for Zack to respond and ask questions.

Kara responds and reflects on social media aftermath.

Opportunity for Zack to respond and ask questions.

Both parties respond to the following prompts.

- What's been the most difficult for you? (Kara, then Zack)
- Lessons learned (Zack, then Kara)
- Where do we go from here? Creating agreement. (Kara, then Zack)
- Closing round. (Kara, then Zack)
  - What's becoming clearer to me is . . .
  - I just want to say . . .

Check-in post dialogue (Facilitator checks in with each party individually after the dialogue)

The Agreement
As a result of their supported dialogue, Kara and Zack reached a simple agreement that honored the healing achieved and opened up a pathway to move forward with a sense of closure and more peace.

- Kara and Zack chose to engage in an informal resolution process with a shared goal of healing, learning, and growth.
- Both parties completed a series of individual restorative sessions to prepare for a facilitated dialogue between them.
- They ultimately engaged in a supported in-depth restorative dialogue and have agreed that their mutual goals were achieved without any need for additional remedies.
- Based on the agreement of the parties, there are no additional measures to complete within the written resolution agreement. As a result, no further process is available with regard to the allegations in the Formal Complaint.

They both reflected on the experience and gave me permission to share their summaries of the experience.

Kara's Reflections (Shared With Permission)

Almost every sexual experience I have had until recently was not consensual. Time after time again a boy would touch me in a way that I did not want or assert himself inside me after I winced in pain or repeatedly told him no. I would wake up the next morning as if nothing happened. I assumed the pain, discomfort, and icky feeling were all an inevitable part of sex. I never told anyone. I certainly did not want to take legal action because that was overwhelming and scary and sounded time consuming and publicly humiliating. But I also didn't confide in friends or family, for similar reasons. It was a secret. Even to myself. I didn't want to admit to myself that it was real either.

This year, I was sexually assaulted by someone I had many mutual friends with. Although I did not know him personally, because of how our groups on campus were interconnected, news became rapidly public; for a few weeks, my life revolved around people asking me if I was going to press charges or how I was feeling. Some people told me to get him kicked off campus. Some people didn't believe my story at all. The feeling of a boy's unwanted fingers hurting me from the inside out was nothing new, but the public concern for the outcome was. I felt pressure to do something and stumbled upon adaptive resolution.

I was hesitant to be so vulnerable in a meeting with a stranger who they told me was the "facilitator" and the man himself who had gotten us into this mess. But the process ended up being one of the most reflective and productive experiences I've had. The safe environment allowed us both to honestly figure out where we went wrong and how to move forward. Being able to talk through the situation in a nonconfrontational environment made both of us much more comfortable and willing to work things out. We both walked away feeling not only like better people, but like things had been made right with each other.

If I could recommend this to every girl who has been sexually assaulted or raped, I would. It prioritized healing and understanding over actual accusation and encouraged both parties to grow from the experience, rather than dwell on it. I am extremely grateful to my facilitator and the process for giving me such a safe environment.

Zack's Reflections (Shared With Permission)

I chose this process because I felt as though it would foster a calmer, more communicative environment to deal with and resolve the conflict at hand. I was hoping to learn more about the issue and grow as a person to develop the skills necessary to understand how the conflict arose and help others in the future facing the same problem.

The process had so many benefits that the traditional Title IX hearing process does not have, and simultaneously avoided the intense environment of a hearing. The experience was truly beneficial, safe, and informative. Throughout the process, there were a series of key moments, but the final supported dialogue at the end really stood out to me. We were discussing very emotional, deep issues, yet the environment could not have been more supportive. I felt completely safe expressing myself and I was truly engaged in a learning experience.

I am confident in saying that at the end we had both grown as people and were able to openly communicate with each other in a constructive way. We each provided a narrative of our experience with the conflict and were able to resolve the incongruities.

I would 100% recommend this process to others. It was extremely beneficial and constructive and provided numerous learning opportunities in a safe, calm environment.

Case Study 3: Deja and Dante

Scene: One week following George Floyd's murder, two Black students, Deja and Dante, were hanging out with mutual friends, playing cards and consuming alcohol. In the wee hours of the morning the male student pushed the female student down to the ground, laid on top of her, and began touching her breasts. She wrestled to push him off and began screaming. Someone heard her and called the police.

Deja: "When the police arrived, I froze. I lost my voice. All I could think was, 'Another Black man could die tonight.' I couldn't speak. I couldn't say what really happened. I put his safety in front of mine and I'm so angry with myself."

What Deja was hoping for: Acceptance of responsibility for what he did. Dante, who was on a full scholarship, was homeless when he wasn't at school. He had very few resources. The world was not a safe place. Deja's consistent threats to resort to an investigation and hearing resulted in him feeling less safe.

During one of our sessions, I asked Deja if anything else would help her heal. She said, "I want him to pay me $1 a day for every day since the assault. I have lost sleep. I haven't been able to work every shift. I have suffered. It's the least he can do." I reached out to colleagues and asked about financial considerations in resolution agreements and was advised that it was a slippery slope they wouldn't consider. In my next conversation with Deja I asked her how the few hundred dollars would support her healing. She began to cry and said, "I would paint again. I haven't painted since the assault, and I would use the money to buy art supplies." I spoke with Dante, but he didn't have the resources. The Title IX officer and I both contributed money to help Kate buy art supplies. Other aspects of the resolution agreement were that Deja had the first choice in which dormitory complex she would live in and Dante would not live or visit there.

Lessons Learned: Identities matter. Keep digging deeper to reveal what people need for their healing and do what you can to provide it.

Closing Thoughts

It is important to acknowledge that not all cases of sexual harm are suited for an informal resolution process, much less a supported dialogue. I would like to invite you to consider the possibility that a supported dialogue could be an appropriate option for more cases than we've thought about until now. (See Appendix B for template of a Supported Dialogue.) A policy should never be a barrier to healing. I respectfully challenge any policy or person that states that RJ should not be an option in cases of sexual assault or an option for a respondent in a Title IX complaint more than once. A restorative lens invites us to center the needs of the person who experienced harm. What does the survivor want? What needs do they have? What does healing look like from their perspective? My wish for you and those you support is that you will see new possibilities to focus on healing in meaningful ways.

PART FOUR

REFLECTIONS ON
IMPLEMENTATION

10

ADAPTABLE RESOLUTION

Where Justice and Healing Meet

Carrie Landrum

Restorative Justice if nothing else is a paradigm shift away from a justice of
punishment and retribution towards a justice that heals.
                    —sujatha baliga (Quoted in Robins, 2018, para. 22)

*Land and Practices Acknowledgment: Acknowledgment and deep appreciation
are extended to the many indigenous wisdom keepers (globally, historically, and
currently) who have practiced and shared their restorative ways since time immemorial. Special acknowledgement and gratitude are offered to the Anishinaabeg,
and in particular the Council of Three Fires Niswi-mishkodewinan confederacy
of Ojibwe, Odawa, and Potawatomi tribes, early stewards and caretakers of the land this text was written on in Michigan (a name derived from
the Anishinaabemowin/Ojibwe word for "Great Lake"—Mishigami; The
Decolonial Atlas, 2015).*

*The Three Fires Confederacy ceded land to the University of Michigan in
1817 to support education. Anishinaabeg have been practicing peacemaking and
restorative ways since long before we had those terms and they continue to teach
others these practices. Through these words of acknowledgment reverencing the
Anishinaabeg, their contemporary and ancestral ties to the land, their historical
and ongoing contributions to education and peacemaking, and their place as a
progenitor of restorative practices are respected and reaffirmed.*

The University of Michigan's (U-M) efforts to implement restorative practices in response to campus misconduct really got underway in 2007, the same year I earned my master's in dispute resolution in Detroit and joined the university's office of student conflict resolution (OSCR) in this work. Out of a commitment to serving a diverse student population with differing needs and interests around conflict resolution, and the recognition that a one-size-fits-all approach doesn't actually work for everyone, U-M's conduct and conflict resolution office began offering multiple pathways to the community to address and resolve campus concerns. The new offerings at U-M, ranging from conflict coaching, facilitated dialogue, mediation, shuttle negotiation, and restorative practices, were collectively called *alternative conflict resolution.*

Alternative conflict resolution reflects the idea of alternative dispute resolution, commonly known as ADR. I knew from my studies in dispute resolution that ADR refers to extrajudicial methods of resolving disputes outside of litigation. The two most well-known forms of ADR are mediation and arbitration (Legal Information Institute, 2021). At OSCR, alternative conflict resolution was contrasted as an alternative to the more typical student judicial processes referred to as *formal conflict resolution*, which in its most formal aspect could include an arbitration hearing. I noted that OSCR's formal conflict resolution processes were also ADR. I also noted that *alternative conflict resolution* wasn't very descriptive in communicating what it is or entails. It was directly named for what it was *not*—it was simply an alternative to what was considered standard. The nomenclature didn't communicate to the campus community what it *was*; it was defined solely by contrasting it with what it *wasn't*—an alternative to something else. Not only was this utterly nondescriptive, it was also *othering*. It communicated to the community that something else was primary, and ACR an alternative to it. I wondered: Why can't ACR be the primary option?

Since ACR was outside the dominant paradigm, I advocated for using as descriptive language as possible to communicate to the campus what it is in its own right, not as an alternative to anything. In keeping with the "ACR" language that was in use, and in search of something more descriptive, I suggested we call it *adaptable conflict resolution.* ACR options at OSCR, like mediations, restorative justice (RJ) processes, and shuttle negotiations, are highly adaptable to participants' needs. Participants are empowered to identify their own solutions, and they decide whether or not to enter into a resolution agreement that addresses and resolves the matter *for them*, and they suggest and agree to all the elements of the resolution agreement. I found that one of the many benefits of ACR was its ability to be highly personalized in terms of outcomes as well as the process itself. In RJ processes we ask harmed participants whether they would like to speak first, or hear from the person who caused harm first. We ask participants if they'd like to include any other people in the process as support or as additionally impacted participants. We cocreate with participants the values and terms of engagement that will guide the process. Process and outcomes are highly customizable and adaptable.

ACR thus became *adaptable conflict resolution* and was codified into U-M policy the next time the student conduct policy was amended in 2010 (Swanson, 2010). I facilitated the amendment process in 2009–2010, which updated the student conduct policy in multiple ways, such as modifying it to be gender neutral, changing the language of *complaining witness* to *complainant* and *accused students* to *respondents* and adding intimate partner violence as a violation of the conduct policy. It was additionally stipulated in the policy then that ACR facilitators would be *multipartial.*

The university's commitment to providing more student-centered options to address campus harms led to the inclusion of restorative practices in 2013, *as voluntary informal resolution*, in the university's Policy on Sexual Misconduct by Students. Per the 2013 policy:

> The University recognizes that in some limited circumstances (and never in sexual assault cases) voluntary informal resolution options may, if implemented consistently with institutional values and legal obligations, be an appropriate means of addressing some behaviors reported under this Policy. (University of Michigan, 2013, section VIII)

The restorative options in the 2016 and 2018 policies were called *alternative resolution* (removing reference to *informal resolution*) and tracked closely with federal guidance at the time by not being available for all types of sexual misconduct. In 2019, the university's restorative options were renamed *adaptable resolution* in the Interim Policy and Procedures on Student Sexual and Gender-Based Misconduct and Other Forms of Interpersonal Violence, and the policy did not restrict the types of cases that would be eligible for approval from the Title IX coordinator. In 2021, the university adopted its umbrella Policy on Sexual and Gender-Based Misconduct (applicable to all students, employees, and third parties) and included adaptable resolution in its student and employee procedures, announcing "the use of adaptable resolution under some circumstances for employees who wish to do so to resolve allegations of misconduct through various adaptable resolution practices rooted in restorative justice" (Fitzgerald, 2021, para. 11).

Adaptable resolution refers to a collective of noninvestigatory options under U-M's sexual misconduct policy and procedures: facilitated dialogues, restorative circles or conferences, restorative shuttle agreements, and community-supported accountability circles. The nomenclature of *adaptable resolution* attempts to decenter the investigatory pathways as a primary pathway (adaptable resolution is not an "alternative," simply an option) and it honors the incredible care, thoughtfulness, and even formalism in its implementation by not calling it "informal." In recognition that sexual violence is not a "conflict"—which implies equal roles, rights, and legitimacy of disputants' interests (as mediation processes also assume)—and is instead an act of harm/injustice that calls for accountability, we do not call the process *adaptable conflict resolution* as we do in cases of actual conflict. (Adaptable resolution cases involve additional protocols and procedures, too, like the Title IX coordinator's approval on the front and back ends, which additionally distinguishes them from ACR cases.)

The nomenclature of *adaptable resolution* also recognizes that while restorative practices may technically be considered a form of ADR, not all "alternative," "informal," or "adaptable" resolution processes are necessarily restorative. The adaptable resolution process under U-M's 2021 student procedures includes four options: facilitated dialogue, a restorative circle or conference process, restorative shuttle agreement, and community-supported accountability circles (University of Michigan, 2021). The first two options allow for face-to-face interactions; the latter two do not require any direct interaction between participants (who may also elect more than one option). If any of these actualized options did not repair harm, then they would not be restorative. A facilitated dialogue, for example, may be restorative depending on the quality and content of the dialogue and if harms were actually repaired.

Given current trends that embrace RJ with increasing popularity, many in the RJ field/movement are concerned about the integrity of RJ in the growing number of programs and alternative options that are called "restorative" even when they may not authentically restorative. Being thoughtful and responsible about not using terms like *restorative* to describe programs and processes that may be only partially or minimally or sometimes restorative in process and outcome will support trust and buy-in for restorative practices to grow and prosper. RJ is an ethos with a very specific framework that must be applied responsibly.

Healing Justice

The "justice" system in the United States is incredibly adversarial. It focuses on rules rather than harms, centers on alleged "offenders" rather than victims, and concentrates on punishment rather than repair. Fania Davis (2019), famed activist, civil rights trial attorney, and RJ practitioner, summed up the current dominant paradigm and its relatively recent origins:

> Our prevailing adversarial system is based upon a Roman notion of justice as just desserts. Causing someone to suffer creates an imbalance in the scales of justice, and the way to rebalance the scales is to cause the responsible person to suffer; we respond to the original harm with a second harm. Ours is a system that harms people who harm people, presumably to show that harming people is wrong. This sets into motion endless cycles of harm. Restorative justice seeks to interrupt these cycles by repairing the damage done to relationships in the wake of crime or other wrongdoing and do so in a way that is consonant with indigenous wisdom—Africa's and that of other traditions. Justice is a healing ground, not a battleground.
>
> In Western culture, we are socialized to believe that the desire to inflict counterviolence upon or retaliate against someone who has hurt us or a loved one is innate and that justice has always been done and will always be done in this way. In fact, far from universal or natural, this adversarial vision of justice is a relatively recent cultural and historical construction, arising around AD 1200 with the dawning of the nation–state and racial capitalism. Though restorative justice is new to Western jurisprudence, it is not at all new in the broader sweep of human history. For most of human history, reconciliation and restitution to victims and their kin took precedence over vengeance. This is because restoring social peace and avoiding blood feuds were paramount social concerns. Restitution and reconciliation, not punishment, were overarching aspirations. (pp. 24–25)

The justice-as-punishment worldview permeates U.S. culture and its educational institutions. Most student conduct and Title IX systems are set up to be adversarial, win/lose, zero-sum battlegrounds. They are battlegrounds where nobody wins, and more harm is created. Research indicates that Title IX processes are more harmful than helpful to survivors and are actively damaging to the well-being of those who report, including by contributing to "institutional betrayal" and an increase in posttraumatic symptoms (Lorenz et al., 2021). Disturbingly, students regularly report that their experience in their institution's Title IX process was worse than the original violence they endured (Lorenz et al., 2021). The adversarial battleground of sexual misconduct proceedings is contributing to the vicious cycle of harm, and I have yet to hear about a Title IX investigation or hearing process being "healing." Whereas investigations and hearings pit one side against another, in RJ there are no sides: "To the degree possible, restorative justice seeks a healing for all versus a victory for one" (Davis, 2019, p. 27). As Fania Davis (2019) noted,

"Restorative justice invites a paradigm shift in the way we think about and do justice—from a justice that harms to a justice that heals" (p. 24).

Justice Is a Healing Ground, Not a Battleground

"When I asked students to define justice, most non-Aboriginal students referred to equality before the law or the application of the same rules to everyone. Most Aboriginal students used the term harmony or a synonym of it" (Barsh, 2005, p. 167).

Justice and Healing in the Community

RJ is a relational concept of justice that is not simply concerned with responding to wrongs, but rather with the harm and effects of wrongs on relationships at all levels: individual, group, community, national, and even international (Llewellyn & Philpott, 2014). At colleges and universities, students live, learn, work, and play within intricate networks of relationships. The individualistic nature of sexual misconduct investigations and hearings does not always match well with the relational and communal harms of some misconduct:

> While our modern Eurocentric justice framework focuses tightly on the individual causing harm, restorative justice, consistent with indigenous justice, expresses a more expansive and communal concern by focusing on the needs and responsibilities of those causing harm, those directly harmed, and all other affected persons and communities. Attention to the entire collective distinguishes restorative justice as a communal, holistic, and balanced justice. (Davis, 2019, p. 26)

It is unfortunately not uncommon that one student will directly and indirectly affect a large group of students with their behavior. Typical Title IX processes do not address these larger communal harms.

Case Study: Harm in the Community

One case I had involved a graduate student cohort in a professional school. The respondent had impacted a large number of his classmates through a pattern of extremely inappropriate comments. The university conducted an investigation and interviewed multiple witnesses. During the investigation the respondent continued to attend class. His presence affected his classmates, who were upset with the length of time the investigation was taking. Due to federal confidentiality protections, the outcome of the investigation was not shared with the students. When they heard that the investigation was complete, and they saw the respondent still attending classes, they were very upset and concluded that the respondent had not been found responsible or sanctioned. Their perspective was that "nothing happened" to address the misconduct and no justice occurred.

When I was invited by school administrators to explore the potential of a restorative process for the cohort, I was met with enthusiasm at the prospect. The investigation was still in progress then, and a pivot to the adaptable resolution process was considered. Ultimately, the investigation was completed, and the student was found responsible and sanctioned. In recognition of the large communal impact the respondent had caused through his harms, the sanctioning officer included a sanction specifically intended to address and repair communal harm. As RJ must be voluntary for all participants, the sanctioning officer got creative and wrote in two options that the respondent could choose from to fulfill the sanction. In one option, he could meet with the school's key administrator over his cohort and discuss his impact on his classmates and potentially develop a repair plan, and in the other option he could meet with me to explore the possibility of an RJ process involving his classmates.

The student opted to meet with me. When he did, he expressed being "angry, bitter, resentful, and ashamed." He wasn't sure whether he wanted to or actually could face all of his classmates. I told him we didn't need to invite *all* of his very large cohort, that we could explore an invitation to those who made sense and who he was comfortable including. He needed to think about it, and we met multiple times, building trust and creating space for his own emotional processing and accountability-taking. He ultimately agreed to participate in a restorative circle with his classmates. When he said he was ready to proceed, however, I had a different interpretation of his readiness, and we met a few more times to prepare before extending the invitation to selected classmates (those who had participated in the investigation and any classmates with whom they wanted to share the invitation).

In the meantime, I extended an invitation to his classmates to meet with me to discuss harms and needs in the community. The ones who accepted my invitation mostly expressed being upset with the university. They wanted to meet with school leadership to ask questions and express their upset, so I facilitated a community needs circle attended by about eight impacted students, an associate dean, and the key school administrator. When the respondent and his classmates were ready to come together for an RJ circle, I encouraged the respondent in our preparatory meetings to share openly with his classmates (as much as he was comfortable sharing) about what his experience was in the Title IX process, including the finding of responsibility and his sanctions. I reminded him that his classmates were not aware of any of it due to student confidentiality protections and the university's federal requirement to not share his confidential information with others.

In the RJ circle the respondent came together with 25 of his classmates. We established values and passed a talking piece (which was an unfamiliar process for the professional students). About half the group focused on harms by the respondent, and the other half focused on their upset with the university. The respondent shared deeply and vulnerably about his remorse, his shame, the investigation outcome, and even the personal factors that contributed to him engaging in the misconduct. I observed that when the respondent was transparent and vulnerable with his classmates, and offered a sincere apology, his classmates softened toward him and changed their previously entrenched position that he needed to be removed from the cohort. The respondent ended up weeping with emotion; we had agreed in advance that I would call a break if he needed one, signaled through a cue word. When he wept, I called a break, and several of his classmates went over to comfort him. I observed at least one primarily impacted student embracing him.

As it happened, the group never came back together. It is always my preference and responsibility to close out an RJ circle formally, as the closing is an important part of the process. However, sometimes things don't go as planned, and sometimes they end how they need to. The power of that particular circle process was plain to me then, as I watched the respondent's classmates embrace him and express their dismay as they learned that he was leaving the cohort and that that was his last day as their classmate.

The circle process was reparative. It gave the students space to have their questions answered and their hurts addressed in a way the investigation and its outcome could not. It allowed the classmates to see and feel the remorse and shame that the respondent carried. It allowed the students to meet each other in their humanity and in their relationships with each other. The restorative circle created space for the tending and repair of relational harms. The students cultivated accountability with the respondent for breaking the unspoken covenant of their class and their individual relationships. In doing all of this, the circle created space for healing and repair that the investigative process did not. RJ circles like these provide a meeting ground for justice and healing to meet at an individual level as well as a communal level.

This case highlights the application of RJ to meet community needs and address communally experienced harm. It also illustrates the fact that RJ can be implemented as a supplemental process alongside or after a disciplinary process and that doing so can bring healing and repair. Lastly, it demonstrates that faculty and staff can—and sometimes should—be included in the process. When an institution has contributed to harm (including through acts of omission), the institution is obligated to work toward repairing it (per RJ and other principles). Federal obligations require schools to take prompt and effective steps to stop sexual misconduct; eliminate the hostile environment; prevent its recurrence; and, as appropriate, remedy its effects.

> Restorative justice provides an opportunity for those who harm and those harmed to empathize with one another, rather than foster hostility between them and their communities. It encourages the responsible person and the community, where appropriate, to take responsibility for actions resulting in harm and make amends. Restorative justice processes invite individuals and the community to take steps to prevent recurrence. Ultimately, it offers processes where the person harmed and all impacted parties can begin to heal.
>
> Restorative justice elevates the voices of survivors, families, communities, and responsible parties in ways that rarely occur in the adversarial context and, in doing so, aspires toward greater community self-governance by bringing together all members impacted by wrong-doing to identify harms, assess needs, meet responsibilities, and heal and repair harm to the degree possible. It shifts the locus of the justice project from dependence on systems and professionals to reliance on the involvement of communities and ordinary people. It moves us from an individualist "I" to a communalist "we," thereby strengthening communities. Individual and community safety and security emerge from healthier and self-governing communities. (Davis, 2019, pp. 26–28)

The Meeting Ground of Adaptable Resolution

The power of adaptable resolution lies in its ability to adapt the process and outcomes around the needs of participants. Sometimes this may mean using more than one process or pivoting in the middle of a process. As healing isn't linear, the ability to adapt and change course cultivates the ground where justice and healing can meet.

Case Study: Adaptability in Addressing Harms

Another adaptable resolution case I facilitated involved members of a large multipronged student organization. Two students agreed to have sex. She asked him to use a condom, but in the absence of one, she reported experiencing pressure to proceed withone one, which they did. She felt the pressure was compounded by the fact that he was a leader in the organization which exacerbated the power imbalance between them. She experienced trauma around it, and the other members of the organization intensified and magnified the harm through public shaming and harassment. She pursued a Title IX investigation to address the matter, then later opted to switch to adaptable resolution.

Both students agreed to participate in adaptable resolution. (His precondition to participation was that he wouldn't step down from leadership of his organization.) Neither of them wanted to see or directly engage with the other through the process. Accordingly, per their request, I facilitated a restorative shuttle process designed to identify needs and create a resolution agreement that would meet those needs.

Since he was a leader in his organization, she wanted him to take personal accountability as well as communal accountability. He agreed to several pieces of an adaptable resolution agreement that included educational components focused on his organization (in lieu of him stepping down). After I shuttled between them all summer (via email and online meetings), they eventually came to agreement on all the educational and reparative components of a thoughtful and robust resolution agreement. The final sticking point came when he requested a nondisclosure agreement, given his career aspirations. She went back and forth about whether or not she wanted to agree to it, as he was adamant he would not sign an adaptable resolution agreement without one. At the time they were negotiating the nondisclosure agreement, there was substantial distrust on both sides. Her refusal to sign it was interpreted by him to mean that she intended to sabotage his career; his request for her to sign it was taken by her as an attempt to silence her from ever sharing her story, which was an important part of her healing process. In working with them both separately, though, I observed sincerity, care, and copious amounts of good will.

The respondent seemed genuinely dedicated to doing what he could (within his terms) to repair harm and contribute to her healing. They were both steadfast in their desire to find resolution and closure. She considered reverting back to an investigative resolution. They both agreed that that was undesirable, and he offered to meet with her for a facilitated dialogue. He believed that through their dialogue he could help bring her satisfactory closure in lieu of the proposed resolution agreement.

They agreed to meet for a restorative dialogue online. I met with each of them separately to prepare for the dialogue, which was tailored to meet her needs and requests. I then facilitated a dialogic encounter between them that gave her space to share her experience with him and illuminated the lasting harm he had caused her, including social harm in their community. He listened attentively and affirmed what she shared. He took accountability for what he thought he could, and he expressed care and remorse. He professed personal and organizational commitment (regardless of a resolution agreement) to address and repair harm and prevent its recurrence. They found points of agreement, and they found closure. The adaptable resolution process concluded and provided resolution of the matter.

The time we spent working toward a resolution agreement via the shuttle process was not wasted time. During that time, I built trust with each of them individually and worked to build trust between them. We explored areas of agreement and areas of disagreement. I helped him understand the harm. I helped her uncover what she needed for repair and restoration. I encouraged him to be more accountable. I vividly remember one exchange when she'd asked him at the beginning of the shuttle process to step down from his leadership position, which was a nonstarter for him, so he countered by offering to submit himself to his organization's internal accountability process instead. She found that laughably ridiculous and completely unsatisfactory in meeting her justice needs. Through the shuttle process I informed him that she had rejected his proposal. He essentially demanded that she come up with another suggestion to counter his proposal (as that's how negotiations typically work). I let him know that in RJ it is the responsibility of the person who caused harm to repair it, so he needed to do the work of coming up with another suggestion to repair harm. She was clear that she wanted him to step down from leadership to satisfy her unmet justice needs, and as he didn't want to do it, the burden was on him to offer other suggestions. He took some time to think about it and ended up proposing a thoughtful multifaceted alternative that she accepted. This process built a lot of trust between them and demonstrated to her that he was committed to repairing harm. The shuttle process prepared the soil for planting the seeds of repair that ultimately bloomed in the dialogue.

Some students in adaptable resolution choose to focus on a resolution agreement and that's it. Others focus on the terms of a resolution agreement to serve as a precursor to a restorative dialogue or circle process. Some want elements of the resolution agreement completed as a precondition prior to meeting for a dialogic encounter. Others may just want a dialogue or restorative encounter and nothing else. Whatever the path to justice and healing may entail, adaptable resolution can provide the meeting ground.

Where Justice and Healing Meet

Typical disciplinary procedures focus on punishment for those found responsible for policy violations. The focus of the process is on policy (and compliance) and what to do to people who break the rules. RJ instead attends to all of the people involved and impacted. It tends to their needs, and it tends to their humanity. It centers those who were most directly impacted by harm and centers their justice and healing needs. In ideal circumstances, it attends to root causes and initiates transformation. RJ processes (when implemented restoratively) are expressions of care that cultivate accountability and mending and tending. These practices move beyond dichotomies as "restorative justice seeks a healing for all" (Davis, 2019, p. 27).

Creating space for people to be leaders and authors of their own healing and justice is incredibly powerful. Universities aspire to develop enlightened and empowered citizens who will positively impact the world. U-M strives to develop "leaders and citizens who will challenge the present and enrich the future" (University of Michigan, n.d., para. 1). If universities want students to do this, it helps to model it—not just teach it—at a whole-systems level. As Shira Hassan noted to adrienne maree brown (2017) in *Emergent Strategy* (which describes adaptive and relational leadership models, actions, practices, and tools), "The goal is for us to embody these values so that our creativity can guide our healing and our drive for treating each other with true justice. With every experience of healing on our own terms, we also begin to heal the generational wounds of colonialist justice" (pp. 134–135). In this way, RJ creates space not just for individual, interpersonal, and communal healing and transformation; it also cultivates the ground for justice and healing to meet at institutional levels and transgenerational levels. The question is not whether or not this incredibly powerful healing justice is possible, the question is whether we will cultivate the ground and make space for it when harms happen within our communities. As Michael Petoskey (2020), chief judge of the Pokagon Band of Potawatomi Indians, said "Peacemaking is not about being soft on folks. We do want to hold people accountable to our community standards and to have them be responsible. And we have to be responsible as a community, too."

I echo adrienne maree brown's (2017) sentiments in *Emergent Strategy* and the call to readers as embodiments of love: "I want us to do better. I want to feel like we are responsible for each other's transformation [. . .] the transformation from broken people and communities to whole ones. [. . .] Towards wholeness and evolution, loves." (p. 150).

References

Barsh, R. L. (2005). Evaluating the quality of justice. In W.D. McCaslin (Ed.), *Justice as healing: Indigenous ways* (pp.167–169). Living Justice Press.

brown, a. m. (2017). *Emergent strategy: Shaping change, changing worlds*. AK Press.

Davis, F. E. (2019). *The little book of race and restorative justice*. Good Books.

Fitzgerald, R. (2021, September 23). U-M adopts policy, procedures for addressing misconduct. *The University Record*. https://record.umich.edu/articles/u-m-adopts-policy-procedures-for-addressing-misconduct/

Legal Information Institute. (2021). *Alternative dispute resolution*. Cornell Law School. https://www.law.cornell.edu/wex/alternative_dispute_resolution

Llewellyn, J. J., & Philpott D. (2014). *Restorative justice and reconciliation: Twin frameworks for peacebuilding*. Oxford Academic. https://doi.org/10.1093/acprof:oso/9780199364862.003.0002

Lorenz, K., Hayes, R., & Jacobsen, C. (2021). *"Title IX isn't for you, it's for the university": Sexual violence survivors' experiences of institutional betrayal in Title IX investigations*. CrimRxiv. https://doi.org/10.21428/cb6ab371.1959e20b

Petoskey, M. (2020, August 5–6). *Sacred justice: A very different world* [Keynote]. Indigenous Peacemaking Initiative 2020 Peacemaking Colloquium, online via Zoom. https://peacemaking.narf.org/2020/09/news-peacemaking-colloquium-2020-recordings-are-now-available

Robins, S. (2018, March 5). *The spirit of restorative justice: An interview with Sujatha Baliga*. Daily Good. https://www.dailygood.org/story/1900/thespirit-of-restorative-justice-an-interview-with-sujatha-baliga

Swanson, K. (2010, May 9). Coleman approves amendments to Student Code. *The Michigan Daily*. https://www.michigandaily.com/uncategorized/coleman-approves-amendments-student-code/

The Decolonial Atlas. (2015, April 14). *The Great Lakes: An Ojibwe perspective*. https://decolonialatlas.wordpress.com/2015/04/14/the-great-lakes-in-ojibwe-v2/

University of Michigan. (n.d.). *Mission*. https://president.umich.edu/about/mission/#:~:text=The%20mission%20of%20the%20University,present%20and%20enrich%20the%20future

University of Michigan. (2013). *University of Michigan policy on sexual misconduct by students*. Ann Arbor, MI.

University of Michigan. (2019). *The University of Michigan interim policy and procedures on student sexual and gender-based misconduct and other forms of interpersonal violence*. Ann Arbor, MI.

University of Michigan. (2021). *The University of Michigan policy on sexual and gender-based misconduct*. Ann Arbor, MI. https://sexualmisconduct.umich.edu/wp-content/uploads/2021/09/sgbm-policy.pdf

University of Michigan. (2021). *Ann Arbor student procedures*. https://sexualmisconduct.umich.edu/wp-content/uploads/2021/10/Student-Procedures-for-Ann-Arbor.pdf

U.S. Department of Education. (2020). *Know your rights: Title IX requires your school to address sexual violence*. https://www2.ed.gov/about/offices/list/ocr/docs/know-rights-201404-title-ix.pdf

II

REFLECTIONS ON STARTING A RESTORATIVE JUSTICE PROGRAM

Ish Orkar

As a restorative practitioner, I have deep respect for the pathways that emerge when we take the time to thoughtfully ask questions. So perhaps it's not surprising that when I was asked what it is I wish I would have known before starting a restorative justice (RJ) program, I knew the answer right away: I wish I would have asked more questions. I'm not suggesting these are the "right" questions to ask, but I hope that sharing the ones that formed along my journey may offer insight into ones that might be useful in yours.

Are Values and Practice Aligned?

Alignment of values is not enough. I learned that the aspects of program development that everyone will agree are important may still be a struggle to implement because of competing priorities. In the early planning stages of any RJ program, I strongly recommended that the RJ program have both proactive and responsive components, with a ratio of 80/20. Everyone I spoke to thought this was an excellent idea. There was no push-back, no reasons raised to suggest it was not reasonable. Yet—it became clear that the priorities of the program partners conflicted with this ratio. A focus on response to harm is what folks naturally think of when they imagine a conflict resolution program. It conjures images of quick fixes and proverbial trophies that can be displayed in a glass case. Anyone who does this work knows this is the furthest from reality, even in the cases where RJ is used successfully as an intervention in response to harm. But it's a myth that is hard to dispel.

Where Will You Call Home?

Think carefully about where you will build your program. Anyone building a house knows that scouting out the land and building on a firm, secure foundation is the most important step of the process. Somehow, in the excitement of having a proposal approved, gaining buy-in from key campus partners and enthusiastic student engagement, it's easy to forget to pay attention to this very important question. There are valid reasons for starting an RJ program to address sexual misconduct in student affairs. Some universities will house programs in the same office that responds to complaints of other harms, including discrimination and harassment. Few universities have a center exclusively dedicated to restorative practices, but having a center that can function as a real "center" for the campus community has remarkable benefits. It signals that these practices and tools are for everyone: faculty, staff, and students. It doesn't, by association, instantly impute other identities onto the program. For example, if it's housed in a residence life office, it may not be perceived as accessible to students who live off campus. If you truly want to transform culture by starting an RJ program, think boldly about where you need to be situated on campus to effectuate real change.

Who Needs to Know, and at What Cost?

Commonly referred to as *confidentiality*, this topic is typically framed as an agreement between participants in a circle as a reminder that we have entered a sacred space and want to establish guidelines to ensure the greatest degree of comfort and safety possible. But what about those outside of the circle who haven't signed onto any such agreement? I refer to these as the *want-to-know group*, because who *wants* to know is different from who really *needs* to know. And for those who need to know, a follow-up question should be: For what purpose? I learned that I could not have anticipated the degree to which the program would be bombarded with want-to-know requests. This could be a request for information for publicity and publications. It could be wanting to know points-of-entry issues and the demographics of those seeking to benefit from the practices. It could be for documentation purposes and risk management. It could look like wanting to know who and why individuals selected restorative practices instead of well-established processes and procedures that afford existing offices greater control over both people and outcomes. In sexual violence cases that become known to university administration, the university is mandated to take great interest in the individuals involved, the harm that occurred, the information shared, and the outcome.

Advance consideration of how you will handle this pressure will go a long way in setting the program up to clearly delineate at the beginning the process of—and boundaries—of knowledge sharing.

What Is Your Relationship With Campus Advocates?

Invest in your relationship with your sexual violence response office, and build trust with advocates; it will go a long way in establishing trust with students. If the staff trusts you and your program, they will refer students to you, and they will uplift the benefits of RJ in the underground communication networks across campus and social media. Having their buy-in, support, and respect is key. Here's the caveat: While both of your programs center the person who experienced harm and are trauma informed, there are distinct and important differences. Being too closely linked to the advocacy program may be harmful to socializing the ways in which restorative practices are countercultural to the punitive model of viewing harm. I remember a conversation I had with an advocate in the early program development stages. As I explained intake to the advocate, the information was at first enthusiastically received, and then the advocate asked, "But who's in the room for the survivor? Who is on the survivor's side?" The first thought that popped into my head was: What if there aren't sides? The use of the word *side* reminded me that I had neglected to consider the degree to which restorative work is a paradigm shift even for those who have always centered the harmed person in their work.

Are You Centering Impact Over Intent in Written Form?

I'm thinking both about the choice of language used and where information about the program resides. Universities may want to use the terms *complainant* to refer to the person who experienced harm and *respondent* to refer to the person who caused harm so it flows seamlessly in the current lexicon of terminology. And those terms are, quite frankly, shorter and easier to say! But that doesn't mean using the same language used in other processes won't have consequences. Similarly, programs may want to include information about a restorative response to harm option in the same policy manual as other processes. I strongly recommend that you resist the urge to succumb to the pressure here. If at all possible, I would recommend you explain restorative options available to the community in a separate guide so it's not placed within a policy that has a punitive framework and accompanying language. Beginning the program by setting the right tone will pay off in the long run.

What's in the Air?

Have an awareness of the campus climate and how that may affect the launch of a new initiative. If there's a prevailing narrative regarding restorative practices, it would be helpful to know so you can address it directly. This will help inform what work needs to be done with education, training, and outreach. You will need to ask: What messaging might be most effective? The campus climate may be particularly hostile to beginning an RJ program. The community may have recently experienced a much-publicized harm and may feel they want vengeance, retribution, punishment. While launching an RJ program may be exactly what a campus in this situation needs, it's important to move with an awareness that some may view the program as the antithesis of what would meet their needs. Others on campus may be enthusiastic about the program, but only because they expect it to solve all the problems instantly. Neither of these perspectives will set a program up for success. Consider a campus environment where a campus has tried other methods of addressing harm without success. Maybe this is a campus where folks feel particularly disconnected after years of experiencing the distancing effects of the pandemic. Beginning a program in this climate has the potential to really resonate with what the community is seeking. Your challenge (and opportunity!) might be to think of ways in which you can help the campus community envision a new model. As it is when one travels to a new and unfamiliar country, being introduced to a new way of thinking, being, relating, and resolving tension may cause the community to experience culture shock. Anticipating this in advance may be useful.

Who Are Your People?

Think internally, and externally in your local community as well. On campus, you may be surprised who is willing and excited to come alongside you in this work. You may find people of all disciplines, of all backgrounds and professional identities who deeply value restorative principles and want to partner with you to transform your community. So let them know who you are! You will find them, and they will find you, and you will instantly have ambassadors of this work infiltrating every unit, department, discipline, and corner of campus, and your program will be better for it. I do not believe it is conscionable to do this work without a connection to the community in which your campus resides. You never know when you may need to consult with an external practitioner for a fresh perspective on a matter. Or you may need to refer cases to someone who does not have a connection to the institution, either at the request of those involved or because you know they would be better served by someone with more distance from the university. Also, what if the person harmed or the person who experienced harm would feel more comfortable working with a practitioner who holds identities that differ from yours? What if you are either the only practitioner, or one of two practitioners, at the university? Having a network of restorative practitioners and colleagues in the community who can meet the needs of those you are working with is invaluable. Community engagement is not only a core principle of RJ, it enriches you, the practitioner, as well. Working on a university campus can quickly result in a very myopic perspective that may impact your ability to think creatively about restorative options. Remember that institutions are co-opting restorative practices. Think about what accountability looks like. Have you thought about collaborating with indigenous practitioners? In what ways are you actively addressing what Edward Valandra in *Colorizing Restorative Justice* (2020) poignantly identified as the first and second harms? I believe we have an obligation to bring these truths to the forefront of our work as practitioners in any setting. Restorative justice needs to be practiced in and with community. Without this engagement, offering restorative practices in a campus vacuum keeps you in a higher ed bubble and denies yourself the growth and renewal opportunities that abound when you form deep relationships with other restorative practitioners in the community. Find your people. They are waiting to support you.

Is It Sustainable?

Think about what would happen if the leaders who championed this initiative shift focus and resources (human and financial) to other priorities. What if all the campus partners who were ambassadors for your program transition to more demanding roles or leave the university altogether? Do you have a system in place to recruit additional support and community? Many of the prior questions (are values and practice aligned, where you will live, who are your people) are connected to this one. If you've been thoughtful every step of the way, then you will not only get your program off to the right start, but you will also be actively working to ensure its enduring legacy at the university.

Who Am I?

"Who am I?" is a common restorative practices tool used to dig deeper into self-awareness and an understanding of one's relationship to the self and others. It is rare that in launching a new initiative everything goes as planned. When that has happened in my own experience, I found myself asking this question frequently: Who am I? I come from a family of farmers. For generations, ancestors on both sides of my family have grown not only their own food but have had surplus to sell and share with others in the community. Yet as an urban dweller for my entire adult life, I struggled to feel connected to this aspect of my lineage, my identity. Who am I when things don't go as planned? Who am I when I feel my vision and dreams cannot be realized? Who am I as an RJ practitioner, as a leader and innovator, when I feel as though I have failed? Here is what I learned by asking myself "Who am I?" over and over and over again. I learned that when you regularly sit in circle with people who recognize your humanity and cloak you with care and wisdom at your lowest moments, things become clear. I learned the answer to my question, but I did not reach this insight on my own; it was in communion with the Restoring Community weekly circle practice I belong to. It was in belonging that I realized the truth. I am a farmer. It would be natural to view farmers as foolish. At first glance, it appears as if they simply dig a hole, throw something in it, and walk away. One might ask, "How in the world do they expect to achieve a positive outcome?" But we know better. We know that there was careful selection of a plot of land. That the soil needed to be fertile. That environmental conditions needed to be evaluated and anticipated. The farmer chooses a hospitable climate where the elements will allow seeds to thrive and not be destroyed. This is what was true for me: In beginning a program, I was planting a seed. This is what I learned with the help of my restorative community: It is enough to plan the seed. You may not see your humble beginnings through to harvest, but that does not make your contribution any less valuable. In my culture, farming is communal. A few people are digging, others water the plants, yet even more helpers weed. In the right relationship with the earth and others, your farm will thrive. You can't do it all by yourself. Find your people. You've done your part. Give yourself permission to move on, if needed.

Who Am I?

Yes, I'm still asking. I'm still curious and striving to be brave enough to be vulnerable. Who am I? A new realization came to me only moments ago: I am a seed. I am reflecting on how, over the past several months of struggle,

I've felt at times as though *I'm* being buried. That I've been shoved 6 inches under the earth, feeling confined and claustrophobic in the soil. Sometimes from that perspective, a helping hand can seem like it's only pushing you further underground. It can be a very dark and lonely place. This is what I wish I would have known: This journey is not about launching a program. It is about changing hearts and minds. Remember that you are not the program. Do not become so enmeshed with your professional identity or your affiliation with any specific institution that you lose perspective. Remember that you began this work because you are committed to living and sharing restorative principles and values, whether you are formally doing this work at an institution or not. Who am I? I am relishing this time under the earth. It is cool and quiet here. I am grounded, rooted. I am preparing for what's next. I cannot wait to hit the surface and grow.

In my experience, I couldn't launch the program of my dreams. But I realize now that something better happened: I and the campus community were able to learn, grow, and heal. Writer Lisa Olivera says, "Sometimes, healing looks less like finding the answers and more like tenderly meeting yourself in the questions" (Olivera, 2019). This was true for me. And I hope the act of reflecting on these questions is useful to you as well.

Acknowledgment

The views and opinions expressed by the author are solely her own and do not reflect the views and opinions of her employer.

References

Olivera, L. [@_lisaolivera]. (2019, November 26). *Sometimes, healing looks less like finding the answers* . . . Instagram. https://www.instagram.com/p/B5VeAYzAcKE/?hl=en

Valandra, E. C. (Ed.). (2020). Undoing the first harm: Settlers in restorative justice. In *Colorizing restorative justice: Voicing our realities* (325–370). Living Justice Press.

12

SYSTEM-AWARE CONSIDERATIONS FOR RESTORATIVE RESPONSES TO CAMPUS SEXUAL MISCONDUCT

Jasmyn Elise Story

This reflection invites restorative practice facilitators to consider incorporating a systems-aware approach to their campus processes. A systems-aware approach describes techniques that accomplish the following: acknowledges historical and structural harm, addresses internal policies that sustain systemic harm, communicates an awareness of the somatic impact of systemic harm, and utilizes frameworks to capture systemic harm alongside emotional and communal harms. This approach invites the participant to share their story from the conjunction of their intersecting social identities.

Systemic harm describes the impact of structural inequities and cultural narratives that create a disadvantage against a group of individuals. Systemic harm holistically impacts the individual due to its social, economic, and physical reach. In *Anti-Racist Psychotherapy*, David Archer (2021) called on mental health practitioners to apply an approach "that is meant to eliminate the suffering caused by this socially constructed sickness by treating the mind, body, and spirit of those impacted by it" (p. 5). This statement should extend to all care professionals, including practitioners of restorative practices. Restorative work should always leave room for the impact of socially constructed inequality that manifests as direct violence, structural inequity, or cultural narratives. Individual members of social groups deemed subordinate or nondominant may experience a culmination of adverse systemic experiences (i.e., education, health care, criminal justice; Archer, 2021). Archer stated that these experiences "impact the recipient's neurobiology, including their [hypothalamic–pituitary–adrenal] axis functioning and other nervous system changes, which lead to further mental health vulnerabilities" (p. 69). The impact of systemic harm on the individual warrants attention from practitioners of restorative practices, especially those addressing sexual misconduct.

Evaluating one's internal policies is crucial to a systems-aware approach, from internal-facing documents to email correspondence with participants. An institution may start this journey by revisiting its intake forms and procedures. Are the forms disseminated to participants aligned with established best practices around gender and racial identity? Do they allow participants to self-identify? The entry fields of an intake form may not seem of great import, but it is in the details that we communicate our understanding of justice. Applying a systems-aware approach to internal policies around campus sexual assault involves

- acknowledging the reality of systemic harm
- revisiting established policy
- reviewing official and unofficial procedures
- investing in professional development around structural/historical harm
- dedication to best practices shared by various experience or identity-specific advocacy groups
- building partnerships with accessible healing, education, and care professionals

The American education system has inherited a long legacy of harm. The identity-based exclusionary practices of the past may be lingering in the established procedures of the present. A systems-aware approach acknowledges this possibility and looks to seek and amend internal policies to ensure alignment with community-informed best practices.

Dialogues around trauma-informed care regarding sexual misconduct often include the direct violence of the incident, adverse childhood experiences activated by the incident, or trauma experienced during a traditional justice process. This work invites facilitators of restorative justice processes for campus sexual misconduct to expand their focus to include the impact of structural and historical harm.

The experience of sexual misconduct is colored by the experience of gender, ability, class, age, race, nationality, and more. The harm central to initiating a justice process is often the focus of the restorative inquiry. The harm connected to a policy or boundary violation may also be related to an inflamed structural/historical harm. *Inflamed structural/historical harm* describes a violation that evokes or alludes to structural or historical violence. In an example of nonconsensual touch at a department party, a student shares that their lab partner's inappropriate comments began with statements about his love of their culture and "their people's docile nature." An active listening reflection may capture emotional harms: fear, confusion, and frustration. The restorative practitioner may reflect the physical harm of anxiety, unwanted contact with their body, and sleeplessness back to the harmed party. They may close by exploring the harm to relationships between the parties in the lab and the department. In my practice, systems awareness means listening for what I named inflamed structural/historical harm. In this example, a cultural narrative about the harmed party's perceived identity is the inflamed historical harm.

Practitioners of restorative practices address sexual misconduct by offering a storytelling process that provides the harmed party with a platform to be seen in their whole humanity. In an attempt to restore dignity, it is also the practitioner's responsibility to acknowledge how systemic, historical, and structural harm contributes to the experience of the incident. This work only provides a glimpse of how practitioners and case managers may apply a systems-aware approach to their alternative processes. There are many intersections of experience to consider beyond the few provided as examples in this text. This reflection is an invitation to continue this dialogue and cocreate ways of acknowledging, mitigating, and addressing systemic harm in restorative justice programs and processes. Those impacted by sexual misconduct deserve care that is as robust and holistic as the harm that interrupted their lives.

Reference

Archer, D. (2021). *Anti-racist psychotherapy: Confronting systemic racism and healing racial trauma*. Each One Teach One.

13

IMPLEMENTATION OF INSTITUTIONALLY FACILITATED RESTORATIVE JUSTICE APPROACHES TO ADDRESS CAMPUS SEXUAL HARM

Rachel Roth Sawatzky

In December 2019, I was sitting in circle with other student affairs administrators and practitioners at the close of a multiday training in restorative justice (RJ) for campus sexual harm. The possibilities of what we had been learning had settled on me and another Title IX coordinator, a close colleague from a neighboring school, leaving us both in tears. Maybe the emotion was close to the surface as a result of the personal secondary trauma and daily professional stress we experienced as a result of this work, or maybe we, like many in higher education, were simply bone tired at the end of another exhausting semester! Regardless, the sense of relief at the possibility of a different way to do this work was also moving—an institutionally facilitated process that could honor the experience, voice, and choice of those impacted by campus sexual misconduct.

The setting for this case study was a small, private university, which means that the lessons learned may not be wholly transferable to all institutional types. That said, whether the institution is large or small, public or private, the human dynamics are often very similar. The account is illuminated by challenges in the story of an educational community, around which were simultaneously woven experiences of student success, achievement, and institutional loyalty along with professional valor, endurance, commitment, and resilience on the part of faculty, staff, and administrators.

The journey toward implementation of a possible adaptive resolution (AR) policy and procedure began with an examination of the current campus climate around power-based personal harms indicating challenges related to a variety of global, national, and organizational dynamics, including economic issues, institutional support, and limits on staff capacity; *context* is clearly significant. Further reflection indicated additional considerations and, based on the experience, thoughts have coalesced that may help other practitioners anticipate and navigate potentially turbulent waters, rising above them when possible, in crafting their approach.

Awareness of the possibility for supplemental procedural options for responding to campus sexual harm resulted in careful reflection. Using a collaborative process to build stakeholder buy-in, a contextually relevant RJ-informed campus sexual harms policy and procedure proposal, referred to as AR was developed. The implementation experience developed a deeper appreciation for federal Title IX law and the limits of institutionalized processes for responding to campus sexual harm and fostered a personal conviction of the possibilities a RJ framework could offer. Even more significant was the new awareness of organizational dynamics that can short-circuit the implementation of this type of project and personal leadership lessons that these dynamics indicated.

Case Study Context

Prioritization of and priorities for any social justice initiative are subject to a variety of institutional factors and dynamics at the local, national, and global levels, including various kinds of pandemics, such as COVID-19 and racism. Institutional policy development and implementation often end up being a bellwether for larger realities. National- and local-level contextual realities are among the factors affecting, in this case, the successful implementation of an RJ additive for responding to campus sexual harms.

National Dynamics

Title IX of the Education Amendments Act of 1972 (2020) has continuously evolved through the legislative process from its original design to offer federally mandated non-sexist guidelines on a variety of educational issues to include prohibiting sex discrimination in the form of sexual harassment, misconduct and assault. Through this clarifying process, what is at stake for campuses that fail to adhere to its mandates, guidance, and precedent around relevant subsidiary public policy and social issues has also been revealed. University administrators are required to sustain ongoing attention to an emergent legal bottom line and adroitly renegotiate institutional policies relative to the law, ratcheting up pressure around compliance. Title IX has also been the subject of a political tug of war as successive presidential administrations attempt to reimagine Title IX to reflect their own agenda and politics, necessarily impacting institutional policy implementation, for better and for worse (Stimpson, 2022). In this case, the allowance of the 2020 Final Rule for the use of RJ-informed procedures in responding to potential Title IX violations provided a timely and exciting possibility; a viable opportunity to solve an identified problem; an approach which was in theoretical alignment with the stated values and priorities of the institution; and, conveniently, a framework that was already being applied in other contexts within the university, including in its academic accountability and conduct procedures. However, given the significance of the various contextual challenges described in this chapter, the timing of national level developments was less serendipitous than hoped for within the local.

Institutional Dynamics

Projects to implement new institutional approaches reveal what an institution values and can expose deeper unresolved issues and preoccupations. In this case, it seemed a natural extension to apply restorative approaches to situations of campus sexual harm given the developments in Title IX law at the federal level and the institutional affinity for RJ. However, in the face of significant existential threats, institutional compromises are sometimes made, creative thinking can be limited, and the temptation may be to lean toward a deficit mindset. Those working toward implementation of a policy additive should certainly consider organizational values and context, including its history, current climate, and the community realities being navigated.

Over the past decade, many small to mid-sized schools have experienced strained financial realities on top of pandemic navigation, campus closures, staffing obstacles, and student mental and physical health challenges. Beneath these more universal issues, individual institutions have their own unique and specific dynamics that will impact the timing for implementation of a new initiative. In this case, there was a deep exhaustion in the wake of enrollment challenges, a sustained contractionary period, and weariness after cascading fallout and reputational damage in the wake of scandal. There had also been repeated senior leadership transitions and staff and programming pivots intended to capitalize on emergent perceived opportunities. These local environmental factors produced cycles of dysregulation, limiting the enthusiasm and readiness of the campus community for implementation as stakeholders to the process landed across the emotional spectrum related to their professional wellness, from feelings of overwhelm and vulnerability to resilience.

Maintaining the supportive involvement of key individuals offered another interesting set of dynamics. Clues that some gatekeepers were wavering in their support for the implementation of AR were registered early. These had been articulated as concerns for institutional liability and limited financial and staffing capacity. In one case, a key senior administrator voiced concerns based on the opinion that Title IX is inherently flawed and "building it out with additional processes and options" would only exacerbate these deficiencies, and that, furthermore, RJ was problematic in that it fails to adequately address the power dynamics at the root of sexual misconduct. This individual had been hired after approval had been granted to draft the process and work toward implementation, so it would have been both strategically and practically imperative to invest energy in open-ended conversation about what might work better, in view of the shared awareness that the current procedures were likewise insufficient to adequately address the power dynamics at the root of sexual misconduct and with an invitation to dream together from there.

Sustaining meaningful administrative support for this approach was another dynamic. To really move the needle on these issues, administrative support is obviously imperative, and realistically there were more basic questions of institutional sustainability consuming the bulk of the collective creative energy that could have supported implementation. Reflections indicate an awareness that if administration were able to offer concrete support of AR it could require an uncomfortable level of organizational transparency and less administrative control to shape the narrative, in a time when, due to the challenging enrollment and financial situation, university leadership was understandably risk averse.

Despite these inauspicious indicators, some process-driven amnesia must have resulted from the energy and optimism required to mount the various phases of the project. To be fair, midway through the implementation experience the potential challenges actually appeared to be less problematic than early memos seemed to anticipate and outcomes would later indicate, as various campus partners were engaged in the process in helpful and meaningful ways and the challenges were thought to have been resolved through various strategy sessions, communications, meetings, and successful presentations. When individuals named capacity limitations, identified questions around institutional support, and clarified or withdrew their support, it was an unpleasant surprise for the collaborating partners.

An exciting, legally viable, emergent possibility plus a theoretically relevant and contextually developed strategic plan leading to implementation does not guarantee that it will be effectuated (Ranjbar et al., 2014; Smith et al., 2020). The timing related to this proposal meant approaching various partners with the opportunity to do something more and different than the standard minimum requirements at the end of an extended period of significant volatility and in the midst of a fresh season of unpredictability. As a result of the multitiered institutional challenges and their very real impacts on people, faculty and staff felt limited in their capacity to support the implementation of new policy and procedures. Policy implementation at a local level is inevitably impacted by macro- and meso-level factors, and ultimately these dynamics would prove too much to overcome for stakeholder participation.

Considerations for Implementation

With a stated need for AR related to campus sexual harm, particularly from students, and the support of many key stakeholders, the policy development and implementation process was initiated with theoretical institutional endorsement from relevant administrators and sustained with adequate interest and support at key junctures to justify proceeding with some level of confidence. However, there was insufficient buy-in from the requisite gatekeepers due to the institutional dynamics suggested above. This led to reflection on a series of additional factors for consideration.

Values–Frameworks–Policies

Given ever-shifting and evolving national- and local-level contextual realities, consideration of how to frame RJ for campus sexual harm as it relates to the institution's mission and values can justify and sustain the work through the shifts in agenda-driven national politics and institutional challenges such as financial downturns and resulting staffing and programming developments. When policies are aligned with the fundamental institutional mission, values, and current vision, support from necessary stakeholders results and translates into staffing capacity and other resources (Hopkins, 2015). That said, institutional values congruence is not a prerequisite for implementation of a restorative or restorative-adjacent approach. Consideration should also be given to pilot approaches that can demonstrate the value of restorative interventions before restorative approaches can be fully embraced by the institution. In this case, despite alignment between stated institutional values and an RJ framework, stakeholder familiarity based on its use in other institutional conduct processes, theoretical support by some, and authentic interest from others, consequential commitment was thin, given the various contextual dynamics the institution was navigating. In this case, another approach would have been to pilot a smaller scale introductory program, gaining support along the way and justifying ongoing growth with the programs' alignment to institutional values.

Collective and Campus Strategies

Policy additives and procedural amendments requiring specific champions and creating new task-based (potentially unfunded) mandates may meet resistance if stakeholders are left feeling unsupported. In fact, Karp and Williamsen (2020) urge a "whole campus approach" that "calls for . . . the university to fulfill broader obligations to make amends and change the campus culture" (p. 10). From here, development of new RJ-informed options becomes one piece of the broader campus conversation and strategy. In our case, along with support for implementation from some, a number of community members identified more pressing concerns of organizational dysregulation and resultant challenges to the campus climate ahead of the need for an RJ approach to campus sexual misconduct. Those who indicated their ambivalence for AR at an applied perspective, often said that first—or, at the very least in addition to—a remedies-based, complainant-driven process with a focus on a specific situation between directly impacted individuals, what was really needed was broader institutional culture change around sex and power. In prioritizing this work amidst a variety of larger social and institutional challenges, a whole-campus approach to implementation addresses broader issues in a holistic way, related to challenging campus climates, unstable or inconsistent institutional support, and a lack of capacity to sustain support for the project.

Trust in People, But Not Institutions

Interestingly, as information was gathered and testing of the concept to offer AR occurred in the first phases of the project, students actually indicated their trust in the Title IX office to offer support, empowerment, respect, and fairness to impacted parties, characteristics of a successful RJ-informed approach. One student noted that, if necessary, they were highly likely to make a Title IX complaint to the university because of their confidence in the people who would be managing the process. Yet campus stakeholder trust in the capacity of the Title IX office did not extend to the institutional investigative–adjudicatory processes to deliver outcomes that would meet the needs of impacted students and net satisfactory resolutions to complaints. Students impacted by campus sexual harm indicated experiencing the investigative–adjudicatory processes as disempowering, arbitrary, and bewilderingly unfair. Illustrating this lack of trust, another student articulated that their perception of legal fairness did not match their experience of emotional fairness. They noted a perceived mismatch between how the process works conceptually and how it is experienced in practice. Based on professional experience, and confirmed by students through campus climate surveys and additional feedback mechanisms, the need for something like RJ-informed responses for campus sexual harms was clear. A number of participants specifically named this need; one expressed they would like to see the advancement of RJ options begin to create a new culture in Title IX policy and practice. The proposed AR policy and procedure for campus sexual harms offered an option that was stakeholder driven and institutionally facilitated, indicating to students that the process could also feel more trustworthy and meet their needs for voice, empowerment, and fairness. While many students and some staff were excited about the potential to implement an AR policy and procedure, other responses were more ambivalent.

The lack of trust for the institution and its processes likely contributed to this indifference, which was described as a lack of trust that RJ could offer adequate and appropriate approaches to address harm; concern that choice, equity, privacy, control, and autonomy would not be authentically offered or preserved through AR; and questions about its ability to offer robust accountability processes. Given the recent institutional turbulence, it should not have been surprising that many, especially faculty and staff, held the principal belief that any and all institutional processes were liable to cause harm and skepticism that an RJ-informed option could be any more trustworthy than other institutional processes. Karp and Williamsen (2020) confirm that while "support for restorative justice—including in matters of sexual harm—is growing, many people mistrust that institutions will implement restorative justice with fidelity and in good faith" (p. 12). In fact, one faculty member articulated this very thing: "Participants do not trust the institution . . . by incorporating restorative justice approaches into the Title IX policy, Title IX might co-opt the new option too."

The reality that many will not trust institutional processes should be considered and potentially mitigated through the employment of whole-campus approaches that have seen success when they employ the following blend of components: comprehensive and wide-ranging strategies; early interventions; utilization of mixed methods and modalities; messaging offered at a frequency to reinforce content, but to avoid messages being ignored; employing competent and qualified educators; encouraging strategies which work to build relationships and which are culturally relevant and competent; and, finally, approaches that are "theory driven" and incorporate methods for evaluation (DeGue et al., 2014).

Theoretical, But Not Practical Openness

As the proposed AR procedural option was developed and drafted, various campus partners and stakeholders were engaged in a series of conversations. Along with wholehearted conceptual support from students and many faculty and staff, stakeholder feedback also represented the full range of openness to the opportunity from an applied perspective. Some regarded the proposal with confusion; some with a lack of trust; and some with caution: What does it mean that this process is "complainant centered?" and would this new process be adequate, appropriate, robust, timely, supportive of complainants, trauma aware, just, and culturally competent? When the rubber hit the road, key administrative and other gatekeepers offered theoretical interest, but not practical support, with resistance attributed to staff capacity and a perceived lack of institutional support. Many small and mid-sized universities will face capacity and other challenges hampering implementation of new or amended policies and procedures. Moreover, the perceived or real need of administrative leadership to mitigate liability and capacity limitations in the short term can overwhelm the need to address incalcitrant institutional shortcomings, even beyond the need for more restorative approaches to addressing campus sexual misconduct, including tumultuous organizational histories, a fundamental lack of trust in institutions, the necessity for institutional culture change over the long haul, and financial and staffing reinforcement to increase resiliency at all of these levels. Drawing on evidence of the ways that this approach can gain efficiencies over time, has the potential to address the capacity concerns while also building both theoretical and practical institutional support.

Crafting the Approach

The reality is that transforming institutional systems does not happen quickly or seamlessly. It is hard. But movement, growth, and change are possible despite the challenges. In assessing the opportunities for forward momentum, honest consideration of site context, stakeholder commitment levels, and staff capacity should foreground collaborative and courageous dreaming about what may be possible. This can look like a lot of different things: reimagining the traditional investigative–adjudicatory approach that incorporates some restorative elements, offering a restorative-adjacent approach, or piloting a full-fledged RJ-focused approach.

At the midpoint of this project I met with Howard Zehr, the "father of restorative justice." In retrospect, the significance of that conversation feels quite powerful given its remarkable relevance to how the project ended up coming together. As we talked, I named the fact that I had gone into this process with the assumption that RJ-based additives would be eagerly welcomed but was surprised that, on the one hand, many in the campus community were relatively satisfied with the status quo, and on the other hand, many were ambivalent, skeptical, or overwhelmed by the idea of something new. Given this reality, I articulated questions regarding the necessity, practicality, and viability of implementing RJ approaches, regardless of their appropriateness: "Are these concerns valid, or am I too simply feeling overwhelmed? We need something to the right scale—not overengineered to the point that it's irrelevant for the context. Are there too many challenges to make this worth it?" Zehr responded with compassion and challenge: "RJ can happen with persistence, and it's difficult, especially when you have an imposed structure like Title IX to navigate. But I hate to see us just give up and accept what is, when we can offer more." He went on to suggest that instead of thinking of specific programs and practices, a helpful way forward is to begin by simply applying the framework: "The framework is really the most important."

From my current vantage point, this answer seems refreshingly simple: "Bring the questions of who's been hurt; ask, what are their needs, and whose obligation it is to address those needs to each situation, and then get as creative as you can to try to address those things." In other words, Zehr suggested, the basic restorative formula provides a go-to starting point. In higher education contexts, RJ's three-question framework can be applied, for example, in navigating a standard investigative–adjudicatory Title IX process, in working with students as part of a conduct process, or in accompanying individuals through a campus survivor support service program. "It might not be a structured program, it may be something you work out on a case-by-case basis . . . based on how you answer the restorative questions," he said. Before a fully developed additional RJ-informed approach to campus sexual harm can be developed, an analysis of opportunities to weave an RJ framework to undergird current compliance and support structures offers a starting point, beginning in ways that are appropriately scaled for particular settings. "So, it doesn't always mean that there are restorative structures or programs in place, but it does mean a kind of creativity where we ask people the right [restorative] questions and try to find ways forward step by step," Zehr reflected.

If the conditions are amenable to the development of a newly focused approach, momentum should be guided by the development of a strategic plan that pays attention to those larger campus climate issues, in order to support, or cultivate a broader culture of, respect and intolerance for abuses of power. In developing this strategic plan, short- and long-term goals should be kept in mind. Strategize using measured and intentional stages toward development, and resist the urge to allow long-term goals to minimize and overwhelm the short-term wins. Experience indicates that this is a long-term project that will see false starts and missed opportunities along with gains. The encouragement is toward *horizon thinking*: Consider cultivating an expansive view and the stages and phases that might take you there, establishing modest goals that can build momentum for the bigger steps forward through smaller wins.

Consideration should also be given to appropriate timing for those stages and phases, with a recognition that this will be an iterative, evolving process with flexible timelines. Approaching partners with the opportunity to do something more than, and different from, the standard minimum required will likely fail to net the result you are after, particularly if this happens during a period of significant volatility or in the midst of seasons of unpredictability and shifting or opaque institutional priorities. Going too far too fast can result in resistance. However, if roadblocks emerge, take heart: "No" may actually mean "Not now."

In the meantime, establish commitments from all necessary campus stakeholders, partners, and gatekeepers. Verbal support is not enough. Active endorsement, underlined by the dedication of financial and staffing capacity, is paramount, particularly when proposals challenge the status quo and when headwinds take the form of historical, financial, and environmental challenges. Just as the strategic plan and timeline will evolve, the process to gain buy-in and shared ownership will be an ongoing and emergent experience too, with various thought partners leaving and entering the process at different points. Ensuring clear, sincere, broad-based understanding and support from university administrative levels and key gatekeepers of any new social justice initiative is vital and will need to happen on a rolling basis, making good personal and working relationships fundamental.

Bridging the divide between theoretical modeling and neat frameworks and our messy, unpredictable campus realities requires flexibility, creativity, patience, and a clear commitment to strategies that are accessible to all campus partners. Where administration and others remain theoretically supportive of the concept for possible future consideration but not able to conceptualize it in the present, consider and capitalize on the ways in which RJ is, first, able to be integrated into preexisting structures and modes of operating and, second, might gain efficiencies down the road by its implementation. Centering the conversation and strategy around the ways that RJ authentically aligns with institutional values and educational objectives and can actually build capacity over the long haul may sway the hearts and minds of crucial advocates.

Conditions

In a National Association of Student Personnel Administrators Research and Policy Institute Issue Brief entitled *Five Things Student Affairs Administrators Should Know About Restorative Justice and Campus Sexual Harm*, Karp and Williamsen (2020) identified five potential roadblocks to the rollout of a RJ mechanism for responding to campus sexual harm: (a) lack of vision for RJ, (b) lack of planning, (c) lack of training and coaching, (d) lack of support, and (e) lack of investment. Our experience tested this checklist and suggested two additional prerequisites, nuancing their list: (a) an institutional growth mindset cultivated by administration to support and affirm innovation, creativity, collaboration, and transparency and (b) careful hiring of competent, compassionate, and connected practitioners who share a vision and commitment toward implementing this approach. Karp and Williamsen (2020) indicate the need to "proceed thoughtfully and carefully: Build widespread support, plan for incremental implementation, and garner the resources necessary to properly train and mentor practitioners" (p. 11). Without capacity and resourcing; with questions about institutional support; philosophical differences, liability concerns, and a misalignment between aspirational identity and facts on the ground, a given strategic plan will not be implemented, regardless of its creativity, comprehensiveness, or appropriateness and in spite of its need. Unresolved contextual dynamics will pose a significant challenge, if they persist, to shape campus culture, modes and mechanisms of operating, and relational realities and when they result in strained human capital and fragmented trust among campus community members.

In preparing to offer a more formal institutionally facilitated RJ-informed approach for campus sexual harm, the following should be kept in mind:

1. Contextual issues, including national realities and institutional factors such as economic realities, leadership developments, and dynamics that will impact the timing of successful implementation.
2. Alignment of the proposal with larger institutional value systems and the existence of frameworks to support new initiatives, the compatibility of

the campus climate to support new initiatives, and the practical support of all necessary stakeholders to support new initiatives.

3. Assessment of energy and resilience levels on campus; whether written and unwritten values and existing procedures are amenable to an RJ approach; and what kind of strategic plan should be developed for implementation, considering the long view and the achievable steps that can get you there; and what good timing looks like in the current context.

4. Ongoing commitment and buy-in cultivated with relevant campus partners.

Craft your approach with the following checklist in mind:

- Ensure institutional vision for RJ
- Plan adequately, considering appropriate timing and contextual dynamics
- Offer training and coaching
- Ensure institutional support
- Ensure institutional investment
- Ensure an institutional growth mindset
- Ensure careful staffing by competent, compassionate, and connected practitioners who share a vision and commitment toward implementation

This experience provided the opportunity to exercise personal, relational, and leadership skills, including team development, shared ownership, engagement, and capacity building. It was a humbling reminder that it takes more than a good idea, collaborative leadership, a plan, energy, and enthusiasm to implement something this significant. Whether starting big or small, buy-in from all the right people, a broader context that is ready and able to dedicate time and resources to support the work, and healthy (enough) institutional dynamics to sustain the project ongoing are critical. Successful implementation of a campus program to offer restorative approaches to campus sexual harm would signal a profound institutional cultural shift toward justice, one that arcs toward meaningful care, repair, justice, and accountability. This is the challenge and the promise.

References

DeGue, S., Valle, L., Holt, M. K., Massetti, G. M., Matjasko, J. L., & Tharp, A.T. (2014). A systematic review of primary prevention strategies for sexual violence perpetration. *Aggression and Violent Behavior, 19*(4), 346–362. https://doi.org/10.1016/j.avb.2014.05.004

Education Amendments Act of 1972, 20 U.S.C. §1681–1688 (2020). https://
www2.ed.gov/about/offices/list/ocr/docs/titleix-regs-unofficial.pdf

Hopkins, B. (2015). From restorative justice to restorative culture. *Revista De
Asistenta Sociala, 4*, 19–34.

Karp, D., & Williamsen, K. (2020). *Five things student affairs administrators should
know about restorative justice and campus sexual harm* (Policy Brief). National
Association of Student Personnel Administrators. https://www.naspa.org/report/
five-things-student-affairs-administrators-should-know-about-restorative-jus-
tice-and-campus-sexual-harm

Ranjbar, M. S., Shirazi, M. A., & Blooki, M. L. (2014). Interaction among intra-
organizational factors effective in successful strategy execution: An analytical view.
Journal of Strategy and Management, 7(2), 127–154. https://doi.org/10.1108/
JSMA-05-2013-0032

Smith, C., Hyde, J., Falkner, T., & Kerlin, C. (2020). The role of organizational
change management in successful strategic enrollment management implementation. *Strategic Enrollment Management Quarterly, 8*(2), 31–40. https://scholar
.uwindsor.ca/educationpub/48

Stimpson, C. (2022). Dereliction, due process, and decorum: The crises of Title IX.
Signs, 47(2), 261–293. https://doi.org/10.1086/716653

14

PRACTITIONER REFLECTION

Rachel King

The student sits in the office with a river of tears steadily streaming down her face and neck. Her pain comes from processing how she made her roommate feel so uncomfortable with her advances that now her roommate has been sleeping on a friend's floor. When she's able to speak again, tears still flowing, she shares how meaningful it was for her to be a good friend and roommate and how painful it is to have failed at her first attempt.

—Vignette 1

They had been dating for a few months, spending most of their nights together in his residence hall room. They talked about previous relationships and her reticence to have sex, because of past experiences. One night they were hooking up and, without conversation, he took it farther than they had discussed.

—Vignette 2

Similar to both these vignettes, the students who share experiences such as these with practitioners on their campuses, as countless have with me, show incredible courage and compassion, often willing to be vulnerable with staff, with each other, and with themselves. Yet often when we speak about restorative justice practices on campus, it is presumed that students would never accept responsibility for causing sexual harm to someone or that those impacted would inevitably experience revictimization. Rather, the way in which we make restorative processes available to students, and how practitioners facilitate those opportunities, dramatically impacts the extent to which students feel they can speak openly, construct a path toward repair, and ultimately have their needs met.

When we create the space, students have a great deal to teach us about what it can look like to restore dignity. Through facilitating restorative processes in response to gender-based harm on campus, I have deepened my understand of the following:

- Restorative processes are not linear.
- Identity is always at play.
- "Accepting responsibility" is complicated. And critical.
- Destigmatizing help-seeking requires intentionality.

Restorative Processes Are Not Linear

When individuals navigate the aftermath of sexual harm, what they want and need may fluctuate. An impacted student may initially express interest in sitting down with the individual who caused them harm and later determine that moving forward no longer includes that dialogue. Those responsible may also shift their desire to engage in a restorative process, at times influenced by an increased awareness of how their behavior was experienced. This fluidity is not a sign of failure of a particular process but rather a reflection of the evolving needs of the participants. To maintain the integrity of restorative processes, such that they unfold with authentic voluntary participation, institutional policies and practices need to anticipate and accommodate these evolving preferences and ensure that practitioners' desires and opinions do not supersede those of the people directly involved.

Identity Is Always at Play

Not only do individuals carry their unique identities and power dynamics into restorative processes, but intersectionality impacts how and whether students access college and university reporting and resolution processes, including restorative justice. Transparent policies and practices, ensuring equitable access to restorative options, will reduce the risk of bias that is inevitable in systems with broad administrative discretion. This is not to be construed as revoking facilitators' responsibility to students to assess readiness to enter into dialogue, or the need for institutions to actively participate in crafting outcomes that address community needs. Utilizing restorative processes in response to sexual harm as a form of social justice does, however, require a level of cultural humility that is integral to effective practice.

"Accepting Responsibility" Is Complicated—and Critical

In my experience, students' accounts of what occurred between them are often not all that dissimilar. Perspectives differ, and levels of understanding as to one's own actions and feelings, and those of the other student, may vary. As essential as it is to allow for students to disagree with a report that does not represent their experience, it is equally as critical to recognize how campus systems make it difficult for individuals who have caused harm to acknowledge ways in which they feel responsible. Achieving the validation and sense of justice restored sought by many impacted students often requires this acknowledgment. What motivates me to advocate for the availability of restorative processes is the conviction that students deserve space to accept responsibility authentically, a stepping stone to accountability and repair, and institutions have an opportunity and obligation to all involved to create such spaces, without infringing on students' rights.

Destigmatizing Help-Seeking Requires Intentionality

Campus practitioners have an extraordinary opportunity to shape students' understanding of restorative processes and, in turn, their path forward. Students likely lack familiarity with restorative frameworks, and their initial conversations with campus staff can dramatically impact the way in which they engage with their institution and with each other. Some responsible students' ability to engage in accountability may hinge upon campus practitioners' verbalizations of the potential that they may have caused harm and, if so, asserting a desire to see them learn, grow, and deepen their understanding of the impact. This multipartiality is integral to helping those who have been harmed have their needs met. It can also present optical challenges for administrators, who face enormous pressure internally and externally to equate justice with punishment and affirm values through permanent exclusion. In practice, systems that lack flexibility to meet the wide array of student needs and leave students uninvolved in decision making risk perpetuating the underreporting prevalent on campuses and sustain the pervasive cultures of sexual violence. Regardless of whether students reintegrate into their campus community or the community beyond, how practitioners destigmatize help seeking by those who cause harm without minimizing the impact of problematic sexual behavior requires transparency, sensitivity, and courage that rivals that of our students.

15

CASE STUDY

Restorative Justice for Campus Sexual Misconduct

Frank A. Cirioni

In 2015, I was serving as a new director of student conduct at a small private residential liberal arts university in the Pacific Northwest. Prior to my arrival, a college senior named Belle (pseudonym) reported an incident of campus sexual misconduct to the university's Title IX coordinator. Belle reported the following: When she was a first-year student, she met another first-year student, Jim (pseudonym), during new student orientation. Jim befriended Belle, and the two started hanging out regularly. One day, Jim invited Belle for a ride off campus in his car. After driving around the neighborhood, Jim parked the car in a private area away from onlookers and asked Belle if she would like to smoke marijuana with him. Belle agreed, and the two smoked a joint together in Jim's car. They then talked for awhile before Jim did something unexpected. He exposed his penis to Belle and asked her to perform oral sex on him.

Belle told the Title IX coordinator that she was taken aback by Jim's actions. She was very high, and the situation felt surreal. Belle felt trapped in Jim's car and isolated from her campus community. She felt pressured to perform oral sex on Jim. Afterward, Jim drove Belle back to campus, and they parted ways. They did not speak or hang out again that year.

At the time of the report, Belle was starting her fourth year at the university. Three years had passed since the incident with Jim, and Belle was still experiencing pain from that unhealed wound. Belle asked the Title IX coordinator what her options were, and they explained that a formal investigation and hearing process was available for student-on-student sexual misconduct cases. The Title IX coordinator would assign a Title IX investigator to Belle's case to conduct interviews with Belle, Jim, and any other students who may have information about the incident. The Title IX investigator would then prepare an investigative report for the campus's sexual misconduct board. The three-person sexual misconduct board was composed of university faculty and staff. The board would review the investigative report; hear the opening and closing statements from the complainant, respondent, and any witnesses (if available); and have the opportunity to ask questions of all parties involved. At the conclusion of the hearing, the board would deliberate in private and then render their decision in writing. The board would issue findings for the respondent (responsible or not responsible) and, if the respondent were found responsible for one or more violations, would also impose sanctions, including, but not limited to, suspension or expulsion.

Belle agreed to participate in the formal process; however, she had one request: She did not want Jim to "get in trouble." Instead, she wanted Jim to understand the harm he caused her, change his behaviors, and not repeat them.

As the director of student conduct, I was responsible for facilitating the sexual misconduct board hearing for Belle and Jim. We gathered in a private room in the basement of the university library after 5:00 pm. The individuals present for the hearing were the complainant, Belle; her support person, Anwen (pseudonym); the respondent, Jim; the three faculty/staff panelists; the Title IX coordinator; and me. Over the course of the 3-hour hearing, I distinctly remember how challenging it was for Belle to share the harms she experienced through her opening and closing statements. I remember Jim crying as he told the hearing board how his actions that day were a "mistake" and something he would never do again. I also remember observing the hearing panelists deliberate for almost an hour on what the "best" sanctions would be for this violation of policy. The hearing board found Jim responsible for violating the university's policy and imposed three sanctions: (a) suspension from the university for one academic term, (b) disciplinary probation for one academic term upon his return to campus, and (c) regular check-in meetings with me to monitor his progress.

I remember meeting with both parties in person, respectively, to share the outcome of the hearing. While Belle felt validated that her harm was acknowledged, she was emotionally raw from the hearing process and displeased with the punitive outcome for Jim. His temporary removal from campus did not meet her needs, and she worried about how the time away from the university would impact his academic plan, behavioral development, and overall student success. When Jim learned of his suspension, he wept in the Title IX office and pleaded for a different outcome. I did my best to console him, and I assured him that I would facilitate his return to campus in the fall and see him through his potential December graduation. In the end, neither party was satisfied with the outcome, and the experience left a bitter taste in my mouth.

At the start of the following semester, I was surprised to see Anwen, Belle's support person from the hearing, in the student conduct office requesting an appointment to see me. I welcomed her into my office, closed the door, and asked how I could help. Anwen told me she wanted to report an incident of campus sexual misconduct. Like Belle, Anwen's incident also had occurred in her first year at the university. Anwen had met another first-year student, Sameer (pseudonym), during new student orientation. They exchanged phone numbers and saw each other a few times during the first weeks of the fall semester. Sameer had shown interest in Anwen, but Anwen did not feel the same way, so she let text messages go unread until he eventually stopped texting her.

Later that semester, Anwen and Sameer attended the same off-campus party at a fraternity house. Anwen and her friends were in the basement, hanging out and dancing, when Sameer noticed her from across the room. He approached her; Anwen recalled Sameer smelling of alcohol and appearing to be under the influence. Anwen remembered chatting with Sameer and catching up with him about the semester and learning about his intentions to join the fraternity that was hosting the party. Anwen told me that while she was speaking with Sameer, her friend group had left the basement, leaving her alone with him. Anwen described how Sameer had encouraged her to dance with him, remembering from earlier conversations that she was an avid dancer. As they danced, Sameer would pull her farther and farther away from the crowd, until the two were in a secluded nook. Anwen recalled Sameer kissing her, and she was OK with that.

Anwen said she had the clearest memory of what she was carrying that night: Chapstick. She had purposely left her wallet, student ID card, keys, and phone with a friend so she could have a carefree night at the house party. This thought, she told me, had turned to dread when the party ended and she realized she had no way of getting home without her friends. Sameer, who was now holding her hand and guiding her out of the fraternity house, was happy to provide her with accommodations in his on-campus room. Anwen felt wary about the idea and suggested they walk back to campus to see if they could access her residence hall by following someone else into the building. When they reached campus, Sameer instead guided them to another building that he had access to, and the two made out in the lobby while Sameer insisted that Anwen spend the night in his room. At one point, Sameer promised Anwen, "We won't have sex." Reluctantly, Anwen followed Sameer to his residence hall room, where he quickly shooed away his roommate and cleared his twin-size bed for Anwen. Anwen remembered Sameer returning from the bathroom and sliding into the bed behind her, letting his large frame weigh on her body. She described how he proceeded to grab her breasts and buttocks, before taking her hand and placing it on his erect penis. Sameer then asked Anwen to perform oral sex on him.

Later that morning, Anwen left Sameer's room and waited outside her residence hall for someone to enter or exit the building so she could gain access. She told her roommate about the party and Sameer, without sharing intimate details. Anwen shared that in the immediate aftermath of the assault, she considered entering into a relationship with Sameer, just to rationalize the incident as a college "hookup." But as the weeks went by, she found herself avoiding Sameer, until they didn't see each other at all. It was not until their junior year that they would see each other again at a new student orientation team leader training. Anwen recalled being alone one day when Sameer approached her and asked if they could talk about "that night." Sameer acknowledged that what happened was wrong, and Anwen asked him why. Sameer said, "I raped you," and Anwen replied, "You assaulted me." The two parted ways again, and Anwen told me her memory lingered on that day regularly.

Anwen told me that she wanted to disclose this incident to me because she remembered hearing me talk about restorative justice when she served as Belle's support person. She had read about restorative justice and wanted to know if that was possible for her case. I told her we could try, and she said, "I want Sameer to know how much he hurt me, but I don't want him to be suspended or expelled. I want him to learn and to be better." The next day, I spoke with the dean of students and asked for his consent to facilitate a restorative justice process as an "informal resolution" under our existing policy. The dean approved, and I began my outreach to Sameer.

When Sameer arrived in my office, I could sense the overwhelming weight he was carrying. He kept his head down, avoided eye contact, and spoke in almost a whisper. Despite his body language, Sameer accepted responsibility for his actions immediately. He expressed remorse for hurting Anwen and causing her so much pain over the past 4 years. Sameer recalled the conversation they had had junior year at new student orientation training, and said he knew this day would come. He asked me what he could do to make things right. He offered to leave the university and turn himself in to the police if that's what Anwen wanted. I told him what Anwen wanted was the opposite of what he suggested. She wanted him to stay at the university and graduate at the end of the term, as scheduled. But what she needed from him were accountability, empathy, understanding, and personal growth. I asked if Sameer would be willing to take that journey with us, and he agreed.

Over the course of the next 5 months, I met with Anwen and Sameer, respectively, for preconference meetings. For Anwen, we met almost weekly for an hour at a time, sometimes longer. For Sameer, we met once or twice a month to prepare for the conference and to complete some preconference work that Anwen had requested; specifically, Anwen wanted Sameer to read her journal entries from after the assault, as well as personal notes, poems, and letters, and a handful of academic essays, that she had written over the past 4 years about the assault, her feelings, and the lingering impact of the incident. Anwen felt strongly that for Sameer to understand the depth of his impact, he needed to read it in her own words.

A few weeks before graduation, Anwen, Sameer, and I met in a quiet meeting room on the second floor of the student union for our restorative conference. Anwen and Sameer decided to meet without support people or other involved parties; it was just the two of them, with me serving as the facilitator. The conference took about 2 hours without breaks. Anwen and Sameer had drafted an agreement that included the following obligations for Sameer to complete: (a) Sameer would write Anwen an apology letter that was informed by the personal and academic works she had shared with him and the restorative conference; (b) Sameer would write a personal essay about the incident, the restorative conference, and what he had learned through the process and submit it anonymously to the university's magazine on sex and gender; (c) Sameer and Anwen would present their story together in person at an upcoming Green Dot Bystander Intervention training program for student leaders; and (d) Sameer would give a presentation on toxic masculinity to young men from the local high school during the fall term. The three of us signed the agreement, Anwen and Sameer exchanged phone numbers so they could stay in touch regarding the completion of the assignments, and we departed the meeting room.

Following the conference, Anwen and Sameer went above and beyond in fulfilling their agreement. Sameer wrote Anwen an apology letter that validated her experience, accepted responsibility for the harm he had caused her, and committed to making serious behavioral and lifestyle changes that would ensure this would never happen again. For Sameer's personal essay, Sameer submitted a two-page article that was published in the spring edition of the campus magazine and included his real full name. When I asked Sameer why he did not submit it anonymously, he insisted that taking responsibility for his actions meant putting his name on the essay and letting the campus community know what he had done to Anwen 4 years ago and what he had done now to seek forgiveness and restoration. In preparation for the bystander intervention training, Anwen and Sameer prepared a script to read to the student participants. The script alternated between Anwen and Sameer, each sharing their perspective at the time of the incident, and all the ways they wished their friends and classmates had intervened that evening to prevent the incident from occurring. The emotional weight of their story and the vulnerability in which they shared it was incredible. I was speechless when they asked me to coordinate with the university to have their presentation professionally recorded so it could be shared at future training sessions for student leaders. Finally, Sameer and I spent the summer designing a presentation on toxic masculinity for high school students that also served as the inspiration to create a weekly men's wellness group at the university called "The Men's Alliance." Sameer served as our first special guest speaker, and he invited several of his fraternity brothers to the group throughout the year to share their lived experiences and talk openly and honestly about the challenges facing young men at college.

After graduation, I stayed in contact with Anwen and Sameer. We celebrated their accomplishments, including new jobs and the start of their careers, and we talked about the new cities they moved to and the new people they were dating. I would ask one if they were keeping in touch with the other, and they almost always responded with "yes." The following year, I was introduced to a journalist who was recording a podcast called *Reckonings*, and she expressed interest in doing an episode on restorative justice. I checked in with Anwen and Sameer, and they both consented to a series of interviews with the journalist, first separately and then together. The result was a beautiful, emotional, and moving episode entitled "A Survivor and Her Perpetrator Find Justice" (Lepp, 2018). You can listen to the podcast episode and hear Anwen and Sameer in their own words as they share the healing power of restorative justice. Years later, their story would be featured in Peggy Orenstein's *New York Times*–best-selling book, *Boys & Sex: Young Men on Hookups, Love, Porn, Consent, and Navigating the New Masculinity.*

References

Lepp, S. (2018, December 3). *A survivor and her perpetrator find justice* [Audio podcast]. Reckonings. http://www.reckonings.show/episodes/21

Orenstein, P. (2020). *Boys & sex: Young men on hookups, love, porn, consent, and navigating the new masculinity.* HarperCollins.

16

PRACTICAL INSIGHT TO LESSONS LEARNED

Jake Dyer and Kasey Nikkel

This reflection is not a philosophy on the philosophy of restorative justice (RJ). This is student affairs professionals sharing practical insight from lessons learned trailblazing RJ at Luther College. Through our experiences as student affairs and Title IX practitioners, we have come to believe that RJ can work for your most egregious and serious allegations of sexual misconduct, regardless of institutional size. These reflections are what we wished had been shared with us when we started.

I (Kasey) am a former assistant dean of student life, chief conduct officer, and chair of the hearing board; my job in conduct was often black and white, although never easy. The role is to uphold community standards of our institutions' policy, provide fundamental fairness in the process, and provide meaningful interventions to educate our students on healthy choices and personal accountability. Sanctions were often set off institutional precedent and developmental needs.

As the chair of our hearing board cases, I saw many Title IX cases often following the same format, with Student A adamant they *did not* give consent for the behavior to occur, and Student B adamant the cues and signals they received *did* constitute consent, and both were telling their truth. Case after case we continued to see a consistent outcome; no one was ever happy with the results, even if the outcome was what they desired (for a respondent: "not responsible" for a complainant: "responsible." suspended.). This often left both parties with feelings of frustration, disappointment, and even resentment and anger at the institution.

I served as chair on an emotionally charged Title IX case. The board found that, based on the information available to them, they could not determine whether the policy had ben violated; therefore, the respondent was found not responsible. The complainant was hurt by the decision. In the complainant's senior year, she was involved in another Title IX incident with someone she would have called her friend. She said she could not do another hearing but had just heard about something called *restorative justice*, and she would like to try it with her case. At the time, I was hesitant to do this. I believe in the work of the board, we were hesitant to pursue this because hearings, regardless of the outcome, are an educational process. However, we are striving to be complainant driven and, to honor her request we decided to proceed as best as we were able with our primitive version of RJ, drawing upon principles found in *The Little Book of Restorative Justice for Colleges and Universities* (Karp, 2019).

After lots of documents, waivers, and all things compliance-related, we proceeded with what was our first RJ circle at Luther College. In a quiet campus house setting, the complainant vividly told the harm that had been bestowed upon her by someone she trusted. The respondent responded by demonstrating heartfelt remorse and what appeared to be a sincere apology with no justification and no defensiveness. At the end of our journey together, I was unsure how the complainant felt about the experience, and I was unsure how I felt about the experience. A couple of days later, she arrived in my office with her advocate to review and sign her RJ agreement document. She was so grateful for the process and said that was what she needed, for him to hear what he had done and how it hurt her, and for him to say he was sorry. She felt resolved and was ready to finish her final semester on campus. When she left my office, I walked to my vice president's office and said, "This might be something, this might actually work." He was familiar with David Karp's work on RJ in higher education and quickly responded, "Well, let's get you trained."

I was able to attend one of Karp's RJ facilitator trainings to further my understanding and skills. This was my takeaway: It was no longer about what I (a college official) wanted but what the parties needed for meaningful resolution, and my job was to listen. RJ is unique in that facilitators lack control over the outcome but work to offer and facilitate the process.

Upon my return, we started building the infrastructure of what it takes. In small schools, we know everyone and everybody wears a variety of hats. We began pulling individuals who had established roles within student life and Title IX: Enter my good friend, colleague, and co-RJ facilitator, Jake Dyer. As a case manager, throughout his professional career Jake has emphasized collaboration and community-driven engagement to foster a campus climate of inclusivity and well-being. He also is one of our trauma-informed Title IX investigators. Jake has the ability to be in the moment and to lean into the difficult topics with an empathetic and calming disposition. If this sounds like someone you know at your college or university, recruit them immediately as an RJ facilitator. These facilitators should be able to understand the complexities of our students, be comfortable navigating the gray, and have a high emotional IQ as well as be nonjudgmental.

At Luther, we started with low-hanging fruit, bringing in RJ questions to all conduct meetings driving at the intent but prioritizing the conversation around the impact of the behavior on our community. When an opportunity presented itself for me to transition fully into the work of sexual misconduct as a Title IX coordinator, I took it. We continued to pioneer RJ, securing a policy and protocol just before the new Title IX regulations landed.

Our first case was a textbook case: The parties were long-term romantic partners with a series of nonconsensual experiences. The complainant knew what they wanted out of the experience and had no community expectations, which made it feel like an easy win. In the cases that then followed, the parties didn't have the same level of care and appreciation for each other, and many of the cases made us second-guess ourselves every step of the way. We had debriefings after meetings with parties leaving us (as facilitators) wondering if one or both of them would stop participating. The continual adversity forced creativity and innovation and made us lean into the process. Our ultimate goal is to create an environment conducive to learning and healing. Today, we often internally reference our own cases as case studies; we are learning this never feels linear.

The more we do, the more we learn, and the better the experience we can work to create. Every case, individual, complexities, and details need to be individually tailored for RJ to be successful. But our biggest role is to listen deeply to identify the needs and desires of the parties. As practitioners, we are striving to manage realistic expectations. When we started, we would say, we are changing behavior through empathy and storytelling, and it is healing for the complainant. While we wish the previous statement were true, our role as facilitators is to intentionally create a safe space of reflection and dialogue. In that dialogue there is a requisite for a respondent's personal responsibility.

Jake and I have compiled in the list below and in Table 16.1: tips of the trade and tough lessons learned so far.

- Get good training; lots of people are talking about RJ, but specific higher education practice is different. Talk to your colleagues in the field about what/who they would recommend for training. The focus should be a practical foundation answering "real" questions and being honest about failures.
- Role model and be adamant on "I" statements—continuously remind.

- It goes without saying to separate the behavior from the respondent as a person.
- Avoid Zoom if safety precautions allow. There are body cues that are present in the prep work and conversation that are hard to duplicate. If Zoom is unavoidable, ensure cameras are on with a focal point image, while including prompts in the chat for viewing.
- Comfortable chairs, a homey hosting site, and an aesthetically pleasing focal point help put the parties at ease.
- Create a way to introduce the process to parties (with handouts or a video to watch). With all the hats we wear, we don't have the time to create presentations/media for RJ, but we do use a YouTube video as a soft introduction to the parties.
- During the conference we do use visual aids by listing harms. Pro tip: Use different colored markers for the complainant, respondent, and support persons.
- Be clear in the expectations of the support person that this is not about them. They can speak to harms and harms witnessed but it is not their process.
- Don't be surprised if a respondent does not include a support person.
- Some may try and direct you to utilize RJ on less egregious violations. It is a complainant-driven request, and both parties voluntarily agree to participate, so there is no reason you can't use it for your most complex and serious cases. It is the parties who can pose the greatest risk to the case, not the previous behavior.
- Be intentional with expressions of gratitude in preconference meetings that encourage and affirm their contributions. Example: "That was moving and really powerful."
- This is heavy work—recognize that, like all the other work we do, it takes on emotional labor.
  - FACILITATOR: Your role is a trauma-informed approach to challenge and support the students. Your mind will be flooded with the continual thoughts of what will be most impactful and helpful for all parties in RJ until a resolution. As a facilitator, be observant of the well-being of all parties and be checking in throughout the process.
  - STUDENT: Preconferences are difficult to work while navigating the demands of being a student (athlete, employee, musician, etc.), yet there are continual conversations about what you put in is what you can get out; this will reaffirm their agency in the outcome.

TABLE 16.1

Case Reflections: (The Headscratchers)

The Denying Respondent	The Facilitator's Response
A denying respondent uses terms like "I don't remember" and "I was drunk/high/etc." but sincerely wants to be part of the process. A student may not want to admit or talk in detail about what would happen stating they "couldn't remember."	We help them understand how that language can minimize and what can be done or said to validate is something we are continuing to work through. A successful solution has been to have the respondent read through the complainant's detailed allegations while simultaneously expressing how that feels in response.
The Defensive Respondent	**The Facilitator Response**
Instead of a typical conversational demeanor of a respondent we previously had in preconferences, we have noticed shorter responses, changes in tone, tartness, and unwillingness to engage with some questions. Physically, we have noticed crossing arms over the chest, poor eye contact, and an individual physically pushing themselves away from facilitators in the circle. *At times, they are distrusting of the process and critical of the questions asked of them.	We think it is important to identify the behavior(s), and allow them an out or an opportunity to lean in. Example: *At the end of yesterday, we noticed you were frustrated and/ or defensive in your body language and answers. We got the impression you didn't want to be there; can you help us understand if you want to continue with this process? Please know you are in the most difficult stage of the process in reflection/accountability. The RJ conversation does have more expressions of hopefulness and resolution, and we hope that is your experience as well. Just a reminder this is a voluntary process, and we need to know: Do you wish to continue at this time?* Note: At times, this has also presented with a complainant (see "The Harmful Complainant" section)

The Dissatisfied Complainant	The Facilitator Response
This individual has concerns about the sincerity of the words the respondent spoke, frustrated with their lack of emotion.	Ultimately, Title IX coordinator, as outlined by our policy, gets the final say on if they believe the RJ conference was a success. This is an example of language we utilize (if necessary) in agreement letters: *If the parties did not reach an agreement, then at the request of the complainant the case could proceed with the formal grievance investigation. However, the facilitators believed both parties participated fully in good faith; both parties were dedicated to the process of personal reflection in sessions with facilitators and on their own. The respondent did demonstrate ownership in accepting full accountability for the harm caused to the complainant; thus, meeting the expectations of a successful process.*
	We also share preconference observations of the respondent who in preparation did seem genuine in their emotional reflections. Additionally, this would create equity for a neurodivergent respondent where social cues can be misread by a complainant.

The Harmful Complainant	The Facilitator Response
This complainant *may* contain oppressed social identities yet believes their own harmful behavior can be justified. An example could be not taking accountability for their behaviors because of the institutional power/privilege of the respondent. This complainant may vindicate themselves because the intent of their actions is to disempower, and thus the harm to the person does not matter. The complainant may gravitate toward the RJ language but is utilizing the process to determine blame while remaining virtuous.	In our experience, we are the gatekeepers and may not get to the final phase of the conference, with this we need to be transparent; communicating a resolution may not be possible through RJ.
	We believe RJ (especially those related to intimacy) is not a platform to right societal wrongs, yet sometimes our students will carry these expectations into the process. As facilitators, be prepared to have the conversation that moves beyond blame and shame, emphasizing personal accountability for our actions. In RJ, a party who persists in their request that the inappropriate behavior was justified or deserved is not an appropriate candidate for the RJ circle. When this response becomes cyclical it will only exhaust the facilitators and harm the other party because they are not seeking to understand or taking active accountability for their actions.

(Continues)

Table 16.1 (*Continued*)

The Nonexpressive Party	The Facilitator Response
Respondent was not able to reciprocate emotions being expressed by a complainant in a circle yet desired to express empathy.	This could be a few things; once a respondent was so overprepared that the emotions were processed in the preconferences, leaving the RJ circle lacking in those raw expressions. While they didn't emote, the language was clear, and was fully engaged; facilitators reaffirmed on breaks this was OK, and they were committed to listening and sharing.
	In a different case, for an unexpressive party, facilitators have utilized a feelings wheel to help the party find their words to express, also being mindful that creative accommodations should be explored.

The Outsider	The Facilitator Response
This type of individual may be on the fringe of their community, yet they want what we all strive for: a sense of belonging. This can come into play when working with groups, teams, or organizations.	It is vital for the success of the conference that members of our community are treated with respect and dignity, so be in tune with dismissive reactions yet honor different perspectives. Sometimes giving voice to the voiceless can be done in other ways. Example: Have all the parties prepare a written statement speaking to harm; after these are collected by facilitators, other members of the circle can read the anonymous statements so harms can still be expressed, heard, and valued.
	As a note, this process may not help the outsider become an insider; in fact, we have seen this process in groups have an isolating effect.

Note. RJ = restorative justice.

"Tentative Structure" at Luther

Once the complainant has requested a restorative response, the Title IX coordinator approves, and the respondent agrees, this is our process.

- We will prepare for 3 weeks and then work for an RJ conversation in the fourth week. Meeting 1 captures raw responses to the questions, in Meeting 2 we lean into those responses, and Meeting 3 is a rehearsal for the conference, being mindful of the parties' momentum.
- Both facilitators participate in all meetings. Meetings are 1-hour appointments.
- With three preconferences, we have seen fatigue wear on a respondent leading up to the conference. We are still monitoring what is the "right" amount of preparation. (We have had no-shows from both parties.)
- We schedule an additional 30 minutes after the student meeting for us to debrief and think of questions to lead into for next time and discuss overall observations.
- We are exhaustive note-takers in preconferences. This helps us in overall preparation and helps mitigate any surprises in a highly emotional space during the RJ conference. Those notes are then highlighted and bolded in areas that we think were most significant and powerful. Typically, the notes are shared with the parties after the second preconference. Our facilitator observations are taken out but added to the facilitator script.
- We use a standard conferencing script, based on Karp's (2019) book.

We utilize prompts at the beginning of each meeting. We use these opening prompts:

1. Creating comfort in the uncomfortable
2. Making facilitators human and relatable
3. Practicing skill building on listening and storytelling (with senses and emotion)

Days 1–5: Formal Complaint of Allegations

Meet with the respondent to review the Notice of Allegations and Request for RJ and the supportive measures provided. (Typically, we give a respondent a weekend to consider their participation.)

Days 7–12: Preconference Meeting No. 1: Review RJ Agreement Form (Overview of Policy, Expectations, Etc.)

We start with a breathing exercise or muscle progression, then start the dialogue.

- First Prompt: Express a favorite holiday memory that may include relatives, food, decor, gifts, or music.
  - After a prompt we ask, what body language did your support person or facilitators do that made you feel heard?
  - We again emphasize that part of this process is to be intentional with our listening in preparation for RJ, not to be thinking of what we are going to say next but about the details surrounding the other's narrative.
- Facilitators ask the RJ questions, capturing raw responses to the questions; facilitators take notes.
- Finish with a comprehension of the process. The first meeting can be an emotionally taxing day for the student, so be sure to check-in.

Days 14–19: Preconference Meeting No. 2

We start with a breathing exercise or muscle progression, then start the dialogue.

- Second Prompt: Tell us about a time when you were sick or injured and how someone took care of you and how that made you feel (vulnerability).
- Facilitators lean in from the parties' previous responses in week 1. We believe that to "lean in" means that a party has shared something of great value or a meaningful reflection. These positive engagements will prompt the facilitator to use phrases such as "that was powerful, tell me more about that," "we appreciate the reflection, is more you can share with us" or "help me understand."
- We start to gauge what they hope will come from the process, reaffirming agency in the outcome. Any fears or concerns that are present can help us be proactive in our risk assessment.
- We find it important to inquire if there is anything else they plan to say or ask of the other party. Having this information can help with controlling the risk (no surprises).

Days 21–26: Preconference Meeting No. 3

We have found complainants do not always need a third meeting because they feel ready, and facilitators agree.

We start with a breathing exercise or muscle progression, then start the dialogue.

- Final Prep Prompt: Tell us about a time when you failed someone. How did you feel at that moment; were there any actions you took to make amends?
- For a respondent this can be a great opportunity to reflect on personal experience what is/has been the most impactful and meaningful for apologies, and at times we have reversed the prompt to assist in this goal.

RJ questions are asked in a rehearsal-like format. We review whether they need any additional support or accommodations. We discuss what to expect for the conference.

Days 28–34

- If there is evidence from the preconferencing that both parties are participating in good faith and the dialogue can be successful, we move forward with RJ.
- During RJ conference week, facilitators are prepping the final script with additional notes from all parties, including support persons.
- The email below is sent to the parties and support person:

Final email to each party (and their support person) with the following details:

- The seating will be arranged by the facilitators.
- Please bring your own water bottle.
- Tissues will be brought, but we encourage individuals to bring their own things that bring you peace, such as a stress ball or fidget spinner.
- If beneficial to you, we encourage you to bring your own notes to ensure you can say all the things that are important to you, but facilitators will actively be trying to assist you in this process with prompts.
- Support persons are encouraged to monitor their direct party and request a quick break from the RJ conversation if it would be helpful.
- Parties themselves are also able to request breaks from the conversation.
- A facilitator will assist the parties in exiting the space.
- If you need assistance in communicating with faculty, coaches, or work-study supervisors on the day of or next day to prioritize self-care, please reach out. (This can come from student engagement vs. Title IX)
- This is and will remain a voluntary process.

As an introductory practice (similar to our warm-up prompts in the prep work), we are asking each individual (parties, support persons, and facilitators) to bring an item of significance for you and be prepared to share in the RJ introductions why it is important to you.

We truly appreciate your dedication to the preparation for this conversation,

I am hopeful we will have constructive dialogue ending in a positive resolution.

RJ Conference

The Vegas rule is: What is said here, stays here; what is learned here can leave here. (We heard this in a training once and have used it in our practice and scripts ever since.)

- We follow our script's prompts to begin the structure of the conversation. We allow the complainant to choose if they prefer to speak to harms first. At times, per complainant request, we have removed the phrase "Tell us what happened from your perspective."
- At times, people can be wild cards. This is where the facilitator relationship comes into play, helping redirect the conversation to the goals of why we are all participating in this process.

Days 34–45: Post RJ

Facilitators draft RJ agreement letters.

- A challenge we have is adequate time for postcare follow up; ideally, we would be following up with all parties; however, we do refer students to complete our online assessment.
- At a small institution, RJ is not embedded in the culture; simply offering the process at times is not enough to sustain the initiative. We have been strategic in sharing outcomes that can speak to the educational principles of the process to defend the value.
- Then we follow Karp's (2019) assessment guide, adding our custom list of learning outcomes specifically created for each party (based on role) to address skill building from the process (answers: yes, no, I don't know)
  - I developed effective communication skills for engaging in difficult dialogue.
  - I was able to demonstrate reflection on harming behavior.

- ○ I think the solution(s) created will prevent harmful reoccurrences.
- ○ I believe the process helped restore the harm caused.
- ○ I believe the process helped restore trust within the Luther community.

The more we do, the more we learn, and the better the RJ experience we can work to create for our students. We know this is a lot; this process is intentional; it is a commitment, but it can and does work.

Reference

Karp, D. R. (2019). *The little book of restorative justice for colleges and universities: Repairing harm and rebuilding trust in response to student misconduct.* Good Books.

17

OBSERVATIONS AND REFLECTIONS FROM A RESTORATIVE JUSTICE PROCESS PARTICIPANT

Elizabeth Larky-Savin

I am a white, bisexual, Jewish woman who was raised in a wealthy suburb of Detroit, Michigan. Some of my identities gave me immense privileges as I explored the possibilities of restorative justice. Other identities put me at a disadvantage and taught me to question systems and institutions as they do not serve all equally.

With gender-based violence specifically, I have a long history of incidents to pull from. Like many other bisexual women in society, I experienced some of the gendered violence that is normalized in our society, like sexualizing young girls; catcalling; public nonconsensual groping; stalking; and stigmatizing public displays of nonheteronormative, nonmale sexuality. When I was a child an adult man groped me, in my teenage years I was sexually manipulated and taken advantage of by my first intimate partner, and in college I was the poster child of every parent's worst nightmare of what happens to their daughter on a weekend night. For most of these encounters the person would exit my life and I would get a therapist. But after I was raped by a peer I trusted while drunk and unconscious in his bed, I had to try something different.

As a college student in STEM and humanities and the daughter of a lawyer, I did what I knew how to do: I researched my options. For me, this meant reading the State of Michigan's laws, studying how local laws were ruled on in court, understanding the recent changes to the implementation of Title IX under the Trump Administration, understanding my school's policy on student and teacher sexual harassment and assault, and drawing on the lessons I learned on the Truth and Reconciliation Commission of South Africa in response to apartheid from my Race and Ethnicity course.

After weighing my options, I hesitantly chose the university's restorative justice adaptable resolution pathway. I empathized with my perpetrator and wanted to find a solution that may benefit both of us. Walking into the process, there was a small but loud part of my mind that didn't believe my own experience. The voice made me question my memory and blame myself. I allowed some hope in a process where his education and accountability directly helped me let go and retake my power. My backup plan was to press local charges and undergo a formal university investigation. I placed some faith that I could win a court case with a good lawyer and evidence of him admitting to the assault over text.

My pathway had three phases that built upon each other. In the first phase, he would go to an alcohol education program. The school frequently referred students to this program, which offered intervention for high-risk behaviors around alcohol and other drugs. A large factor in the rape was that he didn't understand my level of intoxication because extreme drunkenness was normal for him. He was an alcoholic and needed help. The second phase was a program where he would meet with a facilitator who encouraged him to think differently about alcohol, masculinity, and sex through the lens of healthy masculinity. In one of our early conversations, he told me about a paper he had to write for his introductory English course on masculinity. When he told me what he wrote, I realized he embraced a lot of toxic masculinity, some of which oppressed his self-expression. In order to get anywhere in a conversation with him, he needed to see beyond a chauvinistic caricature of being a man. The third and final phase was a meeting where we would speak face to face. I wanted him to be in a state of mind to come to the table truly open to talk.

In the midst of this process, I'd learned the current university policy indicated that my files would be deleted after 7 years. A part of me felt that my experience was so unbelievable that a physical record grounded me, and losing a paper trail scared me. Thus, I kept personal copies of the records and related documents. Though unlikely, I wanted a copy of my record on the off chance someone else spoke up after me and he wasn't held accountable.

In the beginning of the process, I allowed myself to be burdened by meticulously planning out what I wanted to happen in all possible scenarios. My adaptable resolution facilitator, Carrie, tried to gently push me to focus on my desires and personal goals for the process. But I was focused on how to change him. For me, the fact that I grew and healed from the process at all was an unintended consequence. As my plan started playing out, I transitioned from using mental to emotional energy to process feelings I could no longer suppress. I began experiencing combinations of emotions that were more nuanced than I had the tools to process, and I leaned heavily on my therapist. I truly don't know where I'd be without her and Carrie.

There were two pivotal points in my journey. The first was when I wrote an impact statement and had Carrie deliver it to my perpetrator. After meeting with Carrie multiple times, she'd told me that he didn't know why he was there or what for. She asked me to write an impact statement that she could give to him to put this process in context. I assumed he knew nothing regarding the incident and took the time to give a step-by step explanation of what he did and why it was wrong. I carried a lot of guilt, and believed I shared the blame in my rape. Sitting down to consciously disprove that to him also unconsciously allowed me to trust myself. While that letter was a way to share information and express rage to my perpetrator, it also turned out to be an act of self-love and care. The second pivotal point was when we had a face-to-face conversation. I was able to tell him how he had hurt me and how it stayed with me in the form of posttraumatic stress disorder and internalized trauma that impacted my ensuing relationships. While he didn't actually apologize, he acknowledged I was impacted and committed to doing better.

We were able to agree on the conditions of moving forward; we would act as if we did not know each other, especially in shared classes, and we would not talk to each other. But there was one thing he asked me about the future that stuck with me. He wanted to be sure this would not follow him. I took a moment to be surprised and said, "That's up to you." I explained that the point of this was so that I didn't spend my life following and monitoring him. But there were records in place that I hoped would hold him accountable in the future.

Restorative justice isn't perfect. Not everyone has the tools, support, situation, or willingness to advocate for themselves. At the beginning of my testimonial, I called out my privileges and disadvantages. I did this because providing background on me helps us identify the pattern of who this is available to and who we are leaving behind. People not enrolled in school only have the law. And the law is only built to protect young white women from unwanted male penetration. I was left to suffer at 16 when a female raped me. But, more importantly, many people of color, men, nonbinary, queer, quiet, and ashamed people are left behind. When planning my adaptable resolution, it felt like there was a burden on me to know what I wanted and how I could achieve it. I thrive under pressure as long as I have the space to be creative with a solution that truly fits me. Though not available then, I know other survivors who expressed wanting options to pick from rather than being asked to conceive their own path. I also could have prioritized myself. Thinking back, I wished I'd focused less on him and more on me. There, I give myself grace. Additionally, he didn't have to participate. Having participants opt in requires there to be some built in benefit to a perpetrator. No matter what I pursued, I needed closure. He, however, has the ability to ignore. Finally, lasting and meaningful change isn't guaranteed. I have absolutely no idea if he has continued to invest in becoming a better version of himself or if he stalled at where we left off. Regardless, the impression he gave the last time we talked was that this would not happen again.

What I do know is that restorative justice brought me peace. Two years later, I've moved on. I don't linger on what he did to me in the same way that I do my other previous, harmful sexual encounters. I still live with posttraumatic stress disorder, but I have been able to identify my triggers and manage my episodes. I also have been able to use this experience as a foundation to redefine and practice healthy sexuality and healthy relationships. There is still so much of my story left to write. But restorative justice allowed me to keep writing.

18

REFLECTION

STARRSA Active Psychoeducation Implementation Recommendations

Jim McEvilly

I am a clinical social worker and antiviolence practitioner, working primarily within the university campus context, and was incredibly excited when I was first made aware of the Science-based Treatment, Accountability, and Risk Reduction for Sexual Assault Active Psychoeducation (STARRSA AP) program. The primary reason for my excitement centered on two factors. First, prior to beginning my work with the STARRSA AP Program, I had exclusively focused on supporting survivors of gender-based violence within various roles (e.g., advocate, case manager, crisis response team member, Title IX process support). The STARRSA AP program appeared to address a critical need many survivors had shared with me over the years, and that is, that they did not wish to have strictly punitive measures brought against the individual who harmed them, but they did want some form of intervention that would decrease the likelihood of the individual engaging in similar harmful behaviors in the future.

Second, and relatedly, the STARRSA AP program appeared to have the potential to address a significant gap that existed within the interventions available to campus-based practitioners in engaging individuals who had perpetrated harm. Within my own experiences, two primary options for intervention measures (typically resulting as sanctions from a formal Title IX investigation/hearing process) existed: (a) disciplinary measures (e.g., transcript notation, removal from activities, suspension/expulsion) and/or (b) low-intensity, generalized "educational measures" (e.g., reading a book about sexual violence, completing a reflection paper, completing a reflection conversation with a university employee). While both these approaches were understandable, given the resources campuses had access to at the time, they both failed to provide the individualized, structured, long-form, and best practice interventions we knew were required to effectively address the perpetration of instances of gender-based violence.

From utilizing the STARRSA AP program for several years and completing 35+ cases with the intervention, I can confidently attest to the fact that the intervention does fulfill both of my initial hopes. The STARRSA program provides a meaningful educational and behavioral intervention that can meet the needs of many survivors, when requested in a restorative justice response or as part of a sanction in an investigation-based response. Unexpectedly, the STARRSA AP program also has proven useful and effective in preparing some individuals for participating in a restorative process. Through the program's focus on communication skills, healthy relationship psychoeducation, and strategies to navigate complex emotions/thoughts/behaviors, it proved to be a natural preparatory measure in some restorative justice cases. With these points in mind, I would like to offer several insights that I developed while implementing the STARRSA AP program that would have been incredibly helpful when I first began utilizing the intervention. The following list is not exhaustive, and the takeaways are reflective of my own individual practice style and may not necessarily prove to be of utility to all practitioners.

Insight 1: Take the Time to Build Rapport

Under the original organization of the STARRSA AP program, Module 1 contained a single session that was utilized to allow for orientation to the program and assessment of participants' learning needs. For me, transitioning too quickly into assessment and then intervention felt like not enough space was allowed for trust and rapport to effectively develop between facilitator and the participant. Initially, the majority of participants that I partnered with, within the STARRSA AP program, came to me following a Title IX investigation and hearing process. The investigation and hearing process, by its very nature, centers fact finding and adversarial cross-examination. Participants to the adversarial process can take a position of defensiveness, and mistrust between parties is common. As a representative of the university, many participants began the STARRSA AP program transferring these same perceptions to myself and the intervention I was seeking to implement. Most participants were assigned to the STARRSA program and were nonvoluntary, which typically requires more intentional engagement, trust building, and development of buy-in to the educational process. To accomplish these goals, in the first several sessions I took the time to effectively orient participants to the program, provided clarity on confidentiality, ensured an understanding that this was distinct from therapeutic interventions, that it focused on values and goals, and it provided space to focus on holistic wellness for the student.

This approach allowed the participants necessary time to become comfortable within the program, which decreased defensiveness and encouraged openness and transparency during the assessment stage. Second, it allowed more time for rapport development and demonstrated the facilitator's commitment to centering the students' needs/interests by exploring their own individualized values and personal wellness. Last, it also provided the participant an opportunity for investment in and cocreation of the intervention process, thus increasing feelings of buy-in and trust. It has been known for decades among interpersonal practitioners that one of the most essential elements of an effective intervention is the quality of the rapport that exists between the participant/client and the practitioner. Prioritizing rapport development and allowing for a longer period of engagement proved incredibly beneficial from my own experience.

Insight 2: Core Learning Concepts

The second insight I took away from the STARRSA AP program was the significant opportunity, following the effective establishment of rapport, to imbue and thread core learning concepts/outcomes into the actual facilitation of the program. For example, it is intended that STARRSA AP participants will increase their understanding and utilization of consent and consent-focused skills. A critical opportunity that exists for STARRSA facilitators is the opportunity to role-model consent skills in session, and there are many ways to accomplish this throughout the intervention. For example, following the implementation of the program's Baseline Knowledge Assessment I would create a proposed tailored learning curriculum based on the student's specific needs. The curriculum would include the number of sessions, the topic of each session, and how sessions would be ordered. Prior to implementing the curriculum I would review the proposal with each participant; explain my thinking on why certain topics were included; and explore whether the student had any questions, concerns, or requested adjustments (requests for changes were exceedingly rare). The review process I completed with participants centered and conveyed (a) respect, (b) transparency, (c) communication of need, and (d) the creation of space to explore actionable alternatives. These four concepts are critical to the development of full and authentic consent. Similarly, within the structure of each session there are opportunities to allow for consent, whether it be inviting the participant to sit where they feel most comfortable, asking permission prior to transitioning topics, or checking in on how a participant is experiencing a particular topic during a session.

Insight 3: Identify Allies and Opportunities for Learning

I found it incredibly helpful and meaningful to look outside the university to identify potential allies and learning opportunities. It's important to note that community-based practitioners have been facilitating educational and behavioral interventions with individuals who have perpetrated harm since at least the 1970s. There exists a wealth of experience and knowledge outside of the university setting; for example, within my own community there existed two community-based programs focused on engaging individuals who have perpetrated intimate partner violence. Strong relationships with such programs, which provide opportunity to consult, refer, and provide mutual support, can be incredibly useful. Additionally, it proved very worthwhile to engage in professional development opportunities specifically focused on engaging individuals who had perpetrated harm. Following my first few months utilizing the STARRSA AP program, I attended the annual conference held by the Association for the Treatment of Sexual Abusers, where I learned about additional interventions, assessment techniques, and general best practices that would prove invaluable during future interventions.

Insight 4: The Reflective STARRSA Facilitator

Last, it is critical for individual STARRSA AP facilitators to assess what they are bringing into the space with their participant. Though the AP program is not a clinical intervention, I do believe it can be useful for facilitators to develop skills around both active listening and motivational interviewing, if they do not possess these skill sets already. Additionally, it is critical that facilitators examine and address their own biases or preconceived notions pertaining to individuals who have perpetrated harm. Within my experiences, the range of participant presentations was incredibly varied. While some participants have presented as consistently resistant, many others were engaged and reflective and practiced high standards of self-accountability. Centering the individual, we are working with and seeking to recognize the various nuances that make up not only their unique behaviors but also their humanity; this is critical to an effective intervention.

19

TRANSFORMATION

Kendra Svilar

I told my 9-year-old daughter I was trying to write something about why I do the work I do now. I was struggling to find a way to begin. She thought for a minute and said, "You wanted things to change." I looked at her and smiled. Encouraged, she continued, "You wanted people to feel better." And, unsolicited, "You seem happier." As I took a few notes, she told me I needed to make sure she was adequately cited. Her observations are accurate, thoughtful, and deeply appreciated.

I had been an assistant prosecuting attorney, a director of student conduct, a deputy Title IX coordinator, a Title IX coordinator, and a civil rights investigator—in that order—while on my professional journey. The work felt important at each step along the way, but eventually it seemed like I was brokering transactions: Title IX- and Title VII-compliant transactions. That felt incongruent with why I wanted to do the work. I wanted to be part of a process that helped facilitate transformations, not broker transactions.

The knowledge and skills I had acquired were legalistic and, frankly, inadequate to help support repair, connection, and prevention. The tools I had often could not reach the suffering and anguish people had experienced. Worse, the investigation process in which I engaged sometimes exacerbated the harm. And once the parties had an outcome, they still had hard work to live into the institution's decision. They often had little direction or support from the school on how to do that. That felt, well, bad.

I wanted to offer a space where people could explore the harm they experienced without judgment. I wanted to center human dignity no matter the outcome. And I wanted people to come away feeling seen, heard, and that they mattered. As I widened my lens on what was possible, my colleagues introduced me to restorative justice and STARRSA AP (Science-based Treatment Accountability and Risk Reduction for Sexual Assault Active

Psychoeducation) as resolution options that could work together. Something in me locked into place, and a clear, certain voice tugged at me, telling me, "You want to do that."

So, I pursued every training I could attend and tried connecting it to my work as an investigator. I got certified in restorative conferences and circles. I read books. I practiced restorative approaches in my personal relationships. I used them in my professional capacity to facilitate dialogues during training and to conduct educational conversations. I bent the ear of my colleagues about how I could get into the work while still trying to hang onto all the things I thought I knew about how to respond to civil rights concerns.

Meanwhile, I was becoming less engaged in investigative compliance efforts in my "real job." Stuffing myself into what felt like a small space started to really hurt. I realized I needed to take a leap and expand to commit more fully to restorative justice work. I decided to quit my full-time job as an investigator so I could explore restorative practices. I started facilitating RJ cases in educational and employment settings. I also served as a contract civil rights investigator in the K–12 arena.

The transition contained so many sites of learning. I learned that we all need empathy, connection, and accountability. We need a community of care whose members will come alongside us to support, challenge, and tend to us as we grow—during a restorative process or after an investigation. I also learned that carrying heavy armor to hide my vulnerability did not make me stronger or smarter. Allowing my vulnerability to influence my decisions took a lot of strength. I learned that facing the people or things that hurt you without your armor takes bravery and commitment. And choosing to be someone you like while confronting hard things requires you to embrace all of who you are, even the things about you that are messy, contradictory, and confusing.

A recent case solidified these lessons again for me. During the restorative process, I felt like a witness to an important step toward healing and growth the parties were taking. It struck me how they were both able to state their needs clearly when the structure and formality of the investigation fell away. The restorative process created a defined space for them to share their needs, get their needs met, and begin to have closure. They were able to create an outcome that met their individual needs based on their wisdom about their experiences. They allowed their vulnerability to guide the process when it was hard. They chose to be present to the harm and to take an intentional step toward healing. Their meaningful, difficult work reminded me that transformation is worth the risk.

20

PRACTITIONER REFLECTION ON THE RIPPLE EFFECTS ACROSS COMMUNITIES

Erik S. Wessel

I feel like I am being blamed for all the sexual harm that has been experienced . . . my hope is to show people who know me that I am truly the person they have come to know . . . and to those that don't know me, that the present story does not articulate who I was then, nor who I am now.
—Paraphrased from personal student correspondence

The college community was suddenly in turmoil. It was early that very week an urgent conversation with community administrative leadership was convened to better understand the situation and source recommendations on how best to proceed. The upheaval arose from an anonymous email distributed broadly across the community via an internal listserv that was accessed by someone external to the community. The email, received by the entire community, thrust a newer member of the community into the spotlight and levied allegations of past sexual misconduct that allegedly had occurred while this person was a member of a previous educational community. Although not small enough for this student to be well known by all, the community was close-knit enough that their presence was observed and felt. The temperature rose. The fear, among some within the community, was all too real for them. College administrators began fielding calls for action, including the removal of the student—and the clock began ticking. This may sound familiar to some because it is a fact pattern with great potential for replication across all college communities.

Campus sexual misconduct (CSM) creates ripples within communities that drive secondary experiences of harm, fear, and community unrest.

In addition to our efforts to effectively respond to individual and interpersonal effects of CSM, the impact across community requires us to consider the ways in which we provide effective support structures and resources for mitigating the reverberation of harm. This is particularly salient when the occurrence of CSM is rooted in close-knit campus subcommunities. This community-level harm is further complicated when the secondary experienced of harm, fear, and unrest builds from the inclusion of a new member of the community who is perceived to have committed CSM while part of another community—and this fact pattern provides the backdrop for the following reflection from the field.

Those accused of CSM, whether found responsible or not, will inevitably depart their present community and join another. Often, that receiving community is another institution of higher education who, ideally, would receive sufficient disclosure to make an informed and appropriate decision on admission. These deliberations on individual admission decisions become part of the educational record and thus are not transparent to the community—and therein lies an all-too-common problem. Where the student community comes to learn of that student's past, and where information available lacks often-critical contextualization, the narrative may begin to be filled in by the larger community. This undercontextualized narrative may, understandably, drive further harm, fear, and unrest within communities. How, therefore, might we begin to address these issues on our campuses as they arise? In the following, I offer a brief reflection based on my own observational experiences in situations such as this.

Establish Proactive Transparency

Primary prevention of harm is best viewed as the foremost goal in achieving communities free from sexual and gender-based violence. This includes a strategy for the primary prevention of all harm, including secondary harms. The restorative approaches we utilize to work toward this aspiration are inherently a work of cocreation, and thus lend to the establishment and advancement of community trust. In this context, building and maintaining trust requires intentional clarity and transparency on the ways in which an institution receives information and conducts their review of applicants. Such proactive transparency can only serve to improve trust within the community. Although we aren't going to be able to provide specifics on any one particular admission decision, providing contextualizing information on how the institution conducts its review in a manner that prioritizes community safety can be a critical component to mitigating secondary community harm.

Seek Collective Community Expertise and Wisdom

Despite best efforts to provide proactive admission review process transparency, the admission of an individual who has caused harm elsewhere—or those who have been accused of such—may become known to the community by means outside the control of the student or the institution, for example, where a member of the previous community communicates with members of the new community. Or alternatively, where there is information available in the public record that is observed by members of the new community. However it transpires, the narrative that is communicated can grow and extrapolate quickly. In these moments your community will be drawing from the well of trust in systems, community, and people—a well that in many communities is not particularly abundant. These moments require the transition from primary prevention to mobilizing effective support structures—convening appropriate expertise and support resources from across the community becomes essential for an effective and sophisticated response. Larger institutions with decentralized structures and systems may find greater difficulty if points of connection between units have not been previously established.

Offer Empathy

The survivor of sexual and gender-based violence lives with their experience every day. When reminded of this trauma it is understandable that a felt experience of revictimization would be salient. As a community we can and should unreservedly express empathy for the real experience of secondary harm. The expression of empathy does not necessitate judgment on another, and careful attention should be given to ensure it is not interpreted as such. In doing so we rightly hold in appropriate tension the support of a current student who has created—or has been accused of creating—harm elsewhere. Balance is found in holding multiple truths and that providing effective support for all students is fundamentally congruent to our mission.

Communicate "With"

When faced with growing community concern the tendency is to push forward a broadly communicated community response. To be sure, lack of communication of any kind is the worst possible future. That said, communication marked by perceived vagueness may fall equally flat.

To be sure, the path forward is riddled with unintended consequences where leadership pushes forward a community response that is heavy in platitudes and thin on transparency. We've already established that full transparency is often impossible, so where does that leave us? In my experience, the best response is found in restorative philosophy. To communicate in the midst of community concern or crisis is best accomplished by doing so "with" those who are most directly impacted. In one instance, I observed a dean clear their calendar to sit in a hallway to hear the experience, fears, and concerns of survivors. Communicating care through presence offers the best possible opportunity for cocreation of effective community support. It is this very expression of compassion within communities that can move mountains of mistrust.

Avoid Communicating "To"

A common go-to strategy in higher education is to offer a town hall style meeting where concerned members of the community can ask questions of a set panel of university leadership and receive a response to their question. This might seem like a reasonable gesture of transparent goodwill, but it is one that is most certain to achieve the opposite result to what is hoped for or intended. If we follow such an approach to its observed logical conclusion, we find that we are left with a prescribed period of time where community concern is met with often-dispassionate and vague responses. Inevitably, this leaves the community trusting less and administrative leadership questioning what was really accomplished. In such an approach we rightly discern that the community requires our presence, but we miss the mark on an effective strategy.

Lean to Listening Circles

We've established conceptually that a restorative "with" approach is a means by which community trust might be built; however, what might this look like in practice? As we've discussed, a town hall can be a strategy for communicating information broadly but a poor mechanism for communicating empathy and building trust. So, what might be a better approach? In my experience, the answer here is layered and requires deft exploration of need. Such exploration isn't achieved in a vast lecture hall but might be brought into the light through smaller voluntary community circles expertly facilitated to balance power and provide space for emotional expression and for those participating to experience empathetic listening. Put more succinctly, space for one's truth to be heard.

Explore Facilitated Dialogues

In the very real and fairly common scenario that underlies this reflection, those individuals experiencing secondary trauma are likely not the only members of our respective communities who are trying to find a way forward. The past experiences of a student accused of sexual misconduct in another community may weigh heavily on their own ability to belong and thrive. This is particularly true when an external narrative—on which they have no immediate way to speak to—becomes the dominant narrative in their present community context. The narrative of their past now becomes the driving story in their present. In such a scenario they may also possess a divergence of perspective on past events but feel compelled yet powerless to respond to the dominant narrative now saturating their present reality. Human nature doesn't exactly lend to naturally seeking more complexity, and there is danger in a single story. How, therefore, might we intentionally design supportive space for the student accused of sexual misconduct to be further humanized, to add necessary complexity to the story, to express what they have learned and the road they have traveled, and perhaps to express empathy to those who have experienced harm similar to that which they have been previously accused of creating in another community?

Approaching such a scenario restoratively requires such a process to be approached as a voluntary possibility intentionally designed to meet expressed needs. One such expressed need might be for the creation of space to allow additional perspectives to be shared among friend, peer, or affinity groups. A facilitated group dialogue may provide the space for the student accused of sexual misconduct in their past to acknowledge what is theirs to own, affirm who they are at present, and illuminate the person they are striving to become. A facilitated group dialogue can provide a structured and supportive space for a subset of the community to seek additional and important clarity, courageously ask hard questions, and ideally glimpse beyond the present narrative to know more fully the present person.

Multiplying a More Complex Story

It's hard to relinquish control of parts of the story of our life; however, in this type of scenario that may very well be the lived experience already. The dominant single-story narrative travels fast, can ripple across a community quickly, often creates far-reaching harm, and can have staying power. In most communities—but particularly in large ones—it can feel impossible to find equally effective avenues for adding to the story. Facilitated dialogues, although potentially powerful tools for community repair, are not as effective as an anonymous listserv email in distributing a narrative across a community. So, therefore, what solution might we offer? To this, I would suggest that the community itself is the solution that is needed. When utilizing facilitated dialogues as a tool for adding complexity to the story, it is common for those present hearing the story to ask for clarity on what is appropriate for them to share with others. In many restorative processes there exists a preestablished expectation of appropriate confidentiality to the process. However, in this framework there may be good cause to set quite the opposite expectation. In such situations, I've observed those present request permission to and subsequently commit to sharing with others in the broader community their own observations and experience as gained through the dialogue. This, therefore, invites the community into the broader process of restoration: restoration of the accused, restoration of those revictimized, and restoration of the community itself.

The Amend Initiative is a program created by victim advocate counselor Gretchen Casey. Casey (2022b) outlines five lessons learned in practicing restorative justice, across decades, in the space of sexual and gender-based harm (https://amendinitiative.org/what-restorative-justice-offers/#lessons). I find these lessons learned ringing true and offer them, as adapted, for your consideration:

1. *It's important to hear and understand* the context of a person's life to build the most accurate and necessarily complex picture of who they are.
2. *We suffer from our beliefs of others*, which are often built upon an incomplete single story.
3. *People are more than labels.* Like our stories, our humanity is complex and ignoring this complexity perpetuates division and brokenness.
4. *Suffering can be mitigated and prevented* through human connection.
5. *Expanding the pathways for prevention and repair is necessary* for the wellbeing of our communities and to build trust in a way that works toward the promotion of justice and the advancement of peace.

I find that, as a restorative practitioner, like Casey (2022a), "I want to work, create, and live in a world where we are phenomenal at the prevention, recovery and repair of harm and conflict" (para. 1). The hard work before us continues to be finding increasingly constructive pathways to restoration for every member of our community.

References

Casey, G. (2022a, August 18). *What the amend initiative offers.* The Amend Initiative. https://amendinitiative.org/the-amend-initiative-offers-victim-centered-accountability-based-restorative-justice/

Casey, G. (2022b, August 19). *What restorative justice offers. 5 lessons I've learned from restorative justice.* The Amend Initiative. https://amendinitiative.org/what-restorative-justice-offers/

APPENDIX A

Contents

The College of New Jersey (TCNJ) Formal Complaint Form

University of Michigan (Office of Student Conflict Resolution)
Agreement to Participate in Adaptable Resolution

The College of New Jersey (TCNJ)
Alternative Resolution Agreement

Supporting text for these documents can be found
in chapter 5, this volume.

THE COLLEGE OF NEW JERSEY
OFFICE OF TITLE IX
& SEXUAL MISCONDUCT

Office of Title IX & Sexual Misconduct
Formal Complaint Form

Title IX is a law intended to protect people from discrimination based on sex in education programs or activities that receive Federal financial assistance. Under this law, The College of New Jersey defines Title IX Sexual Harassment as three categories of conduct on the basis of sex: quid pro quo harassment by an employee; severe, pervasive, and objectively offensive unwelcome conduct; and sexual assault, dating or domestic violence, or stalking.

The College of New Jersey remains committed to addressing any violations of its policies, even those not meeting the narrow definition of Sexual Harassment under the Title IX Final Rule. Through the *Sexual Harassment, Misconduct, & Discrimination Policy* (hereinafter referred to as *Policy*) the College will uphold a broad scope of sex and gender related violations referred to as "College Sexual Misconduct." Some forms of College Sexual Misconduct may also be considered violations of Title IX as defined by the Title IX Final Rule depending on the nature, scope, and jurisdiction of the alleged conduct. Collectively these types of violations are referred to as "Prohibited Conduct." Given the College's dedication to addressing all forms of sex and gender-based harassment, misconduct, and discrimination, the College reserves the right to investigate and adjudicate all forms of Prohibited Conduct under this *Policy* regardless of any possible Title IX designation(s). Further details can be found within the College *Policy*, which is readily accessible via the provided links and outlines the Party's rights, resources, and the Colleges' processes and procedures for responding to and addressing incidents of sexual harassment or misconduct.

Important to Note: ONLY the individual who experienced the alleged Prohibited Conduct (the Reporter) may use this form to file a Formal Complaint. However, there may be situations where the Title IX Coordinator signs a Formal Complaint on behalf of the College. Examples of such situations include, but are not limited to:

a. Incidents involving a weapon or other forms of physical violence.
b. Incidents involving a Respondent who has been implicated in other sexual violence matters.
c. The Title IX Coordinator believes there may be a potential threat of harm to other members of the campus community.
d. The incident involved more than one Respondent.
e. The College possesses other means to obtain relevant evidence (e.g. security cameras, witnesses or physical evidence).
f. Any other relevant factors.

Filing a Formal Complaint will initiate the specified resolution process related to the reported allegations, which includes notifying the Respondent. Should the allegations change, updated notices will be promptly provided to parties involved. All the information provided in this form will be kept confidential, as applicable by law, and shared only with staff members responsible for addressing these reports and to the extent necessary to implement supportive measures and carry out a College resolution process.

Definitions:

Formal Complaint: a document, which is filed by a Reporter alleging Prohibited Conduct against a Respondent and requesting initiation of a resolution process under the College's *Policy*.

Reporter: is the person who is alleged to have experienced an act(s) of Prohibited Conduct defined within College *Policy*.

Respondent: the individual who has been reported to have allegedly engaged in Prohibited Conduct, and may be subject to an investigation, procedural requirements including proceedings, emergency measures, and/or sanctions as a result of information filed in a report, determined through an investigation, and/or Prohibited Conduct proceeding.

THE COLLEGE OF NEW JERSEY
OFFICE OF TITLE IX
& SEXUAL MISCONDUCT

Office of Title IX & Sexual Misconduct
Formal Complaint Form

Please complete the following sections to the best of your ability -

Reporter's Information		
Name:	Preferred pronouns:	Current role at TCNJ: ☐ Student
Email:	Phone:	PAWS ID: _____
Approved method(s) of contact:	*Choose all that apply:* ☐ Phone ☐ Email ☐ Text Message ☐ Other _____	☐ Faculty * ☐ Staff * ☐ Other _____
* *(If an employee)* Position/title: _____ Dept.: _____		

Details of Alleged Incident	
Date(s)/Time(s):	Location(s): ☐ On-Campus ☐ Off-Campus
Respondent Name:	☐ Virtual Area ☐ Other
Respondent Role at TCNJ: ☐ Student ☐ Faculty * ☐ Staff * ☐ Other _____	Details: _____ _____
* *(If an employee)* Position/title: _____ Dept.: _____	

Please describe your relationship to the Respondent (if any):	Minor at time of incident? ☐ Yes _____ (age) ☐ No

Reported to Police? ☐ Yes ☐ No
If, yes --
Date Reported: _____
Enforcement Agency notified: _____
City: _____ State: _____

Protective Measures obtained? ☐ Yes ☐ No
Active Criminal investigation? ☐ Yes ☐ No
Contact Info for Reporting Law Enforcement: ·
_____

Type(s) of Prohibited Conduct alleged. *Choose all that may apply –*

☐ Sexual Harassment	☐ Domestic Violence	☐ Retaliation
☐ Sexual Assault	☐ Sexual Exploitation	☐ Defamation
☐ Stalking	☐ Gender-based Discrimination or Harassment	☐ Compliance w/ Directives
☐ Dating Violence	☐ Complicity	

For specific definitions of the various forms of Prohibited Conduct, refer to Section II. B. of the College's Policy.

Office of Title IX & Sexual Misconduct

Formal Complaint Form

Basic summary of alleged incident:

THE COLLEGE OF NEW JERSEY
OFFICE OF TITLE IX
& SEXUAL MISCONDUCT

Office of Title IX & Sexual Misconduct

Formal Complaint Form

Anti-Retaliation Statement. You have the right to report any retaliation by individuals and/or groups. The College may take strong responsive action if retaliation occurs and if the College has jurisdiction over the individual and/or group. The College's *Policy* describes retaliation as any adverse action, intimidation, threat, coercion or discrimination against an individual (including students, employees, and Third Parties) for the purpose of interfering with any right or privilege secured by Title IX or its Final Rule, or because the individual has made a report or Formal Complaint of Prohibited Conduct, been accused of Prohibited Conduct, testified, assisted, or participated or refused to participate in any manner in any investigation, proceeding, hearing, or other resolution process under College *Policy*. Retaliation also includes such conduct through associates or agents of a Reporter, Respondent, Third Party, or participant in any investigation, proceeding, or resolution process related to the *Policy*.

Accommodations & Supportive Measures. Should you believe you may require and/or benefit from any Reasonable Accommodation(s) to effectively participate in the College's resolution options, you are encouraged to contact the Accessibility Resource Center ("ARC") directly at 609-771-3199. Reasonable Accommodation(s) are individualized and accord with Section 504 of the Rehabilitation Act of 1973 and the Americans with Disabilities Act of 1992 (as amended). All requests must be made in advance and the Title IX & Sexual Misconduct staff will consider any Reasonable Accommodation(s) recommended by the ARC for persons who are both registered with the ARC and are participating in any meeting or proceeding through the Office of Title IX & Sexual Misconduct. Further, supportive measures are available and can be offered/implemented (as reasonable and applicable) at any point in time throughout the resolution process. Should you wish to discuss the implementation of supportive measures, you may reach out to the Office of Title IX & Sexual Misconduct at any time to discuss your options.

Withdrawal of a Formal Complaint. You also reserve the right to withdraw this Formal Complaint at any time by submitting the request to the Title IX Coordinator in writing. The Title IX Coordinator will consider that request, while also weighing the necessity to maintain safety of the campus community. If upon assessment the Title IX Coordinator determines the College has Actual Knowledge of alleged Prohibited Conduct and signing a Formal Complaint on behalf of the College is necessary, the Title IX Coordinator will sign the Formal Complaint and inform you of this decision to move forward in writing and you can decide the extent to which you wish to participate in the grievance process. You would not be required to participate in the process further but will receive all notices issued under this *Policy* and process.

Dismissal of a Formal Complaint. The Title IX Coordinator reserves the right to dismiss the Formal Complaint, in partial or full, at any time during the handling of a Formal Complaint if it becomes apparent, even if substantiated and believed to be true, would not constitute Prohibited Conduct as defined in this *Policy* or could not have occurred (see discretionary dismissals in Section III, C.: Formal Complaints). Upon receipt of a Formal Complaint, the information gathered will be continuously assessed to determine whether a Mandatory or Discretionary dismissal is warranted. Upon a dismissal, the College will promptly send written notice of the dismissal and rationale for the decision simultaneously to both the Reporter and the Respondent via email. If the behavior at issue would still, as alleged, constitute a form of Prohibited Conduct under this *Policy*, this dismissal for Title IX purposes may have no practical effect on the College's investigation and the allegations of Prohibited Conduct may continue to be addressed under the *Policy's* Procedures. If a Formal Complaint is dismissed for one of the reasons outlined within the College's *Policy*, the Reporter and Respondent may appeal that dismissal using the process described in Section III, F.: Appeals of this *Policy*. Supportive Measures may still be implemented for parties, as appropriate, even if a Formal Complaint has been dismissed.

THE COLLEGE OF NEW JERSEY
OFFICE OF TITLE IX
& SEXUAL MISCONDUCT

Office of Title IX & Sexual Misconduct

Formal Complaint Form

AFFIDAVIT –

By signing this form, I, _____, am requesting that the College initiate the following resolution process to address this matter:

☐ Option 1: Formal Grievance Process

☐ Option 2: Alternative Resolution Process

My signature below indicates that I have read and understand the aforementioned information, as well as my rights and options, and am filing a Formal Complaint requesting the College proceed with the resolution process indicated above. Further, I acknowledge that I have been provided with information on how to access the Sexual Harassment, Misconduct, & Discrimination Policy and have been offered assistance with College resources and supportive measures. I understand that any information I have provided/will provide to the College is true and accurate to the best of my knowledge and may be used in the resolution process and potentially obtained by law enforcement. I understand that Retaliation is prohibited by College Policy and conduct in violation of the Retaliation provision may lead to formal charge(s) and/or the implementation of additional interim measures and/or sanctions. Lastly, I understand that future questions or concerns can be directed towards the staff within the Office of Title IX & Sexual Misconduct or the College's EEO officer, whose contact information can be found below.

_____   _____   _____

Reporter's Printed Name   *Reporter's Signature*   *Date*

Office of Title IX & Sexual Misconduct		EEO
Chelsea Jacoby, Ed.D. Director of Title IX Compliance & Sexual Misconduct Title IX Coordinator (609) 771-3112 jacobyc@tcnj.edu	**Caitlin Babcock, M.Ed.** Assist. Director Sexual Misconduct & Student Conduct Investigator (609) 771-2613 babcockc@tcnj.edu	**Kerri Thompson-Tillett, Esq.** Associate Vice President, Diversity & Inclusion Director of EEO & Affirmative Action (609) 771-3139 eeo@tcnj.edu

---

OFFICIAL COLLEGE USE ONLY:

The Formal Complaint was received by:

_____   _____   _____

Printed Name of College Staff   *Signature of College Staff*   *Date*

[END OF DOCUMENT]

Page 5 of 5

Agreement to Participate in Adaptable Resolution

Office of Student Conflict Resolution I University of Michigan
100 Student Activities Building I 515 East Jefferson I Ann Arbor I MI I 48109
Build Trust. Promote Justice. Teach Peace.   Revised: 1.13.21 (CL)

Adaptable resolution is a voluntary, remedies-based, structured process under *The University of Michigan Interim Policy on Sexual and Gender-Based Misconduct* and related *Student Procedures.* Adaptable resolution is generally designed to allow a Respondent to acknowledge harm and take responsibility for repairing harm (to the extent possible) experienced by the Complainant and/or the University community. Adaptable resolution is also designed to eliminate the prohibited conduct, prevent its recurrence, and remedy its effects in a manner that meets the needs of the Complainant while maintaining the safety of the campus community.

The adaptable resolution process will only be used at the request and agreement of both the Complainant and Respondent and as deemed appropriate by the Title IX Coordinator. In order for the adaptable resolution process to be appropriate both parties must understand and agree to the necessary elements of the process.

By signing below, I acknowledge that I have read, understand, and agree to each of the following:

- Participation in this process is voluntary. Prior to signing a resolution agreement either the Complainant or Respondent can choose to end the process at any time; any other participant can also choose to end their participation at any time;
- Individuals who wish to participate in adaptable resolution must successfully complete preparatory meetings (as determined by OSCR) with an appropriate staff member prior to participating;
- Adaptable resolution does not result in formal disciplinary action against the Respondent;
- Adaptable resolution processes are designed to address harm and prevent additional potential harm. The adaptable resolution coordinator (ARC) may, in their judgment, discontinue an adaptable resolution process when they determine that one or more of the parties have been coerced or where the adaptable resolution process may not have the intended effect. If this happens, the matter may be referred back to the Title IX

Coordinator for consideration of any additional action, for example, closure of the matter or the opening of an investigative resolution;

- I agree that to the extent permitted by law, I will not use information obtained and utilized during adaptable resolution in any other University process (including investigative resolution under the Policy if adaptable resolution does not result in an agreement) or legal proceeding, though information documented and/or shared during adaptable resolution could be subpoenaed by law enforcement if a criminal investigation is initiated;

- I understand that the University will retain, for a period of seven (7) years after the conclusion of the adaptable resolution process, the following records related to the adaptable resolution process: any Agreement to Participate signed by a party or other participant in the process; any Adaptable Resolution Agreement signed by both parties and approved by the Title IX Coordinator; any email communications between the ARC and the Title IX Coordinator or other Office for Institutional Equity staff regarding the use of adaptable resolution in this matter. The University may also retain other administrative records (e.g., emails, database entries, notes related to the completion of a resolution agreement, etc.). The University will not retain beyond the conclusion of the process any handwritten or typed notes made by the ARC in order to facilitate the process. The records retained by the University related to the adaptable resolution process in this matter do not constitute a disciplinary record of any party, but may constitute an educational record of one or both parties.

- Information shared during adaptable resolution will not result in separate or subsequent disciplinary investigation or actions by the University, unless there is a significant threat of harm or safety to self or others;

- By signing a resolution agreement, the parties are affirming that the terms of the agreement (along with any other supportive or interim measures in place) appropriately address the conduct at issue and remedy its effects;

- After the parties sign a resolution agreement, and the Title IX Coordinator or designee approves it, the parties are bound by its terms and cannot pursue investigative resolution regarding the same matter;

- If the parties enter into a resolution agreement, the parties waive the right for an investigative resolution and each party agrees to comply with the terms of the resolution agreement. I understand that failure to comply with a resolution agreement, once signed and approved, may result in the agreed-upon consequences in the resolution agreement, which may include the University placing a hold on the student's account without further process until the terms of the agreement are met;

- If the Complainant and Respondent do not reach a resolution agreement, the matter may be referred to the Title IX Coordinator for further action.

_____

Printed Name

_____

Signature and Date

Alternative Resolution Agreement

Alternative Resolution is a voluntary process within The College of New Jersey's Interim *Sexual Harassment, Misconduct, & Discrimination Policy* (hereinafter referred to as 'Policy') that allows a Respondent in a Prohibited Conduct resolution process to accept responsibility for their behavior and/or potential harm. By fully participating in this process the Respondent will not be charged with a violation of College *Policy*. The Alternative Resolution Process is designed to eliminate the prohibited conduct, prevent its recurrence, and remedy its effects in a manner that meets the needs of the Reporter while still maintaining the safety of the overall campus community.

The Alternative Resolution Process will only be used at the request and agreement of both the Reporter and Respondent and under the direction of the Office of Title IX & Sexual Misconduct. In order for the Alternative Resolution Process to be appropriate both parties must have an understanding and agree on the necessary elements of the process. The following information was reviewed in your original meeting with the Office of Title IX & Sexual Misconduct, but please read through the following elements and initial that you understand each of the following:

<u>Respondent</u>   <u>Reporter</u>

_____   _____   Participation in this process is voluntary and either the Reporter or Respondent can choose to end the process at any time prior to signing the agreement;

_____   _____   Mediation, even if voluntary, will not be used in cases involving sexual assault;

_____   _____   Both the Reporter and Respondent must participate in individual conference meetings with appropriate staff to learn more about the resolution process prior to participating;

_____   _____   The process can only be used once and will not be considered if requested by a repeat Respondent under the College *Policy*;

_____   _____   The Reporter and Respondent must agree to all recommendations laid out in the formal agreement or the matter may be referred to the Title IX Coordinator for further action;

_____   _____   Information documented during this process can be subpoenaed if a criminal investigation is initiated;

_____   _____   Participation in this process does not constitute a responsible finding of a *Policy* violation and therefore is not reflected on a student's disciplinary record;

_____   _____   If the Respondent is found responsible for any violations in the future, this agreement can be considered during the sanctioning phase of that disciplinary proceeding;

_____   _____   The College reserves the right to suspend or terminate the Alternative Resolution Process and revert back to an investigation at any time; and

_____   _____   The Respondent may be charged with *Failure to Comply with a Directive of a College Official* under the College *Policy* for failure to meet the requirements laid out in the agreement.

Educational & Restorative Activities

The following sets forth the actions required to be completed to satisfy the Alternative Resolution agreement.

Educational Activity: Salient Analysis of Interpersonal Dynamics (SAID) Workshop
The Respondent will participate in an individualized three-part workshop (1 hour each - total of 3 hours), hosted by **[name & title of SAID Workshop Facilitator]**, focused on _____ and designed to create a space for those accused of Prohibited Conduct under this *Policy* and/or Violations of the *Student Conduct Code* to examine their behavior and receive contextual information surrounding it with the goal of sparking behavior change, skill-building, and self-reflection. The Respondent should contact the workshop facilitator directly **[email of facilitator]** to schedule the sessions. Once the workshop sessions are scheduled, the Respondent should notify the Title IX & Sexual Misconduct Staff via email of the finalized dates. **All sessions of the workshop must be scheduled (and Title IX & Sexual Misconduct Staff notified) by [insert due date] and completed by [insert due date]**. This workshop is free of charge and the Office of Title IX & Sexual Misconduct will receive general information regarding the attendance and participation of the Respondent.

Educational Activity: Alcohol Education Workshop
The Respondent will participate in a workshop focused on alcohol education and understanding the impact of consumption levels on a persons' decision-making ability. The Respondent will schedule a meeting with staff associated with The Office of Alcohol and Other Drug Support Services [staff name] ([staff email]), who will facilitate the individualized workshop. **The workshop is free of charge and must be scheduled by [insert due date] and completed by [insert due date].** Once the workshop is scheduled, the Respondent should notify the Process Facilitator of the finalized date.

Restorative Activity: Impact Statement
The Reporter will submit an impact statement **that will be shared with the Respondent [in writing, via recording, in-person] during one of the sessions** of the SAID Workshop. The impact statement will discuss all ways in which the Reporter has been impacted and the harm that they believe they've experienced based on this incident. The Respondent will have an opportunity to debrief about the statement with the Facilitator during the workshop & the summative meeting.

Educational Activity: Summative Meeting with Title IX Staff
After completion of all educational/restorative activities, the Respondent will attend a follow-up meeting with the Process Facilitator from the Office of Title IX & Sexual Misconduct. During this meeting, the Process Facilitator will facilitate a conversation to have the Respondent consider how their behavior may have impacted the Reporter, themselves, and the overall community. Additionally, the activities the Respondent participated in will be discussed, including the Respondent's reactions to the completed activities, the overall learning that took place as a result, and the possible impact it has had on the Respondent's understanding of the current situation, as well as future behaviors. The Process Facilitator will also gain feedback about the overall effectiveness of the process. These meetings typically last anywhere from 1-1.5 hours. A summary of the information discussed during this meeting will be shared with the Reporter. **This meeting must be scheduled by [insert due date] and completed by [insert due date].**

Explicit Agreement Between Parties

REPORTER -

By signing below, I indicate that I approve of the Office of Title IX & Sexual Misconduct moving forward with this contract as is and understand the requirements that must be completed on behalf of the Respondent in this case for the Alternative Resolution process (as part of College *Policy*) to be satisfied. By participating in this process, I understand and acknowledge that I am waiving my right to utilize a formal investigation to resolve this matter once both parties (myself & Respondent) have signed this contract. Lastly, I understand and acknowledge that if the Respondent fails to complete the activities set forth above, they may be charged with *Failure to Comply with a Directive of a College Official* under the College *Policy*. I further understand and acknowledge that any sanction listed under the College *Policy* may be imposed upon the Respondent if they are found responsible for *Failure to Comply with a Directive of a College Official.*

Reporter's Printed Name	*Reporter's Signature*	*Date*

RESPONDENT -

By signing below, I indicate that I understand the requirements that must be completed for this Alternative Resolution Process (as part of College *Policy*) to be satisfied, and I also agree to complete the activities set forth above. I understand and acknowledge that if I fail to complete the activities set forth above, I may be charged with *Failure to Comply with a Directive of a College Official* under the College *Policy*. I further understand and acknowledge that any sanction listed under the College *Policy* may be imposed if I am found responsible for *Failure to Comply with a Directive of a College Official,* and that the findings of that case will be shared with the Reporting party.

Respondent's Printed Name	*Respondent's Signature*	*Date*

OFFICIAL COLLEGE USE ONLY:

By signing below, I indicate that a Formal Complaint has been filed by the Reporter requesting to utilize the Alternative Resolution Process. Based on the information currently available at this time, the College has determined that this is an appropriate matter for pursuance of the Alternative Resolution Process and find the educational and/or restorative components outlined above to be appropriate and reasonable. Further, the Title IX Coordinator has approved of me serving as the Process Facilitator in this case.

Printed Name of Process Facilitator	*Signature of Process Facilitator*	*Date*

Template of a Supported Dialogue

Supporting text for this document can be found in chapter 9, this volume.

Logistics:
- Survivor enters first
- Check-in
- Respondent enters

Build the container
- Warm welcome
- Customized reading
- Mindfulness moment
- Agreements
  - Engage authentically and restoratively
  - One person speaks at a time
  - WAIT: Why Am I Talking? Why Aren't I Talking?
  - Honor the learning and leave the stories
  - No recording or off-camera witnesses

What are you hoping for from our time together?
What strength, value, or quality will you lead with?
- Survivor
- Respondent

How might you inadvertently hinder the best possible outcome?
How will you hold yourself accountable?
- Respondent
- Survivor

Survivor: What I most want you to know/understand
- Impact on me

Brief break
- Breakout space for survivor and facilitator and/or support person

Respondent: Empathic response

Where do we go from here?
- Boundaries

Closing round:
- What's becoming clearer to me is . . .
- I just want to say . . .

After dialogue:
- Check-in with Survivor
- Check-in with Respondent
- If applicable, send restorative agreement to school officials

Note. Template created by Toni McMurphy.

EDITORS AND CONTRIBUTORS

Desirée Anderson (she/her/hers) Phd, MEd, was born in San Diego, California. She earned her BA and MEd from the University of Louisville and her PhD from the University of New Orleans, studying the use of campus-based restorative justice (RJ) approaches as a response to racially motivated bias incidents. Anderson is the dean of students, previously associate dean of diversity and student affairs at the University of New Orleans (UNO). Before UNO, she held positions at Saint Mary's College of California, Tulane University, and Texas State University. Desirée serves as an adjunct instructor and a restorative justice trainer and facilitator. She has released book chapters in *Colorizing Restorative Justice* (Living Justice Press, 1999) and *Ethics in Higher Education* (Harvard Education Press, 2021) and founded Lorde & Liberation: Building Transformative Solutions, LLC. She watches an unnecessary amount of TV in her free time, especially K-dramas.

Pablo Cerdera is a restorative justice (RJ) practitioner and educator and has been the associate director of restorative practices at the University of Pennsylvania since 2020. He lives on the Indigenous territory known as *Lenapehoking*, the traditional homelands of the Lenape or Delaware People, in what is now called West Philadelphia. Growing up as a middle child in a cross-cultural, cross-class, and multifaith Spanish and Jewish home, Pablo developed his conflict and communications skills at a young age. He began his professional work at the Legal Rights Center in Minneapolis and has volunteered or worked as an RJ practitioner with Restorative Justice Community Action, the Conflict Resolution Center, the Good Shepherd Mediation Program, and Let's Circle Up. He is committed to sharing the restorative approach and firmly believes in the power to transform harm, promote meaningful accountability, and develop strong and healthy communities through this approach.

Frank A. Cirioni, EdD, serves as the dean of Student Development at Germanna Community College. Cirioni is a student affairs professional with 15 years of experience in campus life, new student orientation, precollege programs, residential life and housing, student conduct, Title IX, restorative justice, and social justice education. Originally from White Plains, New York,

Cirioni is the son and grandson of Italian immigrants. He is a proud first-generation college student and the first in his family to earn a master's degree and doctorate. Cirioni earned a BFA in visual arts education from New York Institute of Technology; an MA in college student personnel from Bowling Green State University; and an EdD in educational leadership, with a specialization in community college/higher education, from California State University, Long Beach. His dissertation, "Needing More to Restore: A Case Study on Utilizing a Restorative Justice Curriculum to Address Campus Sexual Misconduct Cases in U.S. Higher Education," was published in 2021.

Cirioni serves as a restorative justice trainer for the University of San Diego's Center for Restorative Justice and is the founder of Restorative Justice Consulting LLC.

In his free time, he enjoys spending time with his wife, Yulina, and their two pets, Murphy and Eddie. He also enjoys live music, theater, collecting vinyl records, movies, comics, classic cars, and international travel.

Jake Dyer, MSEd, is the assistant dean of student engagement and coordinator of new student initiatives at Luther College. As a first-generation college student, Jake got his BA degree at the University of Wales Trinity St. David in Carmarthen, Wales. He immigrated to the United States in 2010 and has resided in the Midwest since then. His work in higher education began in the Luther College Diversity Center; he then went on to complete his master's in student affairs administration at the University of Wisconsin—La Crosse. While working in various functional areas throughout his career, Jake's focus remains on the systems and barriers that impact students. In his current role he leads new student orientation at Luther College, serves as a case manager, and is an on-call dean for student crisis and emergencies. Jake is a trained restorative justice facilitator and Title IX investigator.

Chelsea L. Jacoby, EdD, currently serves as the director for Title IX compliance and sexual misconduct and Title IX coordinator for The College of New Jersey (TCNJ). Prior to assuming that position, Chelsea served as the Title IX and student conduct investigator for the TCNJ. Chelsea is a leader within the division of student affairs and has the responsibility of overseeing TCNJ's compliance with Title IX of the Education Amendments of 1972 and other laws and rules relating to discrimination and violence based on sex/gender. Additionally, Chelsea has experience conducting and supervising formal investigations and administrative hearings for Title IX and sexual misconduct matters. Chelsea has maximized her professional experience and educational background to develop comprehensive training and educational opportunities (in person and online) for both TCNJ and other colleges throughout the country. Chelsea has also developed informal resolution processes to manage Title IX matters that are grounded in restorative justice and encourage self-reflection, skill building, and the acknowledgment of accountability and reparation of harm. Chelsea holds a doctorate in education (specializing in the design of learning environments) from Rutgers University—New Brunswick, an MS from Kent State University, and a BS from Merrimack College. Chelsea is based in New Jersey.

David Karp is professor of leadership and director of the Center for Restorative Justice in the School of Leadership and Education Sciences at the University of San Diego. His current scholarship focuses on restorative justice in community and educational settings. For his work on campus restorative justice, he was the recipient of the 2019 Leadership and Innovation Award from the National Association of Community and Restorative Justice and the 2011 Donald D. Gehring Award from the Association for Student Conduct Administration. David has published more than 100 academic papers and six books, including *The Little Book of Restorative Justice for Colleges and Universities*, *Wounds That Do Not Bind: Victim-Based Perspectives on the Death Penalty*, and *The Community Justice Ideal*. David is coprincipal investigator for the National Center on Restorative Justice. He has previously served as associate dean of student affairs and professor of sociology at Skidmore College. David received a BA in peace and conflict studies from the University of California at Berkeley and a PhD in sociology from the University of Washington.

Rachel King is a restorative justice practitioner with RK Resolution LLC, specializing in issues of harassment and sexual misconduct in higher education. She has been facilitating restorative justice conferences in community- and school-based programs for two decades and has held numerous roles in college administration, including Title IX coordinator and associate dean of students. Rachel provides training to schools around the country on how to take a restorative approach to cases of sexual misconduct, including through the Department of Justice's Office on Violence Against Women campus grant program and the National Organization for Victim Assistance. She holds a master's degree in higher education administration from Boston College and a PhD in higher education and student affairs leadership from the University of Northern Colorado.

Carrie Landrum lives, works, plays, and dances on land ceded by the Ojibwe, Odawa, Potawatomi, and Wyandot nations at the Treaty of Detroit. She has circled up with Fania Davis, Kay Pranis, Mark Umbreit, and Howard Zehr, among others; has learned restorative practices from sujatha baliga, Timothy Connors, Sandra Momper, Michael Petoskey, Edward Valandra, Robert Yazzie, and others; and has danced restorative practices with Katie Mansfield and Kahstoserakwathe Paulette Moore, among others. Carrie serves the Metro Detroit Restorative Justice Network alongside Angel McKissic, Belinda Dulin, Barbara Jones, and Tashmica Torok. She was appointed as one of the commissioners on the Metro Detroit Truth and Reconciliation Commission on Racial Inequality in 2011 and received a University of Michigan Distinguished Diversity Leader award the same year. She has been facilitating restorative practices at the University of Michigan since 2007, including for cases of sexual harms since 2013. In 2022 Carrie became the adaptable resolution and restorative practices lead at U-M as part of the Equity, Civil Rights and Title IX office, offering restorative practices to university employees and units. Carrie is an internationally known trainer and consultant who ardently guides others on the power of restorative practices to facilitate justice and healing.

Elizabeth Larky-Savin is a survivor of gender-based violence and former participant in an adaptable resolution. In undergraduate school, she played intramural soccer, napped in a hammock in the courtyard, and sat on the boards of a medical bioethics club and the Ann Arbor chapter of Days for Girls. She graduated from the University of Michigan with a BS in biology, health, and society and philosophy. After choosing not to pursue medical school late in undergraduate school, she is looking forward to exploring a career in public health. Currently, Elizabeth works in the health care technology industry as a project manager specializing in inpatient obstetrics and newborn care. Elizabeth sits on the Board of Millennium Soccer Club, an organization that brings youth club soccer to low-income neighborhoods in Madison, Wisconsin. In her free time, Elizabeth enjoys paddle boarding, cycling, podcasts, reading, and watching women's soccer.

Elise Lopez, DrPH, is the director of the University of Arizona Consortium on Gender-Based Violence in the College of Social and Behavioral Sciences and an assistant professor of practice in the College of Public Health. She has worked in public health research and practice since 2004, specializing in restorative justice, adolescent health, substance abuse, trauma, and prevention of and response to sexual violence. In 2016, she was awarded the Abstract of the Year honor from the Law Section of the American Public Health Association for a coauthored paper on restorative justice responses to campus sexual misconduct. In 2017, Lopez served as one of two nonattorney liaisons to the American Bar Association's Criminal Justice Section Task Force on College Due Process Rights and Victim Protections.

Sheila M. McMahon, PhD, MDiv, MSW, LCSW, (she/her/hers) is currently a visiting faculty and director for the Restorative Justice and Catholic Social Teaching Scholars' program at the Center for Restorative Justice, University of San Diego. Her research and practice interests revolve around restorative justice and transformative justice campus-based and community-level interventions to address and prevent sexualized violence. She holds an MDiv from Harvard University. She earned her MSW and PhD at the Rutgers University School of Social Work. McMahon is a licensed clinical social worker in Florida.

Toni McMurphy, a restorative justice facilitator and trainer, specializes in the design of customized restorative processes and facilitating win–win outcomes in emotionally charged situations. She is an expert in creating safe and brave spaces that foster authentic dialogue around harm and accountability and unpack the distinction between intent and impact. Toni is known for inspiring people to bring out the best in themselves and each other in challenging situations and regularly facilitates courageous conversation in a wide variety of settings on myriad topics. Recent projects include facilitating restorative responses to sexual misconduct cases; responding to bias incidents on campus and in communities where racial tensions are high; and facilitating difficult conversations between students and administration, faculty and administration, management and employees, and police officers and people who are incarcerated. Toni recently served as vice president of culture and campus life for the St. Louis College of Pharmacy for 6 years, where she successfully integrated restorative practice in student conduct, Title IX cases, bias incident response, and for numerous conflicts on campus. McMurphy is the founder of Infinite Impact. As an organizational development practitioner for the past 25 years, she has worked with more than 65,000 people in over 230 organizations. Toni is a certified diversity facilitrainer and is certified to teach Crucial Conversations, Unconscious Bias, and the Myers Briggs Type Indicator.

Jessica D. Naidu is the assistant director of the Center for Restorative Justice. She has an MA in higher education leadership and a certificate in restorative justice facilitation and leadership from the University of San Diego (USD). Jessica previously worked with the Office of Ethical Development and Restorative Practices at USD, where she served as a hearing officer for student misconduct, using restorative practices to guide students to a place of reflection and accountability. As part of that role, she also advised students who served as hearing board members for their peers. She has supported cross-campus restorative justice initiatives, including managing program implementation; training campus partners and student leaders; and facilitating alcohol impact harm circles, community building circles for new students, and listening circles to discuss challenging current events. Jessica's action research explored institutional readiness to implement restorative justice for cases of gender-based harm. In this study, victim advocates, conduct professionals, and university administrators at USD participated in stage-matched interventions, evolving through the transtheoretical model of change with a growing motivation to lead policy change that supports restorative justice resolution options for gender-based misconduct.

Kasey Nikkel, MA, is the Title IX coordinator at Luther College. She started her higher education career in collegiate athletics as a volleyball coach, then as a regional director of admission before crossing over into student affairs as an assistant dean of student life and director of student rights and responsibilities. In that role, she served as a case manager and chief conduct officer; coordinated new student orientation; and chaired hearing board cases for the most egregious violations of the code of conduct, including sexual misconduct cases. In 2018, she was trained in restorative justice, bringing the work into compliance with Title IX in 2020. She is hopeful that restorative justice at Luther can create an environment conducive to learning and healing.

Ish Orker is a diversity, equity, inclusion, and belonging professional in the nonprofit sector. She has dedicated her career to supporting and empowering individuals navigating oppressive systems while she simultaneously works toward systems change. For almost a decade, Ish worked as an attorney assisting individuals and families in crisis. She held positions in small firms and in a nonprofit agency that provides free legal and counseling services to survivors of sexual and domestic violence. Prior to her current role, Ish worked in higher education on a team tasked with preventing and responding to reports of discrimination, harassment, domestic violence, and sexual misconduct. A licensed clinical social worker, restorative justice practitioner, and yoga enthusiast, Ish believes that when we intentionally create spaces for authentic connection, joy, healing, and transformation are possible.

Rachel Roth Sawatzky, EdD, is a specialist with prevention, education, assistance, and resources in the Equity, Civil Rights, and Title IX office at the University of Michigan. She has held a variety of student affairs roles, including director of student programs and orientation, associate dean of students, and university Title IX coordinator. Rachel has a master's degree from Emory University, where she studied sociology of religion. She holds an EdD in higher education administration from Northeastern University, where her dissertation considered how institutions respond to campus sexual misconduct and how institutional response mechanisms might be augmented to better meet the needs that result.

Jasmyn Elise Story is an international restorative justice facilitator, doula, and the founder of Honeycomb Justice and Freedom Farm Azul. Named one of *Vice*'s 31 People Making History by Creating a Better Future, they are a dedicated human rights activist with a decade of experience working in the voluntary sector. As the former deputy director of social justice and racial equity for the Office of the Mayor of Birmingham, Jasmyn coled the launch of the State of Alabama's first government sustained women's initiative. This decentralized movement aims to interrupt the cycles of harm plaguing Birmingham's women, children, trans, and nonbinary folk. After completion of their MA in human rights at the University College London, they are currently completing their PhD as a third-generation Tuskegee University student.

Kendra Svilar, JD (she/her/hers), is a restorative justice facilitator and civil rights investigator. She earned her BA in psychology as a natural science from the University of Michigan at Ann Arbor, and her law degree from Case Western Reserve University. She has held various positions at small and medium private colleges, as well as working within a large public university. She has been a civil rights investigator, director of student conduct and community standards, deputy Title IX coordinator, and Title IX coordinator. She has also been an assistant prosecuting attorney assigned to the domestic violence unit and has served within the juvenile division. She got hooked on restorative justice several years ago, attending any training she could find, when it aligned more with her own values and beliefs about how to extend empathy and dignity to all involved in difficult resolution processes. She is currently working as an independent consultant with Restore Resolutions, LLC, and the Center for Education Equity as a restorative justice facilitator and a civil rights investigator.

Joan Tabachnick has developed educational materials and innovative sexual violence prevention programs for national, state, and local organizations for over 30 years. Her primary focus is on preventing the perpetration of sexually harmful behaviors, particularly in adolescents and young adults. Joan created the educational programming for Stop It Now! before starting her own consulting practice. Since then, she has been director of NEARI Press, founding cochair of the Association for the Treatment of Sexual Abusers (ATSA) prevention committee, and is executive director of MASOC. Joan is a fellow of ATSA and of the Prevention Innovations Research Center, and she just completed a fellowship with the U.S. Department of Justice, SMART office, with a focus on preventing the perpetration of campus sexual misconduct. Joan serves on a number of national and statewide task forces, including the National Center for Missing and Exploited Children and Stop It Now!

Her written work includes National Sexual Violence Resource Center publications titled "Engaging Bystanders in Sexual Violence Prevention," and another titled "Family Reunification after Child Sexual Abuse," and a publication through ATSA called "A Reasoned Approach: The Reshaping of Sex Offender Policy to Prevent Child Sexual Abuse" as well as numerous articles and book chapters. Visit www.joantabachnick.com for more information.

Erik S. Wessel, DEd, (he/him) is the Director of the Office of Student Conflict Resolution (OSCR) at the University of Michigan. OSCR is a multidisciplinary office that employs a spectrum model of restorative resolution pathways for campus community conflict and accountability. It is in this role that he has collaborated on the development and effective implementation of adaptable resolution pathways for sexual and gender-based misconduct, as well as building effective psychoeducational intervention tools responsive to sexual and gender-based educational needs. Erik holds a DEd degree in higher education administration from Penn State University with a specialization in counselor education. Prior to joining the OSCR team in 2015, Erik served as the director of the Office of Student Conduct at Ferris State University and worked in student conduct and residence life at Penn State University.

Jay K. Wilgus, JD, MDR, is a lawyer, mediator, educator, consultant, and facilitator specializing in multiparty dispute resolution processes and dispute resolution systems design. He is the founder of Klancy Street. Prior to forming Klancy Street, he served as director of the Office of Student Conflict Resolution at the University of Michigan, assistant dean of students at the University of Utah, and as an attorney–mediator in private practice. Wilgus is a national leader in the field of student conduct and conflict management who is regularly called upon to assist postsecondary institutions, federal agencies, academics, and others seeking to improve institutional responses to student conduct, student conflict, and sexual misconduct. His published work has addressed, among other things, the application of restorative justice practices to student sexual misconduct cases, the use of specialized risk assessment and treatment interventions for college students found responsible for sexual misconduct, and the utility of facilitated dialogue in addressing campus conflict. Wilgus now oversees Klancy Street's menu of law, consulting, and dispute resolution services and provides direct service to clients across the country. He holds an honors degree in communications from the University of Utah; a Master's in Dispute Resolution (MDR) from the Straus Institute for Dispute Resolution at Pepperdine University; and a JD from the S.J. Quinney College of Law in Salt Lake City, where he served as a member of the Utah Law Review. He currently serves as president of the Maine Association of Mediators, cochair of the Braver Angels Alliance of New England, and group leader for a community of practice affiliated with the Center for Restorative Justice at the University of San Diego. He is licensed to practice law in the State of Utah.

Kaaren M. Williamsen, PhD, is Director of Prevention Education, Assistance & Resources (PEAR) Department in the equity, civil rights, and Title IX office at the University of Michigan. PEAR is a new seven-person office focused on providing prevention and policy education for faculty and staff and providing assistance to all 19 schools and colleges as they holistically respond to sexual misconduct in their communities. She has also served as director of the Sexual Assault Prevention and Awareness Center at the University of Michigan. Before this, she served as the Title IX coordinator at Swarthmore College and was the founding director of the Gender and Sexuality Center at Carleton College, where she also served as a deputy Title IX coordinator. Kaaren has masters' degrees in women's studies (Minnesota State, Mankato) and counseling and student personnel psychology (University of Minnesota, Twin Cities); she holds a PhD in organizational leadership, policy, and development from the University of Minnesota. Completed in 2017, her dissertation addressed the limitations of the traditional response to sexual misconduct and the possibilities of restorative justice. She cofounded Campus Promoting Restorative Initiatives for Sexual Misconduct and is a restorative justice facilitator trainer and consultant.

Joe Zichi (he/him) serves as the well-being collective lead at the University of Michigan, where he is responsible for serving as the backbone support for the university's adoption of the Okanagan Charter. Previously, Joe served as the associate director of the Office of Student Conflict Resolution at the University of Michigan, where he was responsible for providing programmatic oversight and supervision of the office. Additionally, Joe was responsible for deciding sanctions and interventions under the Sexual and Gender-based Misconduct Policy. Joe provides consultation and training in adaptable conflict resolution, informal resolution for Title IX, and restorative justice for colleges and universities. He also served on faculty for the Donald D. Gehring Academy with the Association of Student Conduct Administration. Joe holds an MA in student affairs administration and a BA in political theory and constitutional democracy, both from Michigan State University.

Continued from following page

5. To create a strong partnership between scholarship and student affairs practice by developing an avenue for practitioner-scholars to publish their experiences related to gender-inclusive policies in housing and residence life and for others to use these stories to improve their practice.

Administrators, educators, and student affairs staff will find this book useful at any stage in the process of creating gender-inclusive housing policies on their campuses.

Made in the USA
Middletown, DE
12 November 2023

42553470R00166